LANGUAGE, DISCOURSE, SOCIETY

General Editors: Stephen Heath, Colin MacCabe and Denise Riley

Published

Stanley Aronowitz
SCIENCE AS POWER

Norman Bryson
VISION AND PAINTING: The Logic of the Gaze

Teresa de Lauretis
ALICE DOESN'T: Feminism, Semiotics, Cinema
FEMINIST STUDIES/CRITICAL STUDIES

Mary Ann Doane
THE DESIRE TO DESIRE: The Woman's Film of the 1940s

Alan Durant
CONDITIONS OF MUSIC

Jane Gallop
FEMINISM AND PSYCHOANALYSIS: The Daughter's Seduction

Peter Gidal
UNDERSTANDING BECKETT

Peter Goodrich
LEGAL DISCOURSE: Studies in Linguistics, Rhetoric and Legal Analysis

Paul Hirst
ON LAW AND IDEOLOGY

Ian Hunter
CULTURE AND GOVERNMENT: The Emergence of Literary Education

Andreas Huyssen
AFTER THE GREAT DIVIDE: Modernism, Mass Culture and Postmodernism

Nigel Leask
THE POLITICS OF IMAGINATION IN
COLERIDGE'S CRITICAL THOUGHT

Michael Lynn-George
EPOS: WORD, NARRATIVE AND THE *ILIAD*

Colin MacCabe
JAMES JOYCE AND THE REVOLUTION OF THE WORD
THE TALKING CURE: Essays in Psychoanalysis and Language (*editor*)

Louis Marin
PORTRAIT OF THE KING

Christian Metz
PSYCHOANALYSIS AND CINEMA: The Imaginary Signifier

Jean-Claude Milner
FOR THE LOVE OF LANGUAGE

Jeffrey Minson
GENEALOGIES OF MORALS: Nietzsche, Foucault, Donzelot and the Eccentricity of Ethics

Laura Mulvey
VISUAL AND OTHER PLEASURES

Douglas Oliver
POETRY AND NARRATIVE IN PERFORMANCE

Michel Pêcheux
LANGUAGE, SEMANTICS AND IDEOLOGY

Jean-Michel Rabaté
LANGUAGE, SEXUALITY AND IDEOLOGY IN EZRA POUND'S *CANTOS*

Denise Riley
'AM I THAT NAME?' Feminism and the Category of 'Women' in History

Jacqueline Rose
THE CASE OF PETER PAN OR THE IMPOSSIBILITY OF CHILDREN'S FICTION

Brian Rotman
SIGNIFYING NOTHING: The Semiotics of Zero

Raymond Tallis
NOT SAUSSURE: A Critique of Post-Saussurean Literary Theory

David Trotter
CIRCULATION: Defoe, Dickens and the Economies of the Novel
THE MAKING OF THE READER: Language and Subjectivity in Modern American, English and Irish Poetry

Peter Womack
IMPROVEMENT AND ROMANCE: Constructing the Myth of the Highlands

Forthcoming

Lesley Caldwell
ITALIAN WOMEN BETWEEN CHURCH AND STATE

Elizabeth Cowie
TO REPRESENT WOMAN? The Representation of Sexual Differences in the Visual Media

James Donald
THE QUESTION OF EDUCATION: Essays on Schooling and English Culture, 1790–1937

Alan Durant
SOUNDTRACK AND TALKBACK

Piers Gray
MODERNISM AND THE MODERN

Stephen Heath
THREE ESSAYS ON SUBJECTIVITY

Ian Hunter, David Saunders and Dugald Williamson
ON PORNOGRAPHY

Jeffrey Minson
GENESIS AND AUTHORSHIP
PERSONAL POLITICS AND ETHICAL STYLE

Michael Ryan
POLITICS AND CULTURE

James A. Snead and Cornel West
SEEING BLACK: The Semiotics of Black Culture in America

Series Standing Order

If you would like to receive future titles in this series as they are published, you can make use of our standing order facility. To place a standing order please contact your bookseller or, in case of difficulty, write to us at the address below with your name and address and the name of the series. Please state with which title you wish to begin your standing order. (If you live outside the United Kingdom we may not have the rights for your area, in which case we will forward your order to the publisher concerned.)

Customer Services Department, Macmillan Distribution Ltd
Houndmills, Basingstoke, Hampshire, RG21 2XS, England.

Poetry and Narrative in Performance

Douglas Oliver

First published 1989

Published by
THE MACMILLAN PRESS LTD
Houndmills, Basingstoke, Hampshire RG21 2XS
and London
Companies and representatives
throughout the world

Typeset by Wessex Typesetters
(Division of The Eastern Press Ltd)
Frome, Somerset

Printed in the People's Republic of China

British Library Cataloguing in Publication Data
Oliver, Douglas *1937–*
Poetry and narrative in performance. —
(Language, discourse, society).
1. English literature. Phonetic aspects
I. Title II. Series
820.9
ISBN 0–333–47351–5

Contents

Preface

No satisfactory way has yet been developed of teaching people to hear the music of poetry. No wonder the audience for this Cinderella of the written arts remains so small when in school and university so little attention is paid to how students listen to or perform verse lines. Creating notations for stress patterns is no substitute for training novices to hear the melody within a poem's delicately narrow band of frequencies. Until the melody is *heard* it cannot be properly suggested how it unites with meaning and emotional significance.

The first half of this book tackles some of the obstacles in the way of describing how poems can be performed. The second half relates the findings to an overall theory of literary performance, including both poetry and prose narrative. As the field of discussion is extensive, a preliminary guide to the necessarily complex argument will be helpful.

By 'performance' in my title is meant a poem or fictional narrative considered as actually being written or read on one occasion, whether silently or audibly. I do *not* just mean reading aloud but activating the reader's whole response to the work of art: intellectual, emotional and sonic. Generative grammar linguists are fond of referring to the performance–competence opposition, where performance refers to language as a set of specific utterances whereas competence is a distinguishing of the idealised abstract rule structure that underlies performances. As I shall have to keep pointing out, similar distinctions must be borne in mind when we consider the description of poetic music or of narrative structure.

For verse, we can describe the abstract rules presumed to underlie the rhythm or intonation patterns; or we can simply see what happens in a series of individual performances. For narratives, we can create the most sophisticated abstract descriptions of their structure, even to the extent, with modern 'deconstruction', of showing the internal, structural contradictions within the narrative or narrative type considered; or we can simply create a bare logic for what happens inside the head each time the narrative is performed. These are entirely different ways of talking, each with its own value. This book only concerns performance: that is, it deals with literature as an active performing art, sets of individual occasions renewed each time a poem or a narrative is read.

While the distinction between performance and competence grammars is so well established in linguistics, there is frequently confusion in literary criticism between talking about poetry and prose as an art of performance and talking about them as texts whose abstract structures can be analysed. Taking poetry, traditional scansion into classical feet was at one and the same time a laying-down of an abstract rule structure and a permission for almost infinite variation in how those rules might be realised in any one poem or performance of that poem. 'Almost infinite' because no reading of a poem is the same as another in intonation; no stress is ever given an identical weighting from one reading to another; and no syllable is given an exact duration. The simple oppositions between heavy–light stress and short–long durations of such a scansion were tolerant of these variations: the scansion happily confused metrical competence and metrical performance in a way which left the poem free to be judged as a work of art. Most importantly, the confusion permitted the traditional critic to link intuitively a poem's music with its meaning and emotional significance: he could say such things as: 'When I perform the line, I find a tension between the heavy stress specified on syllable 'x' by the abstract metre and the very slightly lighter stress that I actually give the syllable when I read, especially if I raise the pitch. This gives me emotional effect 'y' when I think of the line's meaning.'

(It will be explained later in the book, and in the Glossary, that I prefer to call 'stress' what may be called 'accent' etc., precisely because 'stress' is a portmanteau term.)

There are nowadays various abstract 'competence' descriptions of poetic metric, mostly developed by linguists. These specify exactly where and why stresses may be placed in the line within a given metric. Although interesting for their own sake, they do not allow for the 'almost infinite' variations of 'sloppier' scansions of the classical kind. They are scientific, linguistic descriptions which permit no subtle reference outwards to emotional significance and its interplay with meaning. These matters are discussed in Chapter 1.

Turning to narrative, traditional criticism, which allowed the critic to exercise subjective moral and emotional judgement, was at least able to deal with the text as a work of art; most importantly, it often suggested a real human relationship between the imagined author's mind and the reader's, a relationship in which the necessary subtleties could come into play. Modern 'narratologies' have taught us much about such relationships, as later chapters make clear. What they cannot do is show how poetic form and narrative form aim at the same end. There is too much structural difference between poetry and narrative for the similarity of their task to be caught by any formalistic description. The similarity appears only when the work is considered as performed, when the reader's experience of emotion and meaning at work in space and time is brought *actively* into consonance with that of the imagined author, whether poet or fiction writer. Then moral and emotional reactions must also be considered.

Describing the performance of a literary work necessitates redefining the key terms of the description. To talk of poetic stress in the context of linguistics is one thing: to talk of it in a poetic performance is another, requiring a different definition. In narrative fiction, to talk of deconstructing a text in the rarefied context of that school of criticism is one thing: to experience in performance the actual collapse of a burlesqued narrative back on to itself is another, requiring a simpler logic.

The need for redefinition gives a shape to my argument. In Chapter 1, I make the needed distinction between metrical rule and metrical performance. The first essential is to redefine the term 'stress' so as to include how meaning and emotional significance influence our perception of it. This chapter attempts a preliminary definition of stress which sees it as a minute example of an artistic whole or form and which therefore presents certain spatio-temporal mysteries implicit in artistic form.

In Chapter 2, I try to ensure that we do not lose sight of what poets themselves say about artistic form. The Augustinian sense of time implied in T. S. Eliot's renowned section on artistic form in 'Burnt Norton' is emphasised. Then I test out the definition of stress by displaying machine data of the pitch of poetry readings and find that the space-time mysteries mentioned above cannot be avoided. In particular, it will be seen that 'stress' and 'duration' are paradoxical partners: it is inaccurate to speak of 'duration' as part of stress; rather, stress is a notional 'instant' when the duration of certain sonic elements in a line of poetry is perceived; moreover, the developing meaning and emotional significance of the line must play a part, too, in deciding how heavy we think the stress is. We can tap an instant of stress with a finger but it is also a paradoxical moment, since an instant should have no content. By a sort of mental trick we 'give' this instant a tiny sonic, intellectual and emotional content from the past of the poetic line and from its future considered from the standpoint of that instant. Without this mental trick – akin to St Augustine's description of our experience of time – the stress would be perceived as empty of content, and therefore neither heavy nor light.

Though notionally an instant, a stress is sited by the mind at some point during a syllable. One of the most important factors contributing to a syllable's perceived degree of stress is that of pitch. But everyone gives the words of a poem a different intonation when they read. Unless we can gain some security about the pitch of a given syllable in comparison with its surrounding syllables, no proper idea can be suggested of the degree of any stress in performance. Chapters 3 and 4 show that it is more possible than is often thought to portray objectively elements of a 'neutral' tune to which a given poem can be read. These chapters are easily misunderstood by anyone with a proper repugnance for standardising poetic music, especially by machine. The 'neutral' or 'unmarked' tune is that which the words *would* assume for an average voice in a given dialect when no special emphasis (for example, dramatic or syntactic) is given to the line, *providing there were absolute agreement between different readers about the semantic, emotional and syntactical interpretation*. It is to be thought of rather as the written musical notes for that interpretation and that group of voices and, even so, is ineffable, unattainable. No line can be read aloud without some special emphasis and every reader's voice and every performance have quirks which depart from neutrality. Nor is it true that a neutral reading would be the most talented: talented public readers – like talented pianists – make minor departures from the neutral music precisely to work extra emotional effects upon their hearers. In the same way, a concert violinist must depart from a metronome- and pitch-constant rendition if s/he is to move the audience emotionally. Nevertheless, unless there is, for each performance, an ineffable 'neutral' tune to depart from, such effects would be impossible; and this tune will be fairly standard across many performances. All I am showing is that we can gain quite a close idea of this neutral tune, if we can ask our readers from a broad dialect grouping (broader even than, for example, Received Pronunciation English) to respect the 'natural' music of the words, without adding anything. To appreciate this argument, my readers must depart from that prejudice which insists that either we should obtain a perfect idea of a line's pitch (which a prejudiced reader will scornfully but rightly dismiss as impossible) or otherwise no idea of it is possible at all. The truth is, as the evidence makes plain, that we can glimpse such neutral tunes, unattainable in the absolute though they might be. Departures from them either imply different semantic, emotional or syntactical interpretation or insensitive (usually flat) readings.

If the role of pitch is often poorly understood, so is what happens to the glottis or larynx when a line of poetry is being spoken. Some consonants are voiceless – the vocal chords in the larynx do not sound and the mouth and upper throat form the whispered sound. Other consonants and all vowels are voiced: the vocal chords buzz in the throat. The voiced parts of the line carry the main emotional expression because, as in song, they carry the perceived main pitch and intonation. Furthermore, experiments described in Chapter 4 indicate that the perceived pace of a poem is partly decided by the arrangement of voiced, unvoiced and silent stretches of the line. With a restoration of the importance of voicing and pitch in prosodic description, a unified description (a hierarchy) of the relationship between part and whole, including rhythm, music, meaning and emotional significance can be built up, after generalising the methods of analysis a little more.

In Chapter 5, it is indicated from experiments that good translators have an intuitive sense of such neglected factors as intonation and voicing in the target poem. This chapter also shows that the methods of analysis developed can be applied to poetry in languages other than English.

Chapter 6 opens by specifying this hierarchy of units of sound in a poem, beginning with the notional 'instant' (stress), extending through various units of duration, and ending with the form of the whole poem, as follows:

(a) Poetic stress, an ambiguous entity relating duration and instant, and including elements of meaning and emotional significance. All degrees of stress from the weakest to the strongest must be considered in a full account of a poem's music.
(b) Syllable, the unit which is the main, but not the only determinant of the durations considered as affecting the degree of a single stress. It is also the presumed site of the stress.

(c) Voiced stretches, which, as in a song, carry the perceived pitch. Emotional tonality is importantly expressed through the pitch. Voiced stretches unite the syllable and therefore the stress with the overall flow of the melody and interact with voiceless stretches or silence to create other complicated effects.
(d) Dominant intonation accent at the line's main informational focus, which also focuses the music of the line to a climax.
(e) The line itself as a rhythmic and melodic unit.
(f) Its relationship to other lines, cadences and stanzas.
(g) The notional unity of stanzas and overall poetic form (perhaps never perfect).

The hierarchy fully links the 'instant' (actually, that ambiguous entity, the 'stress') to the overall form of a poem, and unites, according to the definitions created, meaning, emotional significance and sound. Every step of this sonic hierarchy is a smaller or larger example of our perceiving an artistic form both as a succession of moments and as part of a developing whole. The rest of the chapter lends support for these findings by showing how insight can be obtained into the performances of individual poets by applying the methods so far described.

Chapter 7 gives an extended example of such methods at work. A passage by Milton is chosen because his versification is particularly subtle and hard to define and because its syntactical complexity can be related to its sonic complexity. The methods, applied to a much-analysed section of *Paradise Lost*, display elements of Milton's craft otherwise hard to pinpoint.

All this has been heading the same way: to show how necessary were the definitions of poetic stress and music developed during these chapters. Chapter 8 draws this part of the argument together. It deals with possible philosophical objections to the spatio-temporal paradoxes that have been observed in the nature of poetic form and then revises the preliminary definition of poetic stress in terms of this discussion.

Now that a definition of how the 'instant' of a poem relates to its overall form has been developed, a poem's performance can be compared with that of narrative. Because of the constant danger of confusion in a field full of literary and linguistic prejudice, Chapter 9 explains the distinction between 'competence' descriptions of narrative and a description of narrative performance.

In fact, to show the essential of narrative's effect upon us in performance, we need only look at certain burlesques where the author deliberately collapses the narrative structure back on itself. Two examples, in Chapters 10 and 11, are the recognition of 'Chaucer' by the Host in *The Canterbury Tales*, and the entry of Rabelais' narrator into Pantagruel's mouth. These examples are different from a deconstructionist analysis of a text because the collapse of the narrative structure is not purely intellectual and abstract but is felt at each performance of the text; it plays a *blatant* effect upon our feelings, and involves our everyday ego and our everyday language.

The psychological effect of poetry and narrative fiction can now be compared in Chapter 12. This is because both have been considered as performances in which the part and the whole have been given a necessary, seamless connection – at least, considered as Coleridge would say 'in ideal perfection'. Literary form fills the apparent 'instant' of time with mental content, an operation which ought to be impossible and, in fact, is only achieved in a paradoxical way. But because the paradox is infinitely repeatable, literary form allows the reader to think he is sharing this 'instant' with the imagined author of the text. Its full value only appears when the text is activated by a performance, because in the repeatability of a shared mental experience lies the hope that we can enrich our perception and human sympathy. For these reasons this chapter concentrates on our emotional response to literary art.

That is the shape of the argument: I should add a word about the linguistic machinery employed. Why every university department of literature has not got the fairly inexpensive machinery which registers vocal frequency, is beyond me. So many students finish their undergraduate literature studies without having been properly trained to hear the delicacy of poetic music within the narrow band of frequencies it employs. Although there are signs of renewed interest in machine data, its limitations have been more emphasised by literary critics than its uses; much of the technical research into prosody has therefore been left to the linguists, whose scientific approach is not always suitable for application in intuitive criticism. In a standard textbook, Wellek and Warren (1963, p. 169) are understandably sceptical about the value of acoustic metrics for literary criticism. Acoustic and musical–metrical approaches to poetic prosody share, they say, the common defect that they rely exclusively on sound and on a single or many performances of reciters, whereas there are various ways of performing a poem. They usefully add: 'The meaning of verse simply cannot be ignored in a theory of metrics.' This book asserts that emotional significance cannot be ignored either.

Machine traces of poetry readings are a valuable critical aid: instead of the critic or teacher performing the poems inside his head and then making subjective pronouncements about the role of, say, heavy stresses in a line, he can use a machine trace rather like a map to say exactly what parts of the sound he is talking about. Sometimes he may remain quite subjective, putting into his own performance of the poem, as recorded by machine, features that he has already divined in the work. The machine traces, used sparingly, are *still* an advance on vague, subjective remarks about poetic rhythm, and in the university classroom, in my experience, they can be a godsend. More objectively, but not completely so, the critic may try, in ways already referred to, to suggest a fairly neutral tune, or, with different interpretations, tunes, for the verse by comparing different readings. Nothing in this use of machinery takes away the mystery of rhythm and music or of art, unless we become pseudo-scientific where we have insufficient warrant to be.

Readers should note that 'he', referring to poets generally, should be understood as 'he/she' (occasionally employed where not clumsy). The concentration on male poets is regrettable: it is through my own male voice that I gain access to the very finest phonetic details; unfortunately, it has to be matched with those of other men because the machinery cannot match it so convincingly with those of women. Therefore, poems which had already a male voice in them seemed the safest material. (Male and female melodies are similar but this is disguised by pitch levels.)

A final preparatory comment: readers will look in vain for out-of-the-way passages of literature or for the more avant-garde views of poetic prosody in the Poundian and post-Poundian traditions. I have chosen, both for poetry and narrative fiction, as well-known passages as I could – to the point of obviousness – so as to site my discussion as centrally as possible within the public domain, whatever my own working beliefs.

Employing an everyday language where possible, I am hoping to talk to the traditionalists as well as to poets, novelists or critics with modernist, post-modern or high-powered deconstructional views.

Before continuing, the reader is invited first to inspect the Glossary. All translations from the French are my own except where translations by other people are mentioned in the Bibliography.

Douglas Oliver

Acknowledgements

For help at various stages of this project I should like to thank the following: Mr V. J. Cook, Dr J. M. Durand, Professor M. A. A. Tatham, Dr Linda Shockey and Mr R. Jennings, all of the Essex University Department of Language and Linguistics. In the same university, Mr Herbie Butterfield and Dr Angela Livingstone, of the Department of Literature, gave help in conducting opinion polls, and Dr M. T. Wilson, of the Department of Chemistry, gave advice on statistics. Professor H. C. Longuet-Higgins, FRS, Director of the Centre for Research on Perception and Cognition at Sussex University, kindly allowed me to use his real-time speech intonation spectrometer, and Dr Anne Cutler of that Centre showed me its operation. In Paris, Professor Ivan Fónagy, Directeur de Recherche for the Centre National de la Recherche Scientifique (CNRS), has been extraordinarily generous, not least in making arrangements for use of a laboratory; and M. Bernard Gautheron of the Phonetics Laboratory at the Institut d'Études Linguistiques et Phonétiques, gave me expert help in recording the data.

The following figures and tables were originally published in the journals mentioned below:

Figures 3.2, 3.3, 3.4, 6.2, and Table 3.1 *Journal of Phonetics* (1983) 11; Figures 4.1, 4.2, 4.3, 4.4, 4.5, 4.6, and Tables 4.1, 4.2 *Journal of Phonetics* (1984) 12.

Figures 5.1, 5.2 and Tables 5.1, 5.2 *Franco–British Studies* (1986), 1, Spring.

Figures 3.1, 6.2 and 6.3 *Grosseteste Review* (1979) 12.

I thank the editors of those journals, in which parts of the text appear in other versions, for permission to reprint these figures and tables in the present volume.

The following publishers are thanked for permission to reproduce copyright material:

The Open University and P. Howard for Figure 2.1 (redrawn and adapted by me), published in Arts: A Second Level Course, The

Enlightenment, Units 21a–24a, *Haydn in London*, © 1980, The Open University Press.

Excerpt from 'Burnt Norton' in *Four Quartets*, copyright 1943 by T. S. Eliot; renewed 1971 by Esmé Valerie Eliot. Reprinted by permission of Faber & Faber and of Harcourt Brace Jovanovich, Inc.

Professor Anthony Kenny and Oxford University Press for an excerpt from *The God of the Philosophers* (1979).

Yale University Press for an excerpt from Ernst Cassirer, *The Philosophy of Symbolic Forms*, trans. R. Mannheim, intr. C. W. Hendel (1957), vol. III.

Professor Paul Ricoeur and Chicago University Press for excerpts from *Temps et Récit*, trans. K. McLaughlin and D. Pellauer as *Time and Narrative*, vol. I (1984), vol. II (1985), and vol. III (1986). Copyright Chicago University Press, all rights reserved.

Short Glossary

Certain key words have been used in their strict linguistic sense; others, where the linguistic definition would prejudice a discussion of artistic performance, have been used in a slightly broader sense. I acknowledge the influence on this Glossary of Crystal's very helpful *A First Dictionary of Linguistics and Phonetics* (1980).

Duration The length of any discreet item or *segment* (see Suprasegmental).

Formant When the raw wave form is examined by certain machinery the myriad lines representing various vocal frequencies are seen to group into broad bands of nearly similar frequency; these bands are formants. The F_o is generally the lowest of these bands.

Frequency In acoustic linguistics, the number of opening or closing movements (cycles) of the vocal chords per unit of time. The vibrations or pulsations given to the air as it passes through the vocal apparatus.

Fundamental frequency (F_o) A frequency component created by the *vocal chords* and the gap between them (the *glottis*) which gives us our fundamental sense of the *pitch* of an utterance. The glottis produces a 'buzz' which can be recorded. This buzz and, alternatively, the whisper that comes through when the vocal chords are not vibrating are shaped into vowels and consonants mostly by areas of the vocal apparatus higher than the glottis, although the glottal opening plays a role in this. (See below.)

Intonation The rise and fall of the voice; its changes of pitch or melody. As Crystal (1972) has pointed out, intonation itself can be viewed either as a narrow system of *pitch change* or as a broad system which involves several other factors, including tone, pitch *range*, loudness, rhythmicality and tempo (q.v.). My own approach takes the latter, holistic view by and large, though I also use the term (inexactly) as equivalent to fundamental frequency (q.v.). Intonation has often been studied by creating abstract representations applicable to utterances generally, such as symbols for rise–fall, fall–rise, high–rise, and so on. It will be seen that my own system is less abstract than this and more closely related to individual *performance* (q.v.).

Loudness I use this term, as it is simpler than its technical, acoustic correlates, intensity and amplitude.

Performance The active experience on individual occasions of creating or reading (silently or aloud) poetry or narrative fiction. As opposed to the general governing of poetic and other fictional texts by rules or generalisations about structures not specific to a single performance (for further details, see Crystal, 1980).

Prosody The study of verse or prose music and rhythm. More strictly, the study of variations in pitch, loudness, tempo and rhythm. I employ the term loosely.

Quality/voice quality Quality means the pattern of frequencies characteristic of a particular sound. Voice quality means those features of speech which identify particular voices of particular people. They include pitch height, loudness level, tempo and timbre. (In reading a given poem a good reader may adopt a voice quality deemed suitable for it: thus, Yeats may be read with a singing lilt, Eliot slightly ponderously, and so on.)

Quantity A classical term not quite the same as duration: it refers to the durations of sounds and syllables when these are linguistically contrastive. For simplicity, I usually prefer *duration*.

Raw wave form A record by machine of the general frequency pattern of an utterance, including both the fundamental frequency (q.v.) and the other frequencies added by higher levels of the vocal apparatus (that is, parts of the throat and mouth above the glottis).

Stress The experience of 'beat' or of prominent emphasis upon a syllable in an utterance or poetic line – or, at least, apparently upon a syllable. The definition of 'stress' is, in fact, highly contentious, since in any performance (q.v.) of a poetic line there is a contribution to the emphatic pattern from abstract metrical pattern (if present), word 'stress', and the overall 'accent' linked with pitch changes and overall informational focus. I am deliberately combining all its distinctive senses into one, compounded term. This is because my whole concentration is not upon rule-governed metrics but upon what happens psychologically when we think we have experienced a stress upon a given syllable of a poetic line. (Ultimately, this can only be a matter for speculation.) For this, an admittedly muddly term is an advantage; and its use is not in any sense a critique of those kinds of analysis which require greater precision concerning this term. (For further discussion, S. Chatman, 1965, pp. 101–27).

Suprasegmental Some characteristic of vocal sound that stretches over several discrete units of sound (*segments*), such as an intonation contour. I talk generally of effects such as an overall pattern of stress or pitch change or changes in loudness and duration, etc., affecting, say, more than one syllable, and may use the term 'suprasegmental' to refer to them.

Tempo The speed of speech.

Voiced/voiceless/devoiced Voiced is used of that part of an utterance when the vocal chords are vibrating (and producing the F_o, etc.). All vowels are voiced, but many consonants, such as [t], are voiceless, while others, such as [d], are voiced. Voiceless parts of utterances do not give us the normal sense of pitch, although substitute effects can be created in whispering (W. Meyer-Eppler, in Bolinger, 1972) and the complicated frequency patterns of voiceless stretches are important in poetry. Voiced consonants may sometimes undergo *devoicing*, represented by a small circle under the phonetic symbol, as does the [z̥] of 'as' in 'as shown'.

Voicing pattern My own term for the pattern created by those stretches of an utterance when the vocal chords vibrate and those where they do not, either because the sound is voiceless or there is silence.

1

Rule and Performance

In the technical linguistic literature about poetic prosody, the linguists, while very ready to quote each other, rarely pay very much attention to what poets themselves say about their craft. Poet and linguist talk a different language. The poet always has a need for a speculative, working belief in what he is doing; he has to have a dim presentiment that expressing himself in rhythm and music is worth his while. And so he may make subjective, even mystical statements about the technicalities of his craft. But the linguist's is a slow, scientific work which will probably never be able to tell the poet all that he needs to know about his mental world as he creates a poem and experiences its music and rhythm. The poet cannot wait for the scientist.

When linguists study the prosody of poetry or ordinary speech they may examine the physiology of voice production, isolate for special examination acoustic phenomena such as syllabic duration, look at longer stretches of sound such as changes in pitch, investigate the meanings or grammatical structure of words in relation to rhythm, plot the 'informational focus' in a line or phrase, study the emotional significance of prosodic features as reported by various subjects, and so on. All this is of potential relevance to our inquiry. What will not be relevant are the recent linguistic attempts to substitute abstract rule structures for traditional ways of scanning poetry. Because it is an active research field in the same general area I shall talk about, I must be clear why it isn't useful to me.

Linguists can create a serviceable set of rules which will specify how most lines of a metrical poem can be ruled as admissible or not. I shall call this 'rule-governing' the line. It is proposed that for a given metre there is an abstract metrical pattern whose modifications are prescribed by the rules, rather as in generative grammar. The rules apply automatically and will generate all allowable permutations of the basic, abstract pattern; drawing up the rules does not depend on any actual data from performances of the line although performances may be judged by their standard. As W. K. Wimsatt (1971) has explained, this is different from traditional literary scansion into poetic feet, which describes a normal pattern for the metre – let us say, an iambic pentameter – and then admits allowable exceptions according to whether they work or not. The linguists' rules aim at stating exactly which actually realised lines are metrical and which not. To do so, they usually have either to decree that a syllable bears a weak or a strong stress or else that there are certain levels of stress which a syllable may be said to bear, as in the Trager–Smith convention from 0–4 inclusive (Trager and Smith, 1957).

The gulf between literary and linguistic disciplines may be appreciated from the disquiet expressed by Wimsatt, a knowledgeable literary prosodist, at the attempt by Halle and Keyser (1966; also 1971, 1975, 1981) working within the generative school of American linguistics, to rule-govern the generation of the iambic pentameter as practised by Chaucer. The two linguists thought of the pentameter as consisting at base of ten abstract positions (in reality usually filled by one syllable, though not always), to which may be added one or two extra-metrical syllables.

1 2 3 4 5 6 7 8 9 10
x x x x x x x x x x plus x x

They then specified what a 'stress maximum' is: a syllable of greater stress than the two adjacent syllables (x/x). It will be noticed that 'greater' introduces a binary opposition between weak and strong syllables. Briefly, they said a stress maximum (that is, the middle heavy stress) may only occupy even positions within the 10+ positions but that not every even position must be occupied by one. This forms the basis for judging whether the lines are metrical or not. As I'm mentioning this only to omit such approaches from my present account, the details of how such rules are realised within the poetic line can be left aside. Wimsatt's criticism was that with such a metrics the actual, flexible magic of Chaucer's iambic 'feet' would be lost; the lines and syllables would be ruled either in or out, weak or strong. Although certainly agreeing with this, I should perhaps qualify it. While linguistic-generative rules of this kind must seem clumsy to the trained literary ear, abstract rule structures capable of predicting poetic stress placement have their own interest – and more refined models, probably capable of more accuracy, are now in the field (for example, Kiparsky, 1977; Liberman and Prince, 1977). One can imagine the interest of such attempts for psychology, for machine synthesis of speech or poetry, and so on. No problem arises unless anyone should think that the poetic music itself had been explained or the *exact* degree of stress borne by any one syllable specified. That would confuse a purely abstract set of rules with the study of performance.

Literary criticism when studying actual poetic lines would have but a limited use for such rules, if at all, because the writing of a line is as much a performance as the reciting or reading of it.[1] Most likely, what a poet thinks he does when writing a poem enters at least to some extent into what he does in performance. For example, Funkhouser (1979, pp. 381–403) found that the American poet, Randall Jarrell, paid greater respect to the middle pauses in his 'The Death of the Ball Turret Gunner' than did professors of literature or novice readers, thus indicating his respect for the prosodic rules he had assumed he was following. Further, in an iambic pentameter for example, metrical patterns that skirt the borderlines of regularity can be the most fascinating and to rule them in or out according to abstract rules would be poetically trivial.

One may create methods of literary criticism which take some of their data from scientific work without exactly becoming linguistic science itself. I mean by this employing machines to measure, even though imperfectly, the music of poetry, its intonation, loudness, syllabic duration, the moments when the voice sounds in the throat and when it does not, and the frequency patterns created by the various vowels and consonants. Once having done that, however, the literary critic has to remember that his work belongs to the arts. The fullest *rapprochement* between the two disciplines remains that of Chatman (1965). He emphasised that performance (a purely linguistic record), scansion (reduction of linguistic data to the metrical system in one performance), and metrical analysis (the sum of all reasonable scansions), were separate inquiries, and demonstrated this by analysing acoustically and phonemically several machine recordings of Shakespeare's 18th sonnet.

We can get a long way into our subject if we ask what poetic stress is. Let's begin by comparing linguistic and poetic points of view.

Gimson (1973, pp. 94–102), a celebrated phonetician, discussed stress in the context of everyday speech performance. He suggested that there may be some measurable activity in the brain corresponding to our experience of a mental pulse or beat; this is probably the stimulus for our sensation of rhythm. It is, however, a 'speaker activity' which can only be interpreted linguistically by the listener when he consults his 'kinaesthetic memory' – that is, I presume, his memory of equivalent events in his own brain with their mental activity associated with the sensation of stress. It is a matching process, 'a reciprocal action of linguistic recollection rather than an exchange of meaningful signals'.

I am not entirely happy with this, on one or two grounds. First, we can deliberately 'mean' a stress, rather as we mean a word. When the parent scolds the child, 'Now just you listen to *me*', both parent and child can easily anticipate the stress that is to come and know that it will contribute to the communicated meaning. Second, Gimson's 'measurable activity in the brain' may be right – who knows? – but does not explicitly acknowledge a possible mutual influence, not part of the formal linguistic system, between stress and meaning. We might find that a semantically important word is perceived as bearing heavier stress than any of its acoustic features might lead us to expect. It has certainly been found that the stressed syllables in an utterance tend to be those in words of more significant factual content (Cutler and Foss, 1977). As in the parent–child example, stress is often consciously employed, too, for communicating emotion as well as meaning and this may affect our sense of how much a syllable is stressed. Either as speakers or listeners, we may anticipate to some degree many of the stresses that occur in ordinary speech. All this would imply that meaningful signals can be exchanged *via* stress, at least. It is very much a shadow land. However, and this is perhaps Gimson's point, we cannot create a dictionary of the 'meanings of different stresses' because they are extra-linguistic and cannot be satisfactorily specified outside the act of speaking. Allen (1970) puts the point well in discussing the location of rhythmic stress beats in English. His results 'illustrate the nature of stress in English as an element of a performance or speaking grammar of English'. This emphasis upon performance is much to my purpose: the concept we form of a syllable's exact degree of stress is a mental performance which is never exactly repeated and which, as Gimson says, is essentially made conscious by a process of recollection of some kind.

We shall see that there are acoustic correlates of stress, which are usually stated to be *duration, pitch, loudness* and *quality* (see Glossary), with dissension among linguists sometimes about which is more determinant. Marked changes to or levels of any of these correlates in themselves alone do not, however, 'constitute' stress.

Remembering that it is a mental concept, and leaving aside the question of 'kinaesthetic memory', I'm going to try a preliminary definition from my own standpoint in poetry rather than from a standpoint in linguistics. We shall find it very different:

> *Preliminary definition of stress in performance;* A poetic stress is apparently an instant when we unify into a single conception some of our sense of the form of a poetic line's sound as it has been developing over a small period of time. It necessarily involves unifying with our perception of the sound some conception of the meaning and emotional significance of the stress-bearing syllable in relation to the overall meaning and emotional significance of the poem.

This may seem much to load on to the experience of a poetic beat, for the realisations involved may be so minor as to be largely unconscious; a syllable speeds past our ears too quickly, almost, to appreciate. So I do not imply that we are conscious of all the elements which affect our judgement. Syntactical and orthodox metrical influences upon stress are not yet part of the definition but will be when I revise the definition in Chapter 8. We gradually become aware of the meaning and emotional significance of a poem and it may seem nonsense to claim that this awareness centres on stressed syllables. In fact, we cannot limit stress in actual performance just to the obvious heavy beats or to fixed levels of stress as in the 0–4 Trager–Smith notation; all conscious and unconscious comparisons between the relative prominence of sounds in a line grade down infinitesimally even to durations shorter than that of the syllables deemed to bear the stresses. Weak and strong stresses are already structures built from this interplay of minute sonic duration. Stress links the experience of infinitesimal sounds with the wider flow of the music. Even the above definition is incomplete; it asserts, however, that when reading poetry we pattern our understanding into moments of slightly greater awareness, centring on the incidence of major stresses. Put another way, the experience of stress is a tiny experience of artistic form.

2

Musical Form and Poetic Stress

The definition in my last chapter is unscientific and untestable, but is quite close to Coleridge's familiar description of the relation between a poem's individual moments of sound and the overall artistic form (Coleridge, 1920):

> If metre be superadded, all other parts must be made consonant with it. They must be such, as to justify the perpetual and distinct attention to each part, which an exact correspondent recurrence of accent and sound are calculated to excite . . . [A poem] . . . is discriminated by proposing to itself such delight from the *whole*, as is compatible with a distinct gratification from each component *part*.

We add to this a literary critic's statement about a poem's form. This is Northrop Frye (1957):

> The process of academic criticism begins, then, with reading a poem through to the end, suspending value-judgments while doing so. Once the end is reached, we can see the whole design of the work as a unity. It is now a *simultaneous* pattern radiating out from a centre, not a narrative moving in time. (My italics)

There are many problems with Coleridge's description as a whole and I refer readers to Richards's (1950) analysis of them. But we shall ignore particularly the remarks about metre. Coleridge is talking of a complex of intellectual and emotional factors,[1] which he calls by the Horatian word, 'delight', and which results from the consonance between these factors and the individual sounds of the poem; and then a similar delight resulting from unifying all individual parts into the whole. As for Frye, I doubt that we can quite suspend value-judgements and his description concentrates upon a more abstractly formal question than I am comfortable with. Furthermore, if form extends from a centre, we must say that the centre is not locatable, since it is not a simple spatio-temporal point. All the same, he implies that when we unite all the moments of our linear experience of reading a poem we attain a sense of form in which that linear experience still seems active ('radiating') as energising principle. We might put Coleridge and Frye together and say that to see the poem all-at-once involves an active resolving into unity of any 'emotional' and intellectual-semantic 'delight' along with the sounds and rhythm. This must surely mean that within the linear experience we carry out smaller acts of mental reflection in which we appreciate the developing form. This may be done at line endings, of course, but I believe that poetic stresses are also smaller moments of comprehension of this kind.

After reading both poems and novels we pattern a text retrospectively in our minds in myriad ways: recent parts of the text may take mental precedence over earlier, or vice versa; the reader does not wait until the end before acquiring a sense of its form; and the form itself may be either 'open' or only closed ambiguously. None of this destroys a fundamental logic that form has ultimately to be judged against potential closure and, ideally considered, should be perfect in its unity of the linear and the totality. Writers' experiments with open form depend ultimately on its possibility of dynamic closure, although literature can go a very long way into formlessness without destroying itself. Open forms, that is, are usually closed in parts of the whole.[2]

The best-known statement in modern English poetry about artistic form comes in the first of Eliot's *Four Quartets*, 'Burnt Norton'. An apparent drawback in approaching my subject through Eliot is that it obliges me to use words like 'eternity'. But to use the word 'instant', as I shall have to in Chapter 8 when I revise the preliminary definition of stress, will raise similar problems to those raised by the word 'eternity'; so the issue must be dealt with in that chapter in any case. The passage reads:

> Words move, music moves
> Only in time; but that which is only living
> Can only die. Words, after speech, reach
> Into the silence. Only by the form, the pattern,
> Can words or music reach
> The stillness, as a Chinese jar still
> Moves perpetually in its stillness.

Not the stillness of the violin, while the note lasts,
Not that only, but the coexistence,
Or say that the end precedes the beginning
And the end and the beginning were always there
Before the beginning and after the end.
And all is always now.[3]

It will be clearest for my subsequent argument if I relate Eliot's assertions to music in a detailed way, and some readers very aware of his meaning may need patience for the next few paragraphs. It will not matter, however, whether readers are familiar with the actual musical examples or can read music or not.

In Figure 2.1 we see a few bars comprising the main theme of Haydn's *Sinfonia Concertante*:[4]

Figure 2.1

Suppose we have just started listening to the sinfonia concertante and are getting the hang of the vaguely annunciatory passages that begin it. Then we come to this, the theme, now clearly distinguished. Contrasting it with the vaguer opening passages will add meaning to its greater clarity, as it states, according to Howard, a musical question and an answer.

We shall eventually understand that this theme will structure the work, and by the time the last bars of the whole piece have sounded, its formal role will be complete. As Blamires (1969, p. 36) says about a symphony: 'The first bar of the symphonic movement would be strictly meaningless were it not that the last bar already exists.' We might adapt Frye: after we have heard the whole sinfonia concertante the bars which are past and have 'moved' in time are held in our minds as though 'still' but simultaneously continuing to move, and as though each of them existed again in the present moment. Without this 'still' conception of continuing, remembered movement there could be no experience of form. At the end of the piece we try to retain in memory all those moving relationships from bars that were past, through bars that were present, towards bars that were future at given moments inside the piece. It is rather like a ruler with a windowed slide containing a vertical line, except that we have to imagine the window as able to exist in many places or points of formal recognition at once: pasts, presents, and futures are all held *in memory* as though present yet retaining their temporal relationships.

We began by supposing that in our listening we had only reached the above bars, shortly after the opening. To grasp even this fragment's limited form we follow it from beginning to end, and finally conceive its form as an 'answered question', which implies that we retain simultaneously in memory both the sequence of question and answer and this formal conception, 'answered question', in which all the notes simultaneously exist. Let's take note A, marked in Figure 2.1: when we hear it, or shortly afterwards, we sense that the answer is beginning. This is slightly different from reaching the end of the whole sinfonia concertante and looking back, because in the middle of this theme-fragment a contribution has to be made from anticipation. If the whole work finished at note A we should be confused. The question would remain unanswered, a work promising to be long turned out to be short: we would have got the form wrong. Whereas note A's real significance is to begin the answer to the question posed by the main theme in the whole sinfonia concertante.

To grasp the formal status of note A, then, we unify memory, present experience and anticipation of the theme-fragment into a moving-still conception. The input from the past, 'X' of the piece, the present experience, 'A', and the anticipation of the future, 'Y', are imagined as happening simultaneously, with X post-reported (from past memory) on to A and Y back-reported on to it, through anticipation (the back-reporting of a forward-looking search), before we can interpret our hearing of A. Both X and Y point an arrow inwards towards A, which is like a vertical line of the present, so thin that even note A's own durations have to be reported inwards towards the line, or otherwise we do not even know what note we are listening to.

Traversi (1976) supposes that St Augustine is a likely main source for Eliot's passage. Of course, as St Augustine (1930) knew, we cannot bring the present moment, the vertical line, into consciousness: we are always too late to think a present moment: it is experienced as a 'specious present'. Our formal conception of XAY is actually constructed in our (perhaps very short-term) memory, a working model in which the past and future are still reported inwards on to a present instant. But the model pretends that we are still having the experience because its point of unity is pictured in memory as a present moment seen as the Now, even though it has gone by. This is the temporal paradox, because we have just said that we cannot consciously experience a present moment. The paradox of artistic form is such that it represents the experience of the present itself as having a content from past and future, or at least gives us a strong impression of this unity as constantly recoverable.

Ideally considered, note A would then be unified with the form of the whole sinfonia concertante. But no doubt there is no such thing as a perfect work of art. Even an individual note is perhaps never absolutely grasped, because our awareness of it depends upon immediately-past and anticipated sounds even in the minute duration of the note. The mind is working on other matters all the time and dulls reality down slightly. Only the present moment, the instant, unimaginably, would be truly vivid.

(Whenever, subsequently, I use this trite word, 'instant', I am not talking about what Thomas Pynchon calls in *The Crying of Lot 49* 'the religious instant'. We have too knowing a cynicism about such phrases these days. I am talking about an entity difficult to define, a 'notional instant' in which we imagine we unify artistic form. While I think there is a spiritual dimension even to that, my drawing of an example from Eliot implies no religious doctrine about it.)

Before I consider poetry I am going to keep with music because its more obvious melody will help to show what factors give heavy stress to a syllable. My example is a record made in the 1920s by the great Black singer, Bessie Smith, the 12-bar 'Backwater Blues'. The advantage of a blues is this: the verses are in two lines but the first line is repeated. In theory, the repetition should be identical to the first singing of line one: after all, both words and tune are the same. But when Bessie repeats the first line she usually changes the whole musical pattern to draw attention to words or themes that had been neglected the first time. That is, she puts a different pattern of stresses or emphases on to the line. She sings:

> Backwater Blues done caused me to pack my things and go,
> Backwater Blues done caused me to pack my things and go,
> 'Ços my house fell down and I can't live there no mo'.

Rather than give the musical notes for the first line, which would tell us nothing to the purpose, I'm going to sing to myself as nearly as possible what Bessie Smith sings and, as I do so, let my hand instinctively trace a pattern on a piece of paper before me, expressing graphically what I perform and simultaneously hear (Figure 2.2). The rise and fall of the trace will express changes in pitch, the length of any 'hump' the length of a syllable, and the thickness of the line a very subjective impression combining both my sense of syllabic 'accent' and of loudness. The combination is because I find these factors very hard to separate mentally, although I am *not* identifying a perception of accent with a perception of loudness. The word 'accent' here means a main stress in a line resulting from a syllable's being a principal information focus in the overall intonation. As the Glossary makes clear, this book normally uses 'stress' in a deliberately muddled way that includes 'accent' as a major example. Chatman (1965) has distinguished stress and accent acoustically, but in studies of performance to distinguish the terms too clearly would break up the flow of sound being studied. Having acknowledged this, I shall now revert to calling 'accent' 'stress' in my muddling way. A break in my graph shows a conventional break in sound, which is not the same as the voicing breaks I shall discuss in subsequent chapters.

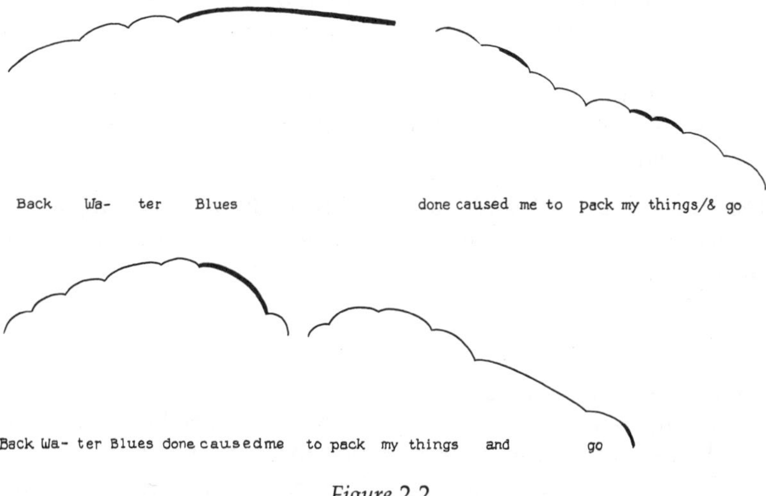

Figure 2.2

When I give lectures on this subject and spontaneously draw these lines on a blackboard while croakily singing, audiences not only agree that these traces match, near enough, their own experience of listening to the record, but also that 'Blues' carries the principal stress in the first rendition of line one, with subsidiary stresses on 'caused' and 'pack'. In the repetition, 'Blues' bears less stress, and 'caused' carries principal emphasis, they say. Now we can ask some questions:

Line One

(1) Why is 'Blues' stressed? Probably because it is part of the song's title, helps to sell the record, emphasises the blues genre and is important therefore for both meaning and emotional response.
(2) What features of its sound, as sketched, help it to appear heavily stressed?
    (a) It is long in duration.
    (b) It flattens pitch after notes that mount towards it; that is, it represents a change in pitch pattern.
    (c) Audiences usually agree from listening to the record that it is louder than the previous and immediately subsequent syllables.
    (d) It is 'blued', partly because of pitch flattening but additionally because of diphthongisation of the vowel and a nasal timbre; that is, elements of voice quality affect our sense of stress.
    (e) The quick syllables before it emphasise its duration.
    (f) It is followed by a pronounced pause; in fact it respects a middle pause in the line.

(Analysis of 'caused' and 'pack' in this rendition would throw up similar features: 'pack', for example, rises in pitch during a general pitch fall.)

Line One (Repeat)

(1) Why is 'caused' stressed in the repeat? Probably because Bessie Smith has already stressed 'Blues' once – no need to do it again; she can select another information focus. So this time the line is going to stress *what* the blues caused her to do: it will emphasise the line's main message.
(2) What features of its sound help it to appear heavily stressed?
    (a) It is slightly longer in duration.

(b) It has a marked downward pitch, with a glide on the vowel.
(c) I believe it is louder.
(d) It is chosen for 'blueing' this time; voice quality added too.
(e) It represents the middle pause but in fact cannot be separated syntactically from 'me'; so there is a brief pause after 'me'.

It will be seen that we have arrived at the linguists' main acoustic correlates for our perception of stress: *duration, pitch change* up or down, *loudness* and *voice quality*. We have quietly added other factors:

(i) The influence of syllabic durations, pitch, loudness (and voice quality) that have occurred both before and after the syllable we are considering seem to affect our sense of how much it is stressed, since they are part of how we measure the change.
(ii) A pause after a syllable can throw back on to it an increased sense of its prominence.
(iii) These effects interact with the meaning and emotional importance of the syllable or word.

I don't think linguists would quarrel with (i) to (ii). It is recognised that our estimates of duration etc. are relative, and this presumably means relative to pauses too. As for (iii), we need to examine this further, although we shall again find support from linguists. I must ask the reader to believe that there is a curious effect with 'and go' in the repetition, where 'and' is given unusual duration. The ear refuses to interpret this duration as a stress signal but takes it as a device of *suspense*, adding a slight drama to 'go'. As I have said, Cutler and Foss (1977) have reported that words bearing higher stress are typically words of greater semantic content; they are also easier for listeners to process mentally. (There is some evidence that pitch discrimination, too, can be affected by the absence or presence of linguistic content.[5]) Therefore, when a stress correlate such as extra duration is given to 'and', which has little semantic content, we may speculate that we scarcely hear the word as stressed but as extended in a suspenseful way. If this, admittedly subjective, statement is credited, there is a negative influence from a word's lack of semantic content upon our sense of its stress.

We may now apply these observations in a preliminary way to three lines from Yeats's 'Sailing to Byzantium', whose theoretical heavy stresses I have marked, with 'irregularities' shown in brackets.

/ / (/) / /
An aged man is but a paltry thing
/ / (/) / /
A tattered coat upon a stick, unless
(x) / / / / /
Soul clap its hands and sing, and louder sing . . .

Figure 2.3 shows what happened when two readers performed these lines (both with a slight Irish lilt) into machinery which draws a trace of the fundamental frequency (F_o) as recorded by two electrodes placed at the glottis.

Since fundamental frequency (see Glossary) gives us our primary sense of pitch, if the voice goes high the pen rises; if low the pen falls. If what is being spoken is a clearly distinguished voiceless consonant or a devoiced one or if there is silence, the pen falls rapidly to zero. For technical reasons, readers should concentrate upon the overall direction taken by the pen line and not upon the very minor zig-zags, or over-sharp dips and peaks of the pen. What results is quite a sensitive trace of the voice's intonation contour, together with a less accurate but serviceable record of how long the durations of the voiced segments of the line are: while the trace is kept above zero the vocal chords are producing 'voice' (the glottis is buzzing), and when it falls to zero we have a voiceless interval – for example at the end of a word or during a voiceless consonant or a transition from one voiced sound to another.

We have, therefore, a visible record of some factors already distinguished as correlates of stress: 'pitch' (actually fundamental frequency), duration (in the sense of length of voiced segment) and pause. Approximate indication of loudness is retrieved from a conventional microphone's raw wave form (taking amplitude), but this is mostly used for checking details. Much of the analysis in this book will be done from the simpler F_o contour shown for 'Sailing to Byzantium'.

Although myself and a linguistics M.A. student who had never discussed poetry with me recorded quite separately, similarities between the directions taken by the pen line for each reader are much more striking than the differences. Except for the third line, the basic patterning into groups of syllables – what I shall later call 'voicing patterns' (see Glossary) – is almost identical. What is also

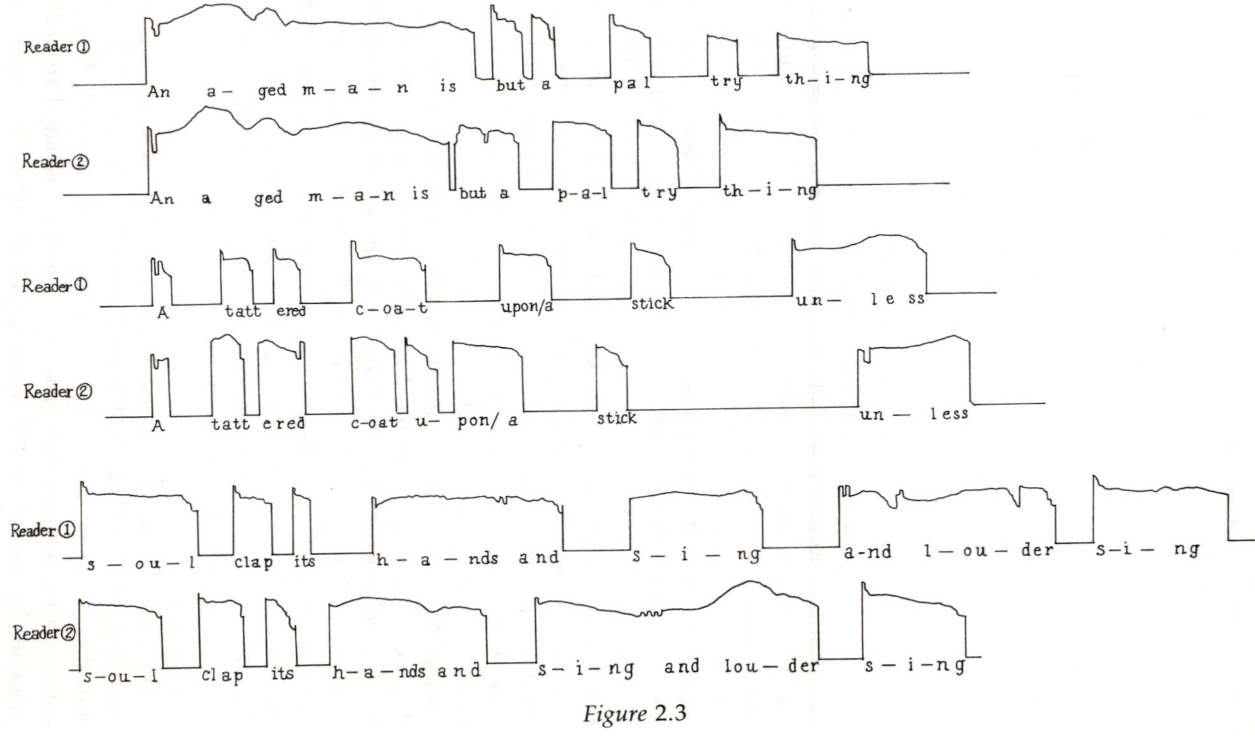
Reader ①
An a- ged m – a – n is but a pal try th-i-ng
Reader ②
An a ged m – a-n is but a p-a-l t ry th – i – ng
Reader ①
A tatt ered c-oa-t upon/a stick un- l e ss
Reader ②
A tatt e red c-oat u- pon/ a stick un – less
Reader ①
s – ou – l clap its h – a – nds a nd s – i – ng a-nd l – ou – der s-i – ng
Reader ②
s-ou-l cl ap its h- a – nds a n d s – i – ng and lou – der s – i – ng

Figure 2.3

remarkable is the very much greater variation of pattern between individual lines of the same poem.

Now let us look at the lines to show how each reader suggests acoustically that a syllable has heavy stress. Comparing Figure 2.3 with the traditional scansion pattern makes plain that syllabic duration and pitch change up or down are often associated with the experience of these stresses. The 'a' of 'aged' is relatively long, especially for reader 1; 'man' is very long, 'pal-' is slightly longer than 'try' and has a sharper pitch change for reader 1 but not for reader 2, while 'tat-' of 'tattered' is neither particularly long nor marked by pitch. The amplitude trace, however, not shown, indicates that it is extra loud.

'Stick' is a special case that is worth dwelling on, for reader 1 uses a different way of stressing it from reader 2. He gives it more duration and longer pitch fall; then he leaves a pause and gives 'unless' long duration. Reader 2 leaves a much longer pause after 'stick', gives 'unless' a longish duration and the word 'stick' itself shorter duration, although a sharper pitch fall than reader 1. Both readers agree in hurrying through the syllables before 'stick'; then they fall in pitch on 'stick' to mark the pause, making it more definite. As O'Connor and Arnold (1973) have noted: 'All statements associated with tone groups containing falling nuclear tones . . . sound definite and complete in the sense that the speaker wishes them to be regarded as separate items of interest.' There is little so far, however, that would seem to indicate a heavy stress. Reader 1 gives 'stick' a marked peak in loudness (not shown) and isolates the word from preceding syllables; whereas reader 2 gives it quite low volume – the word is probably only noticeable because he also isolates it in the line. Intuitively, therefore, one might think reader 1 had given 'stick' greater stress. When audiences listen to the natural voice recordings, they are unsure which reader gives the greater stress, some even saying that it is the shortness of duration in reader 2's version that adds stress to the word. We may see short syllables connoting stress in a phrase such as 'The clock ticked'.

The orthodox acoustic correlates of stress are now looking quite complicated. 'Stick' can be stressed partly by any of the following: duration (long *or* short); pitch change (up *or* down); loudness; coming after hurried syllables; being slightly isolated from those syllables by a pronounced voicing gap before it; having a pause after it; the contrast between that pause and the fast enjambement at the end of the line. This is to say nothing of inter-line effects, such as its assonance with 'thing' in the first line and 'sing' in the third, the sonic echo of [k] sounds with 'clap', and so on. Also, it is semantically and emotionally very important because it is the symbol of distaste for old age. And the pause that comes after it is syntactically important because 'unless' turns the stanza from this distaste into a celebration of age in a transformed state. The reader may sense what a little artistic complex this word has become.

But now we have the familiar temporal paradox which arises in all questions of artistic form and is also known of by linguists in relation to stress.[6] If we wanted to express *exactly* where in the word 'stick' the stress actually occurs we might try to tap it out. (If you get subjects to tap as they read poetry into the machinery it is not entirely satisfactory because they then tend to read in a doggerel way;[7] this does not, however, destroy the essential point.) Probably, they will site the tap at vowel onset;[8] where doesn't matter so much as the fact that they will think it sensible at all to tap at a precise, conceptual point. But at the point chosen the full duration of the vowel and its change in pitch haven't happened yet. Nor has the pause that comes afterwards. And the quick syllables before have already happened. Judged as an isolated point in time, the loudness has no meaning without relation to the loudness of other syllables. And yet we try to tap a single point of time like this:

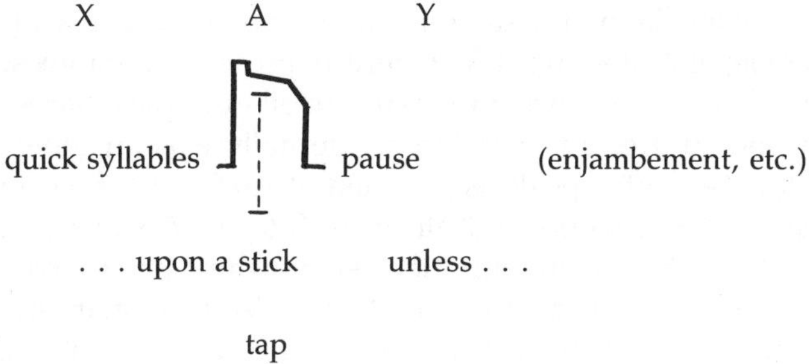

We seem to be tapping a point which has no duration, and whose pitch, supposing it existed, would have no significance unless we compared it with pitches in the past and those yet to come. The same is true of its loudness and, indeed, of its voice quality. We are again creating a model in memory in which X is reported forward on to A, and Y is back-reported on to it.

Let me just set on one side one way of talking about this: scientists sometimes talk of such phenomena in terms of 'bunching' or 'chunking' operations performed by the brain. It is supposed that information is held in a short-term memory store and then 'decoded' in some way at a given moment. Even fast-speed typing has been explained in this way.[9] It may one day prove possible to create some scientific description of how the brain 'reports' a past and future content inwards into a single moment. What remains mysterious is the confidence with which we think we are trying to tap an instant of time; whether that confidence is realistically based or not, it is an immense confidence like confidence about *a priori* truth.

To sum up: what is strange is not that our brains can accommodate all the elements in my description of the forces playing upon 'stick' and rescue from them a sense of a beat made in a rhythmic pattern, for our brains probably always work in ways analogous to this. What is strange is that to express duration and flow of pitch we try to tap a particular point even though it is paradoxical to do so. We keep encountering that ancient question about time: how is it, since the present moment takes no time at all, that we seem to experience the passing of time through a succession of present moments? I have referred to St Augustine's *Confessions*; I might also have referred to his *De Musica* (n.d.) where he was greatly interested in allied questions in relation to music and prosody. As Eliot well knew, medieval writers such as St Augustine and St Anselm claimed that God's mind and God's consciousness of the whole of finite time and of eternity present a paradox which, formally, has a similar structure to the small example of stress: that is, past and future are regarded as eternally existing now – the whole of time, so to speak, is reported inwards. All the events in the past of the universe and all in its future exist in the divine eternal present but again with their relationships preserved.

In *Four Quartets*, Eliot implies that an experience of artistic form is like experiencing the eternal in a finite dynamic. For Eliot's traditional Christianity, the eternal, in the form of Christ, had to intervene in the finite. 'If all time is eternally present / All time is unredeemable,' he wrote at the beginning of 'Burnt Norton'. Nevertheless, for him an experience of artistic form is a hint that there is an eternal aspect of time held in the mind of God: 'all is always now.'

I am not concentrating here upon anything so majestic as

eternity, simply on the tiny phenomenon of poetic stress. A stress is born in time, and in sound, meaning and emotion; but it also stands outside time in a sort of minor, eternal present, a trembling instant which half stands still, partly resisting the flow of the line which creates it. It probably represents a little model of how our minds relate the instant of time to the flow of time; here lies its very great fascination.

3
Intonation Contours

A method will now be established for comparing the intonation contours of different readers of verse. Lines by the Tudor poet, Sir Thomas Wyatt (1503–42) will illustrate the kinds of problem that arise because Tudor pronunciation would not always have been that of a modern reader and because Wyatt seems to have composed by respecting the spoken rhythms of his verse rather than by observing, here, a more formal iambic pattern. Shortly after him, the iambic pentameter became more regular under influence from the Earl of Surrey and later Tudor and Elizabethan Humanists, as Jones has usefully described.[1] This may make it difficult for inexperienced readers to judge intonation so exactly as in a tighter metrics.

> So unwarely was never no man caught
> With steadfast look upon a goodly face
> As I of late; for suddenly me thought
> My heart was torn out of his place.

My first step is to do to the Wyatt what I did to the Bessie Smith song, that is, repeat the verse to myself while letting my hand trace, almost unconsciously, a pattern on a piece of paper before me (Figure 3.1). I shall end-stop the resulting graphs for clarity. I drop or raise my graph line to express my sense of pitch up or down, and I thicken or lighten the line to express where a given syllable seems to represent a region of main stress. I call it 'leaning into' a syllable when, reading, I have that idea of stress as spread over a small region of time. But I have already asserted that stress is something we try to tap at an instant: the ambiguity is caused by the constant dichotomy between stress as an instant whose content is given by duration. If the reader repeats the poem to himself or herself while tracing over my patterns he may see what I've done, even if not agreeing with the way I read.

I shall leave the amateurish look of these traces as witness to the spontaneity of the process and to show the varying pace of the syllables. My main stresses fall on the emotionally and

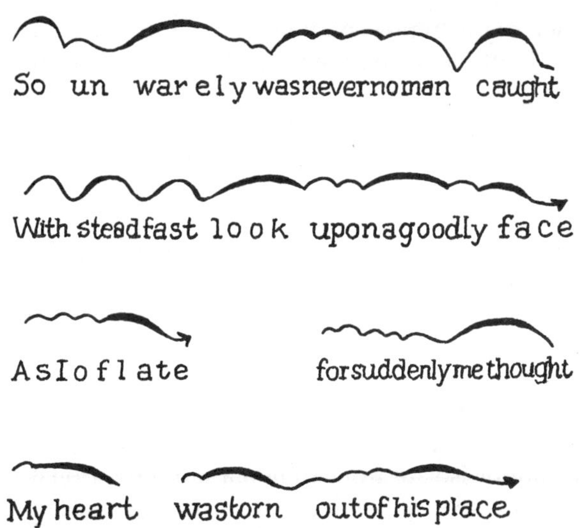

Figure 3.1

semantically important syllables, as usual in the English lyric tradition: 'ware', 'caught', 'look', 'face', 'late' (a special case – see end of chapter), 'thought', 'heart', 'torn', 'place'. The virtue of this inaccurate, impressionistic method is that it deliberately confuses a visible, hand-tracing process and those psychological factors which, using machines, we should have more rigorously to distinguish. I can, here, talk about stress appearing in the hand trace because I have put it there, whereas stress never appears as such in a machine trace. A comparison of these hand traces with those created on machine by reader C (myself) below will show both that my hand trace has meaning and that there is a close relationship between machine records and subjective impression. I created the Figure 3.1 drawing, in its essentials, some years before having recourse to machines.

Now let me remind the reader of the three traces that emerge from the linguistic machinery. The complete set of traces may be inspected in Figure 3.4.

(a) From an ordinary acoustic microphone I register the overall vocal frequencies from all parts of the mouth apparatus, yielding a rather crude representation called the voice raw wave form. This is the fuzzy frequencies in the middle of the traces.

(b) From the same microphone I register 'loudness' (actually 'amplitude' of the raw wave form – see Glossary). This is the top main trace in the figure, ignoring the zig-zag timing spike at the very top.

(c) From electrodes placed at the reader's glottis (Adam's apple) I register the fundamental frequency, F_0, of the glottal vibrations. This gives the basic intonation contour (perceived as 'pitch') and is the bottom trace. Figures 3.2 and 3.3 show this F_0 trace.

My speculative definition of stress now determines the way in which I measure these machine traces for literary critical purposes. We know that we cannot isolate from the data any one acoustic correlate that will exactly specify the degree of stress on a syllable during performance. We cannot even identify a nexus of acoustic correlates – duration, loudness, pitch and quality – which will specify it because stress is conceptual, is influenced by intellectual–semantic–syntactical and aesthetic–emotional factors, and presents space–time problems inseparable from the notion of unity. Linguists would perhaps agree, but think the point trivial since a matter for the privacy of consciousness. Approximate levels of stress will be sufficient for them to create their rules for positional assignment of stress. The poet, on the other hand, in creating the rhythm of his verse line *is* chasing this will-o'-the-wisp of great exactness in our perceptions: his aim is always to develop a perfect ear.

With the previous chapter's caution that in using linguistic machinery the critic is accepting a linear trace to describe mental phenomena that are not linear, we can employ the machinery to suggest what several features of a 'normal' reading of a poem or part of a poem might look like. By 'normal' is meant a reading not marked by dramatic emphasis, accentuation of emotional expression, or unconventional interpretation. All readings will be somewhat marked by these factors. Most of the prejudice against this kind of analysis arises because literary critics rule out definitive specification of pitch but do not see the merits of partial specification.

The methodological principles are these:

(1) Record on the machinery and on tape several readers of the same lines of verse, asking them to read musically but without special or dramatic emphasis.
(2) Test by opinion poll which tape-recorded reading a group of experienced listeners judges to make the melody most aptly fitted to the words of the poem. It is usually not crucial which of these readings is chosen as 'best', but the important thing is to weed out readings that are evidently bad or aberrant. Listeners have little doubt about these.
(3) I generally choose the fundamental frequency trace (pitch) to work on. Loudness tells us little of delicacy and is difficult to measure; syllabic duration is not only hard to measure but depends upon overall tempo, which varies even in two performances by the same reader. Tempo alters inter-syllable relationships and no doubt interacts with intonation. In ordinary speech, for example, recent research shows a large variation in the rate at which the speech is produced, and this is not just because of pausing.[2] Even normalising for tempo mathematically doesn't eliminate this difference in relationships set up by a faster reading.
(4) Respect the limitations of trace (c), which is a not very subtle linear representation and cannot correlate to any conceptual act. The only features we can investigate from it are:
   (i) Pitch.
   (ii) Approximate intervals of continuous voicing, voiceless intervals and silence.
   (iii) Even more approximate syllabic durations at those points in a line where a syllabic division coincides with an interval or marked change in the voicing. (Often, it does not.)
(5) The best reading polled under principle 2, above, is then chosen as a standard against which to match all other readings and a system is developed for matching one trace outline against another, not by using conventionalised symbols but by respecting the actual shape of the intonation contour.

(Linguistic literature is full of the difficulties involved in specifying an intonation contour and different notation systems proliferate. Ladd (1980) gives good coverage of the issues.[3] Other multifarious small technical problems arise, for whose discussion I refer readers to my original paper (Oliver, 1983).)

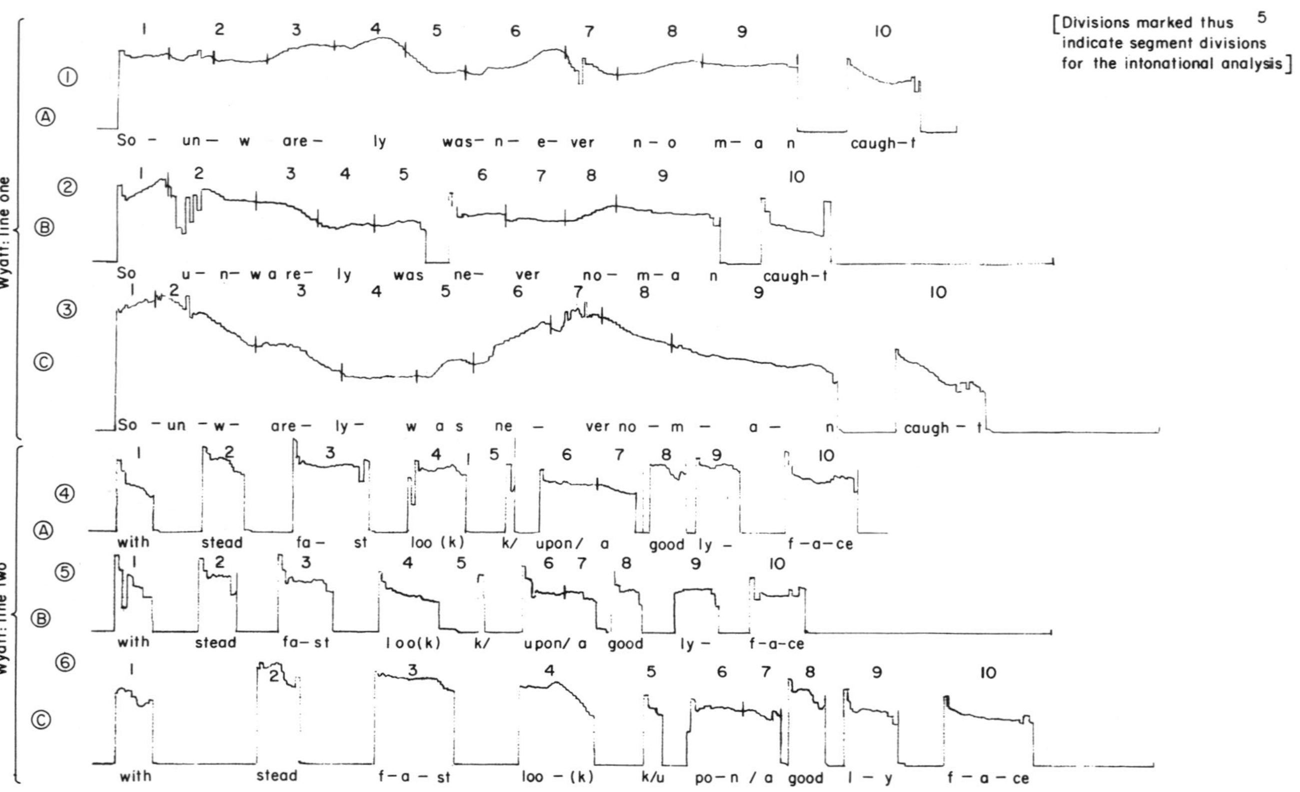
[Divisions marked thus 5 indicate segment divisions for the intonational analysis]
Wyatt: line one
Wyatt: line two
So - un - w are - ly was - n - e - ver n - o m - a n caugh - t
So u - n - w a re - ly was ne - ver no - m - a n caugh - t
So - un - w - are - ly - w a s ne - ver no - m - a - n caugh - t
with stead fa - st loo (k) k/ upon/ a good ly - f - a - ce
with stead fa - st l oo(k) k/ upon/ a good ly - f - a - ce
with stead f - a - st loo - (k) k/u po - n / a good l - y f - a - ce

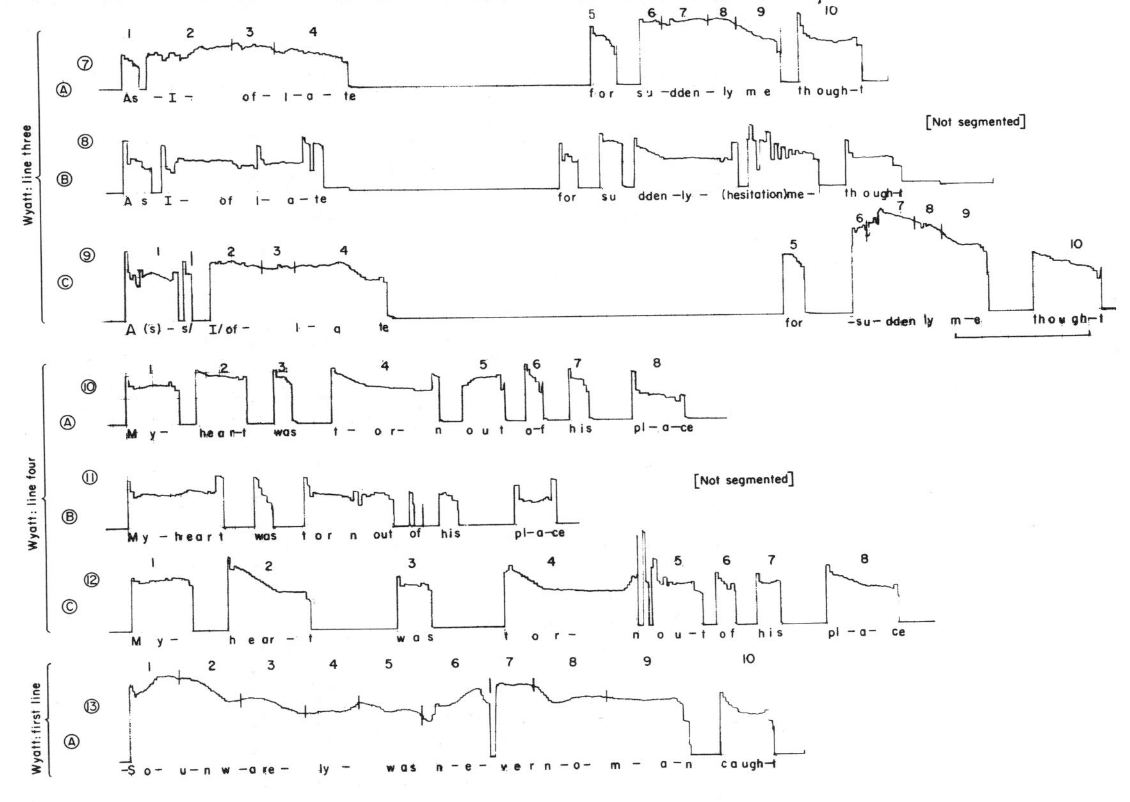

Wyatt: line three
Wyatt: line four
Wyatt: first line
[Not segmented]
[Not segmented]
As - I - of - l - a - te for su -dden - ly m e th ough-t
A s I - of l- a - te for su dden -ly - (hesitation)me - th ough-t
A ('s) - s/ I/of - l - a te for -su- dden ly m-e thou gh-t
My - hear-t was t - o r- n o u t o-f his pl-a-ce
My - heart was t or n out of his pl-a-ce
M y - h e ar - t w a s t o r - n o u - t of his pl - a - ce
S o- u-n w -a re - ly - w a s n - e - v e r n -o- m - a-n caugh-t

Figure 3.2

Wyatt: line one
So un w-are - ly was ne - ver n - o m - a - n caught
Wyatt: line two
with stead fast loo(k)- k/u - pon /a good- ly face
Wyatt: line three
As I - of la- te for su d d e n l y me thought
Wyatt: line four
My hea r t was t - o r n out/of his pla - ce
(omitted)

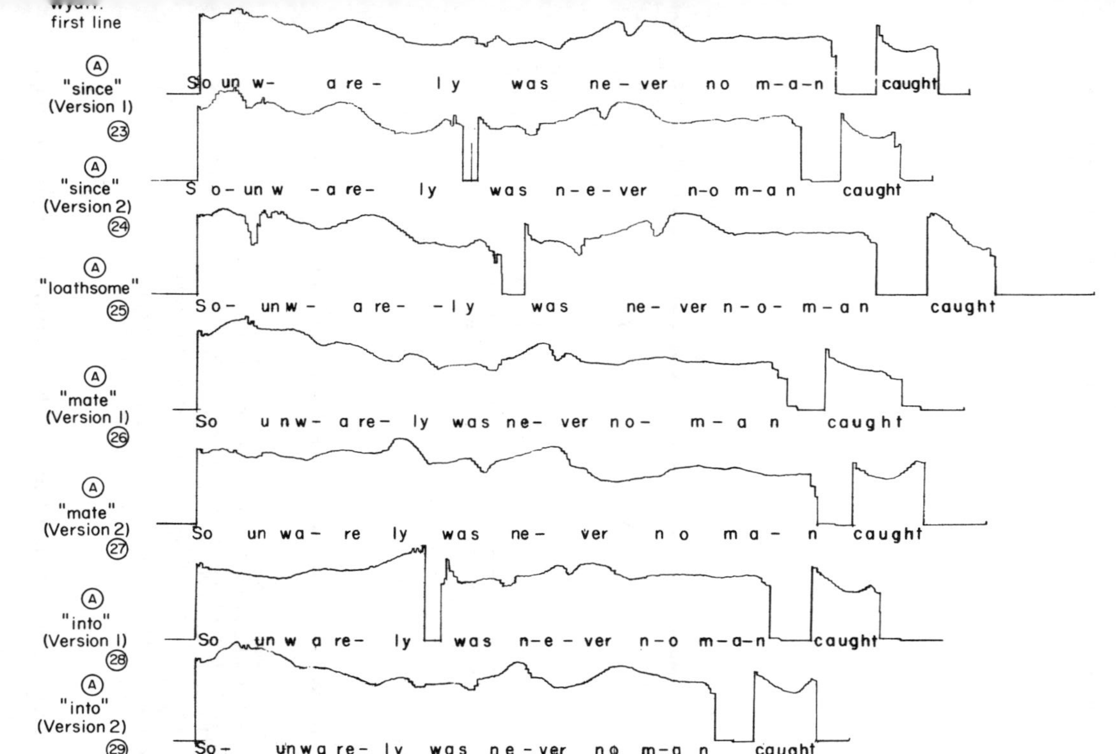
first line
Ⓐ "since" (Version 1) ㉓
So un w- a re- l y was ne - ver no m-a-n caught
Ⓐ "since" (Version 2) ㉔
S o- un w -a re- ly was n-e-ver n-o m-a n caught
Ⓐ "loathsome" ㉕
So- un w- a re- -l y was ne- ver n-o- m-a n caught
Ⓐ "mate" (Version 1) ㉖
So u n w- a re- ly was ne- ver no- m- a n caug h t
Ⓐ "mate" (Version 2) ㉗
So un wa- re ly was ne- ver n o ma- n caught
Ⓐ "into" (Version 1) ㉘
So un w a re- ly was n-e - ver n-o m-a-n caught
Ⓐ "into" (Version 2) ㉙
So- unwa re- ly was ne-ver no m-a n caught

Figure 3.3

Table 3.1

Reader	Reading no.	1	2	3	4	5	6	7	8	9	10	Match to target %
Line 1												
A	1	—	—	/	_/‾	╰	/	\	/	—	╰	15
B	2	/	\	\	_	—	—	\	/	\	\	50
C	3	/	\	‾\	—	/	_/	/	\	\	╰	Target
A	13	/‾	\	‾\	_/	\	_/	—	_	—	╰	55
D	14	\	/	—	—	\ ı	—	/‾	—	—	‾\	25
E	15	/	\	—	∧	‾\ ı	—	/‾	_/	\	╰	55
Line 2												
A	4	\	\	‿	—	|	\	\	\	\	╰	70
B	5	\	\	\	\	|	\	—	\	—	╰	70
C	6	\	\	\	\	\	\	\	\	\	╰	Target
D	16	—	\	—	—	|	—	—	—	\	╯	20
E	17	—	\	\	V	|	—	\	\	\	╯	55
Line 3												
A	7	\	/	—	\	\	\	—	—	\	‿	45
C	9	—	\	—	‾\	\	/	\	\	\	‿	Target
D	18	/	—	—	_/	\	\	\	\	\	‿	65
E	19	\	_/	\	V	\	\	/‾	—	\	‿	30
Line 4												
A	10	—	╰	\	╰	/	\	\	╰			75
C	12	—	╰	\	╰	\	\	‿	╰			Target
D	20	/‾	/	\	\	—	\	\	—			37.5
E	21	—	—	\	\	—	\	\	╰			56.25

N.B. All gradients and durations of gradient idealized within each segment.
For segmentation, see respective graphs.
Average similarities to the target segments in all four lines:
Reader A = 51.25%
Reader A substituting reading No. 13 for No. 1 = 61.25%
Reader B (two lines only) = 60%
Reader D = 36.9%
Reader E = 49.1%
Average similarities, Reader D compared with Reader E (i.e. the two "worst" readings):
54.7%
Line one. Reader D and E are alike in 4 segments out of 10 = 40%
Line two. Reader D and E are alike in 6 segments out of 10 = 60%
Reader C's contour differs from the others at segment 5.
Line three. Reader D and E are alike in 5 segments out of 10 = 50%.
Reader B's reading No. 8 not considered good enough for contour analysis.
Line four. Reader D and E are alike in 5.5 segments out of 8 = 68.75%.
Reader B's reading No. 11 not considered good enough for contour analysis.

Five readers performed the four lines into the linguistic machinery:

So unwarely was never no man caught
With steadfast look upon a goodly face
As I of late; for suddenly me thought
My heart was torn out of his place.

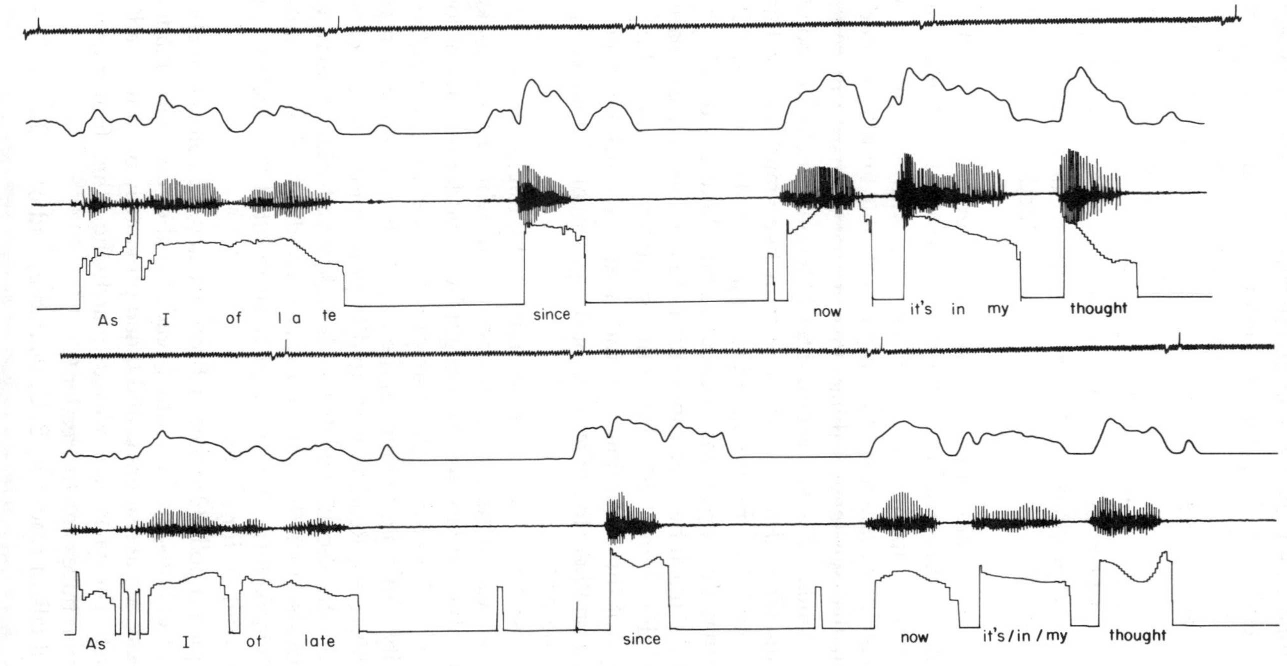
As I of l a te since now it's in my thought
As I of late since now it's / in / my thought

Figure 3.4

The following remarks about the relation between interpretation of a poem's meaning and the intonation contour given it in performance apply to all the experiments described in this book.

There are problems of syntax with the Wyatt, especially in relation to the precise effect of 'So' on the lines that follow. Owing to their linear crudity, machine traces cannot often suggest the delicate nuances of a reader's syntactical comprehension. It is usually inappropriate therefore to bring such nuances into discussion: they remain a matter for orthodox literary-critical analysis.

What I am comparing in the Wyatt, therefore, is not authentic sixteenth-century readings or subtle semantic interpretations. I am simply comparing one machine trace with another. But the improbability of one reader's contour matching another reader's is so high that we may, I think, take it that similarity of contour implies similarity of syntactical interpretation. As Diderot pointed out in his 1767 *Salon*, intonation is finally like a rainbow – an image of the soul itself and the quantity of its accents is infinite.[4] I am aware that this argument is circular, but there is no help for it without a machine that can read minds. However, compare in figures throughout this book the similarity between different readings of the same line with the great difference between one line and another, to get an idea of the potential contour variation in the one poem.

Readers were given a conventionalised paraphrase as follows: 'The poet was unguarded or unaware and, while he was looking steadily at a fair face he was caught by a sudden feeling of love. "Of late" = "recently".' (My paraphrase leaves the force of 'So' in obscurity, but from examining the traces I do not believe it makes any difference.) Readers were told to pronounce 'Unwarely' with stress on the second syllable, although Wyatt himself may well have stressed it on the first. This was to avoid stumbling, unnatural intonation patterns which might have resulted had readers tried to cope with Tudor English.

By opinion poll (30 subjects) it was decided (22 votes) that reader C gave the lines the best tune, reader A the next best, reader B third best, while readers D and E had previously been weeded out as worst. The task now was to match the other four readings' intonation traces against reader C's.

I shall talk of reader A, B, C, D, and E, and of reading 1, 2, etc., meaning by the numbers simply a reading of one line by one of the readers. For example, 'reading 16' in Figure 3.3 happens to be a performance by reader D of Wyatt's second line.

Taking Wyatt's first line, the matching process goes like this. In Figure 3.2 reading 3 is the performance of this line by reader C, whom we have chosen as the target against which to match the other four readings of this line (readings 1, 2, 14, and 15). It will be seen that voicing is continuous all the way up to the end of the word 'man', since the line never falls to zero. Then there is a voicing gap before 'caught', whose significance I shall discuss in my conclusions to this chapter. To create a set of symbols by which reader C's contour can be matched with the others, the contour is divided artificially into ten segments, shown by the vertical, numbered 'cuts' in the figure. The fragment of curve found in each of the resulting ten sections per line of target trace is then conventionalised into a symbol comprising one or two straight lines (or three in the case of some other experiments). For example, a trace like this would be conventionalised into . This captured as intuitively as possible the fragment's essential nature while providing a quantifiable symbol. In addition, a curved, 'scoop' symbol, rising, falling or horizontal , was employed for fragments where the intonation seemed to 'glide' importantly. Trace fragments for the ten sections of the other readings of this first line were likewise conventionalised and the symbols then matched, one for one, against the equivalent fragments in the 'best' reading. An exact match scored 1.0, with proportionate scores for scoops and inexactly matching hinged symbols.[5] Some voicing gaps, marked *, are discounted. Relative height of trace above the line is not accounted for, because although mathematical methods exist to compare relative pitch height, I cannot be sure that starting a reading at high pitch will not alter all other pitch relationships; also pitch nearly always falls, overall, from the beginning of the line to its end and I suspect our ear compensates for this when listening. The aim was more simple: to capture the direction of pitch change.

The results can be inspected in Table 3.1. The two worst readings, D and E, match the target least (36.9 per cent and 49.1 per cent). If there really were a neutral tune, reader A, because judged second best, should most closely match the target or best reading. But the Wyatt example shows the problems that sometimes stand in the way of easy results. In fact, reader A gives an unusual interpretation to the first line, 'So unwarely. . .', and this reduces his degree of matching, whereas his last three lines match target by 63.3 per cent. The question is whether we can do anything about this.

From the tape recordings we find that reader A unusually emphasises the word 'never' in the first line: this is reading 1 in Figure 3.2. The first syllable 'ne-' has a sharp intonation peak (high pitch) while the rest of the line is held relatively flat, so that 'never' becomes the main informational focus of the whole phrase. It is well known that change of informational focus can alter a whole intonation contour, as Halliday (1970) among others, has shown, and here we see such a case. One may hypothesise that this reader had an unusual idea about the semantics, deliberately marking 'never' as the most important word. This is, of course, allowed for in my definition of stress, where intellectual–semantic interpretations interfere with our sense of what we think we should hear.

We can trick this reader out of his fixation upon 'never' by asking him to read several versions of the poem in which the third line has been rewritten. The new third line may read 'As I of late, since, now it's in my thought', or 'As I of late. For, once the loathsome thought', or, to destroy decorum, 'As I was mate: for suddenly me thought', or the nonsense 'Into, into, into, into, into', or 'My heart, my heart, my heart, my heart, my heart'. Sometimes, this throws his attention off the first line and on to the third, so that he reads 'never' neutrally, as originally asked. When he does so the *whole* intonation of the line returns to neutral. From Figures 3.2 and 3.3 we can document a miniature history of his pronunciation of this line. In readings 13, 23, 24 and 25 he achieves an intonation contour very like that of the target reader C's, and again the probability of this being accidental is surely very low, given the scope for variation. In readings 26, 27, and 29 he reverts to his former emphasis upon 'never', while in reading 28 he goes a little haywire. All this checks out with listening to the natural voice recordings.

Further documentation on how this same reader unusually stresses negatives came from the work on Pope that I shall describe later. In his first reading of 'Know then thyself, presume not God to scan' he made 'not' rise sharply in pitch, unlike other readers. However, he stumbled on the word 'sceptic' in a later line and was asked to read again. This time his attention must have been on 'sceptic' because 'not' reverted to a more orthodox intonation pattern.

If we substitute in the scoring one of reader A's orthodox intonation patterns (reading 13) for Wyatt's first line, admitting that this is cheating, we find his intonation pattern for all four lines matches the target reader's by 61.25 per cent; that is, the second best reader follows the best reader most closely out of the five readers. We shall see that where a metre is tighter and there is less scope for unorthodox interpretations even closer matchings between the better readers are obtained. Further, by examining the tables of symbols, one can note where matching occurs and compare those points with the target reader's traces: elements of the neutral tune for a line can be discerned.

From Figure 3.2, then, in which the three best readings are displayed, it can be confirmed that each reader is following approximately the same tune. By contrast, the two worst readers are alike only in that they have a very narrow pitch range and vestigial melody. Why we think these readers worst is partly explained by Uldall's (1961) finding that contours of small range or change are rated by observers as less marked in emotional significance. The best reader, C, seems to have perceived something of the unachievable 'normal' tune and is emphasising it, smoothing out hesitations and increasing peaks and valleys to bring the tune out.

Many different valid ways of reading the lines are possible, as I have acknowledged, and they could even be successfully sung or chanted. We are simply assuming from strong evidence that we can partly distinguish a 'normal tune' from a group possessing a rough consensus about interpretation and sharing modern-English English without very marked regional dialect. It means this: with a rough consensus we can glimpse a reading that would be 'absolute' to such a shared performance: we cannot attain that absolute. And the absolute would be specific to such a performance, rather as we may speak in mystical terms of there being an absolute which appears at each moment of finite time – an absolute different from those other absolutes at other moments of time. Only here a group of performances in which much is shared between readers is viewed as a quasi-single performance with a suggestion that it might have an absolutely 'correct' music. Of course, although I ask my performers not to act the poems as though on stage, I cannot be sure what is going on in their heads. Nevertheless, the 'inherent music' of the line was first discerned long ago by the Germanist, Sievers,[6] and this is why I do not try to overprove its existence, limiting myself to the evidence in this and the following chapter.

Three special syllables will bring further factors to light. Since I was reader C, I can assert that when reading 'heart' in the Wyatt I can deliberately let its emotional significance influence my stressing of it, giving it an extremely open vowel, a sharply falling pitch, and a vibrant timbre (quality). The machine trace, reading 12, Figure 3.2, confirms to some extent what I do, but the emotional element in my response, which is specific to one performance, cannot be measured. If the word were 'hart' = 'male deer', and if it were *not* accorded that usual Wyatt pun – 'hart' = 'heart' = 'dear' – then I should wish to stress it less, even though the theoretical pronunciation of the line would not change. There is an accumulating emotional significance in the poem affecting both our wish to stress this syllable and the way we hear it.

In my stressing of 'caught', both hand and machine traces (reading 3) suggest how I isolate the word, rhythmically, at the end of the line. The voicing pattern is continuous until the end of 'man' and then breaks just before 'caught', as the 'n' changes to the voiceless 'c', with its hard-edge onset. Consequently, the hearer, after the flowing 'w's of the line, whose lack of abrupt breaks keeps him, so to speak, unaware, is suddenly 'caught' on the end there. Readers' machine traces generally show that this voicing gap is well-nigh inescapable. In reading 'So unwarely was never no man' I am already anticipating the 'caught': I may be wrong, the line may go drowsy on me: 'So unwarely were all men unaware'. But to speak 'caught' properly I have to anticipate it to the time the voicing gap before it just right. This implies that voicing patterns (see Glossary) are important.

The case of 'late' in the third line is notable: in my hand trace and in all readers' machine traces there is a marked pause after it, which is not just syntactical. 'Of late' means 'recently', but, semantically considered, the pause makes 'late' almost literally 'late' in that allied meaning, because the word takes its time before the sound resumes quickly with 'for suddenly'. The effect is enhanced by the speed of 'As I of' contrasting with the long vowel of 'late'. Though a routine word semantically, cadentially and in the way it prepares for 'for suddenly', 'late' provides a crucial rest. Expert reading increases the pause after it up to a point of maximum tension (beyond which point the tension dulls). Then 'for suddenly' takes us quickly over the next line break into the emotional centre of the stanza, 'heart'. The stanza's whole cadence has led to this. The machine traces for reader C show it: the 'unaware' sound flow is 'caught' at the end of the first line; regular sound pulses succeed as the talk is of steadfastness; an enjambment helps the brief spurt to the prolongation upon 'late'; that pause then triggers the quick enjambment towards 'heart', and there are twin pairs of sounds, 'My heart' and 'was torn', leading to a quiet conclusion. The stress on 'late', therefore, has its sonic factors – especially duration and pitch fall – but its stress depends upon its role in the whole stanza movement.

The pause after 'late' seems to increase my sense of how much 'late' was stressed, although I have already pronounced the word. This gives us a new concept, which I call 'retrospective stress'; it is what we should expect from my definition of stress in the last chapter. Part of our sense of a syllable's stress is cast back on to it afterwards, not from anticipation but from the real future (the pause). It is a minute puzzle of space–time that we think we heard, back in the past, a certain stress, but are able to add to our sense of what happened *then* by later events in the line. That is, the mind mistimes, if you like, a present experience, the pause, by posting its influence back to the notional instant when the voice stressed the syllable 'late' and by thinking that the influence took place then. It is insufficient just to suppose that this is a customary effect of memory without explaining our apparent certainty that what we actually heard was affected.

(There is a scientific analogy, whose analogical strength I cannot sum up, in which the mind seems to play tricks with its timing of events – as I believe it always does. I refer to Libet and others, reported in Popper and Eccles (1977). Working on electrical stimuli to the skin of the hand and on the brain cortex, Libet and co-workers found that the brain required time, in addition to that of mere transmission skin-to-brain, before the skin stimulus could be reported as experienced. They conjectured that during this time neuronal spatio-temporal patterns were elaborating in the cerebral cortex. But in a second test, under more complicated circumstances, it was possible to ask the subjects more exactly when they thought the skin was stimulated. This event was not thought by them to have occurred after the delay during which the stimulus was processed and entered consciousness. Their conscious report backdated the event to when the stimulus first reached the cortex and evoked an initial response *before the elaboration of cortical patterns*. It is certainly a field for research to see if the brain plays tricks with time in order to form consciousness of a sudden event.)

Durational factors – pitch, loudness, the pause, etc. – before and after the notional incidence of the stress on 'late' are what tell us what happened. Only in this way can the instant of stress be filled with content. For example, a durationless pitch or one sound in the entire universe considered as an endless monotone would have no meaning in terms of pitch at all.

A final comment. From the various traces of the better readings, it will be seen that each line of a poem seems to have a 'personality' connoted by the voicing patterns (informed at more delicate level by syllable formation) and, in a good reading, by intonation contour. This, together with further evidence of neutral tunes, will be examined more closely in the next chapter.

4

Voicing Patterns and the Pace of Poetry

As in a song, it is the voiced elements of a poetic line which bear onwards the line's main melody and help to shape it. During the continuous, voiced stretches of sound, perhaps encompassing more than one word or breaking mid-word, the glottal opening permits the vocal chords to vibrate; and from the glottis originates the F_0 trace that we have been measuring as our primary indication of pitch. The alternation of continuous voicing with voiceless intervals creates what I have called 'voicing patterns', whose intervals are filled by voiceless consonants or transitions or emptied by silence. Our F_0 trace will approximately show us these patterns. I am going to argue that perception of cadence and movement (or 'pace') in verse are partly dependent upon the inter-involvement of the voice's intonation contour with the voicing patterns. As well as studying such factors as a poet's syllable management, literary criticism should take more account of these patterns.

The interrelation of voicing and intonation is a linguistic commonplace and Pike (1945) long ago drew attention to the rhythmic importance of intonation breaks which effectively create the patterns I am describing. I have referred to Funkhouser (1979), who has pointed out how rarely acoustic data has been used in poetic criticism, and has interestingly studied, *inter alia*, durations and pacing in a poem of Randall Jarrell's. But she concentrated upon such elements as syllable, phrase, inter-word pause and overall line duration rather than upon voicing patterns as such. In this chapter it is these patterns rather than the normal literary categories of phrase, word, length of syllable, vowel, consonant, suprasegmental tone units or even of conventional pause that are most in question.

We are only half conscious of voicing durations; yet they interact with intonation to give a poetic line much of its personality in addition to what is contributed by the syllables. Wyatt's first line has an unusually long voicing duration, 'So unwarely was never no man/caught', whereas the personality of the second comes partly from splitting up the voicing into syllables, 'With/stead/fast/look/upon a/good/ly/face', the strokes indicating the voicing gaps. And so on.

Returning to music, when five subjects sang into the linguistic machinery the refrain 'I never promised you a rose garden', the voicing patterns were characteristically as follows: 'I never/promised/you a rose/garden'. Typically in performance, the prolonged 'o' vowel of 'rose' and its voiced [z] almost join up that three-syllable voicing segment, 'you a rose', with the 'g' that follows. By prolonging the vowel in conjunction with the [z], all five subjects were able to vary pitch considerably and thus make the line 'swing', Country and Western style; and the voicing of the consonant made this possible. (Hoagy Carmichael would swing the voiced middle 'ng' of 'old Hong Kong' to create a Chinese tonal effect.) Asked to tap the music's beats on to the microphone as they sang, three of the subjects sited two beats on the vowel of 'rose', the second one very close to the final [z].

The same five subjects read this line by Sir Philip Sidney with characteristic voicing patterns as follows: 'Till her eyes/shine/I live in/dar/kest night'. (A gap after 'Till' seemed optional but the semi-break after 'her' in Figure 4.1 is just a weak signal.) All five prolonged the 'ey' of 'eyes', making its pitch fall and glide, thus creating the poetic equivalent of 'swing'; and they could do this even though the 's' (phonetically [z̥]) is partly devoiced as it changes into the 'sh' of 'shine'; voicing, in fact, usually permits a longer vowel – compare 'cat' and 'cad'. Consequently, the less the 's' is devoiced the longer the vowel of 'eyes' can be made. If the reader taps the beat and prolongs the [a:] part of the 'eyes' diphthong sufficiently he may add an unorthodox, sixth beat to the line, siting it near the 's': this is probably because the action of tapping sets up nearly isochronous intervals. The sonnet in question, 'Lock up fair lids . . .', is addressed to a sleeping mistress. The long vowel helps the intonation contour of 'eyes' to ape that of 'shine' in both glide and duration, while the gradual devoicing of [z̥] merges into the following 'sh'. This intonational pairing of 'eyes' and 'shine', I would say, emphasises the crucial distinction between eyes shut and eyes shining which is the semantic and emotional heart of the poem. As with 'rose garden', we have here an *inter-syllable* transition affecting vowel and consonant voicing duration and doing so in a way which is involved with semantic and emotional interpretation. Both musical and poetic effect are

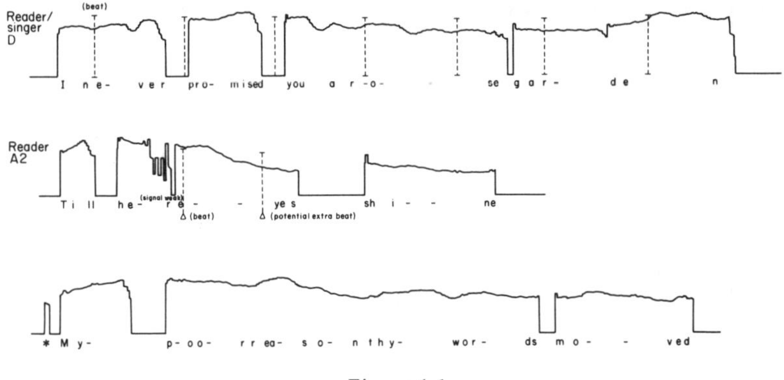

Figure 4.1

shown in Figure 4.1, and I shall return to this example in Chapter 6. It may seem that I am merely talking about syllabic and vowel effects, and we have said that tapping like this is a dubious technique (Loots, 1980). However, the fact that a vowel can be performed so as to bear a double beat (extremely unorthodox in a poem) is linked with the increased voicing duration. And beat is linked with pace. We have a small-scale demonstration at syllable level that it is not just syllable duration that interacts with intonation contour to create stress, cadence and pace; the voicing duration is necessarily involved since it bears the intonation. An example on a larger scale of a voicing pattern employed across several syllables comes from another Sidney poem, 'All my sense thy sweetness gained', whose line, 'My poor reason thy words moved' is shown in Figure 4.1. The voicing gap before 'moved' after a long, voiced segment slightly emphasises the final word and adds to its sense of movement. In our discussion of Wyatt's word 'caught', isolated from a previous long voiced segment, we noticed an allied effect.

Perhaps voicing patterns have been little examined in literary criticism because discussions of a poem's pitch have been hesitant owing to performance variation. As I began by saying, intonation and voicing are intimately related means of expressing emphasis. But now we are trying to create, through our matching procedures, more secure ways of talking about pitch in different readings of the same poem. Establishing elements of neutral intonation contours for a poem by Pope will help us to discuss the interaction between voicing pattern and pitch.

The procedure for matching intonation for the following Pope

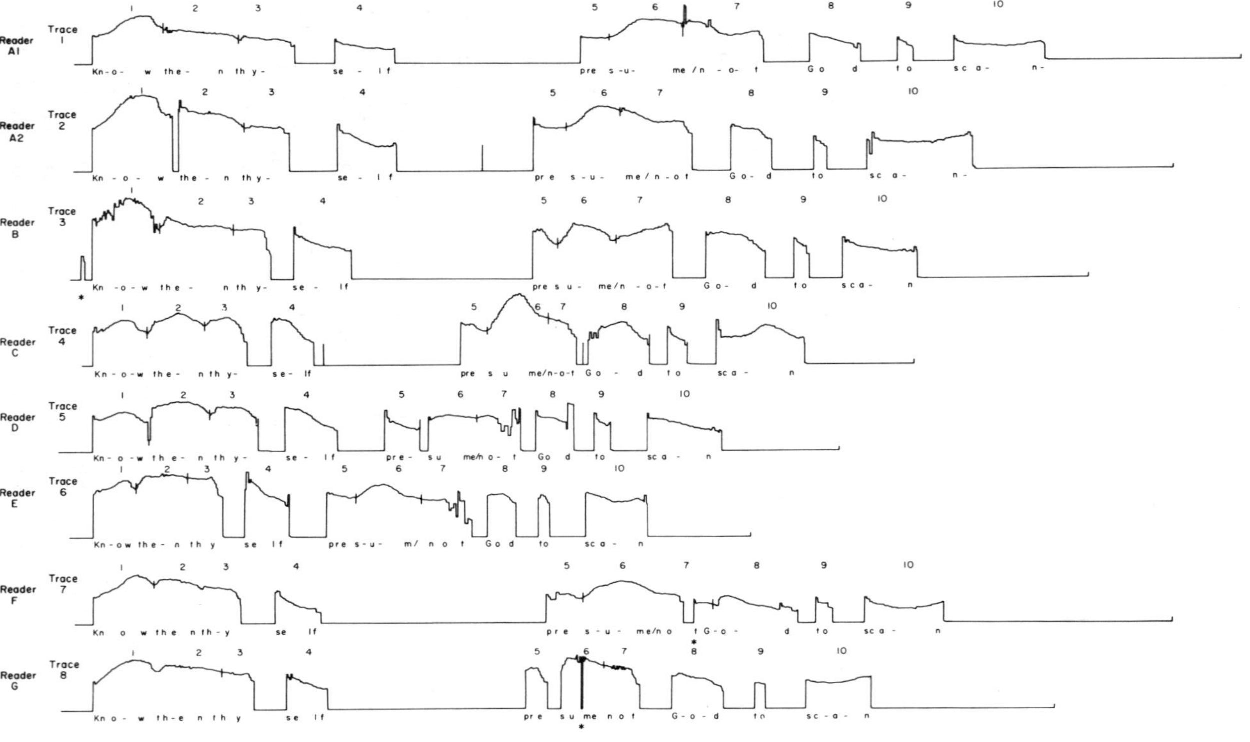
Reader A1 Trace 1
Reader A2 Trace 2
Reader B Trace 3
Reader C Trace 4
Reader D Trace 5
Reader E Trace 6
Reader F Trace 7
Reader G Trace 8

Figure 4.2

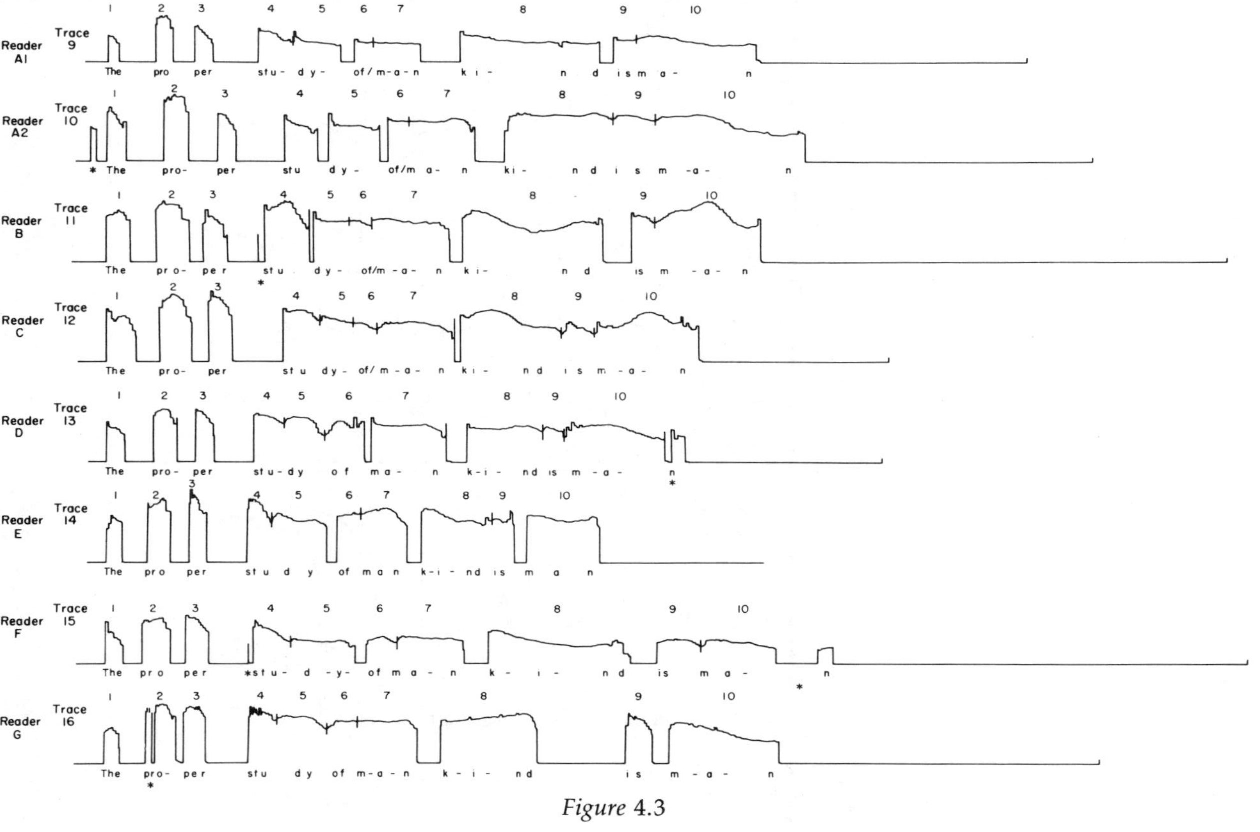

Reader A1 Trace 9
The pro per stu- dy- of/m-a-n ki- n d is m a- n
Reader A2 Trace 10
* The pro- per stu dy- of/m a- n ki- n d i s m -a- n
Reader B Trace 11
The pro- per stu dy- of/m-a- n ki- n d is m -a- n
Reader C Trace 12
The pro- per stu dy- of/m-a- n ki- n d i s m -a- n
Reader D Trace 13
The pro- per stu-dy of ma- n k-i- nd is m -a- n
Reader E Trace 14
The pro per stu d y of m a n k-i- nd is m a n
Reader F Trace 15
The pro per *stu- d -y- of m a- n k- i- n d is m a- n
Reader G Trace 16
The pro- per stu d y of m-a-n k-i- nd is m -a- n

Figure 4.3

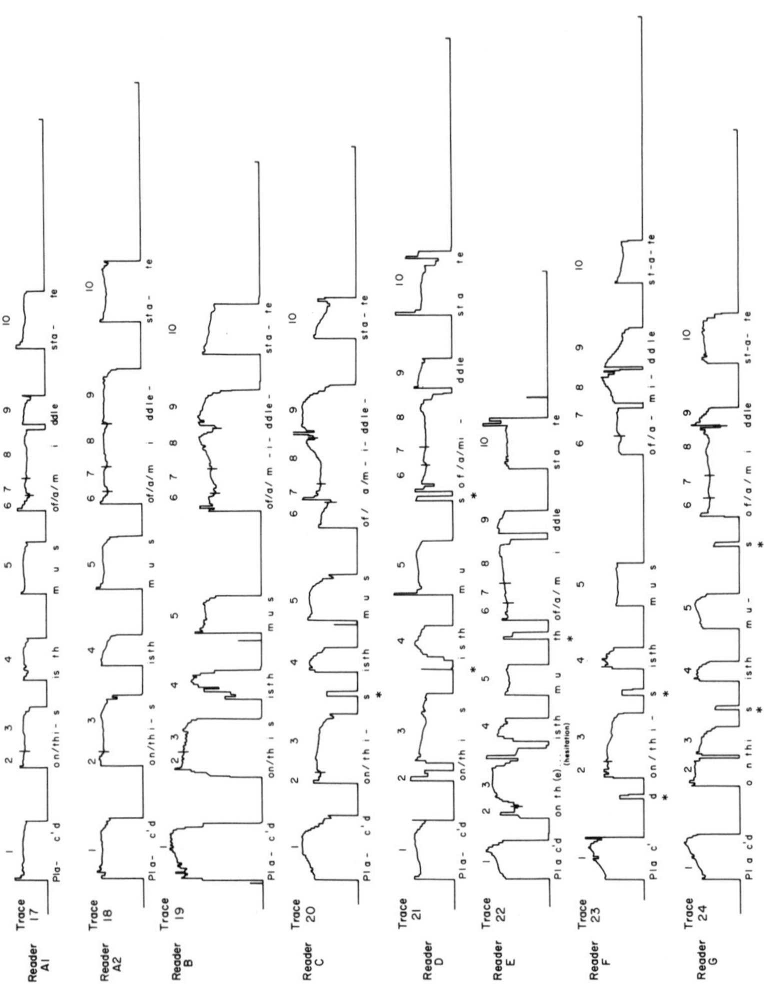
Reader A1 Trace 17
Reader A2 Trace 18
Reader B Trace 19
Reader C Trace 20
Reader D Trace 21
Reader E Trace 22
Reader F Trace 23
Reader G Trace 24

Figure 4.4

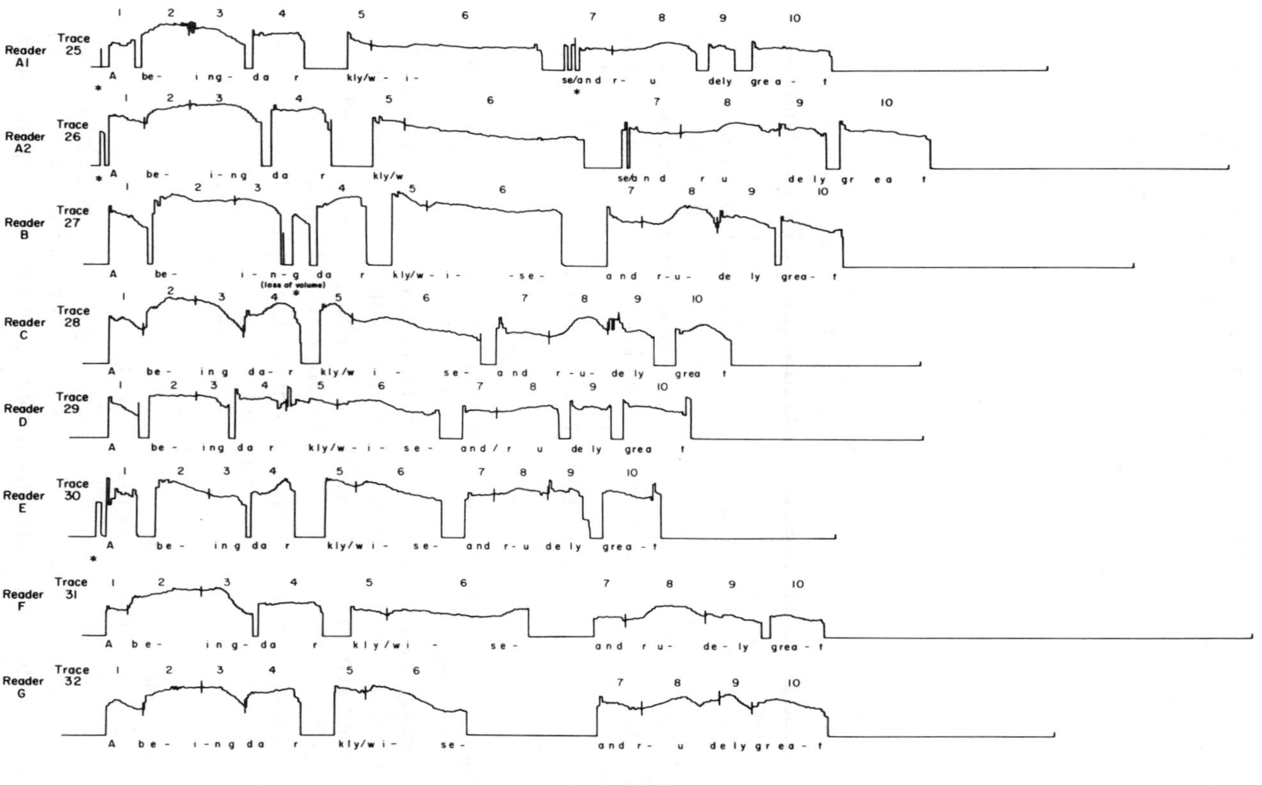
Reader A1 Trace 25
1 2 3 4 5 6 7 8 9 10
A be- ing- da r kly/w - i- se/and r- u dely gre a - t
Reader A2 Trace 26
A be- i-ng da r kly/w se/and r u de ly gr ea t
Reader B Trace 27
A be- i-n-g da r kly/w-i- -se- and r-u- de ly grea-t
(loss of volume)
Reader C Trace 28
A be- ing da- r kly/w i- se- and r-u- de ly grea t
Reader D Trace 29
A be- ing da r kly/w-i- se- and/r u de ly grea t
Reader E Trace 30
A be- ing da r kly/wi- se- and r-u de ly grea-t
Reader F Trace 31
A be- ing- da r kly/wi- se- and ru- de-ly grea-t
Reader G Trace 32
A be- i-ng da r kly/wi- se- and r- u delygrea-t

Figure 4.5

extract was similar to that for Wyatt. In two laboratory sessions seven performers read the opening four lines of Pope's *Essay on Man*, 'Epistle II', into the machinery, yielding eight sets of traces in all, since one reader read twice at an interval of seven months. (See Figures 4.2 to 4.5) The famous lines are:

> Know then thyself, presume not God to scan;
> The proper study of Mankind is Man.
> Plac'd on this isthmus of a middle state,
> A being darkly wise, and rudely great . . .

It was not crucial which of the four best readers in my own judgement acted as target, all being quite similar enough for my purpose. But I wanted to weed out readers D, E and G as targets, because: D was unorthodox in voiced segments, E seemed deficient in melody, and G gave a good but rather dramatic reading with consequent unorthodoxies in voicing and intonation. In an opinion poll, E's was unanimously judged the worst reading and no one judged that D's or G's was the best. I accordingly selected as target the most convenient trace, A2, which had tied at the top of the poll, was my own and thus accessible to my subjective interpretation, and was the highest scorer taking all rankings into account.

I have not contended that two good readers will give the same relative duration to the same segments of voicing. If reader A gives the segment, 'Know then thy/', twice the duration of 'self', I do not suggest that equally good reader B will necessarily observe the same proportions of duration. Quite possibly, his voicing pattern will not even be absolutely identical in how it groups words into voiced stretches, owing to a different sense of pause, tempo and drama and also to relatively different heights of pitch. Nevertheless, the voicing patterns from two readers will be very much alike: the acoustic value of the words imposes this, and a glance at the figures confirms it. This is all that my argument requires; so let us make it plain, as follows:

Taking the target reading as basis and matching the voicing patterns of each reader to it line by line, I give one point to each syllable in the line so that there is a maximum of ten points, and I subtract one point every time a voicing segment in a reading lacks one of the syllables that appear in the corresponding target segment. The results are:

Reader	Percentage of syllables in all four lines taking part in the same voicing patterns as target reading (A2)
A1 (first reading by performer A)	87.5%
B	90%
C	90%
D	67.5%
E	87.5%
F	87.5%
G	72.5%

That is, except for D and perhaps G the voicing patterns are roughly the same and even in D and G there is quite good accord.

Fragments of the intonation traces were matched as previously.[1] Points scored out of the maximum ten per line, together with the percentage match, can be seen in Tables 4.1 and 4.2. The tables show that if we total the percentages for all four lines for each reader, then:

Reader	had an average percentage match to A2 for intonation in all four lines of
B	70%
C	68.5%
D	65.6%
E	51.6%
F	67.6%
G	59.5%

Reader A's first reading (A1) matched an average of 74.4 per cent for intonation against his second reading (the target), which gives some guidance as to how close some of the higher scores were. Reader E was polled as the worst tune and I have called reader G a 'talented alternative', owing to the drama of his rendition, although he still matched quite closely. Including the target (100 per cent) but excluding reader A1, the average match of all readers' symbols to each other was 68.97 per cent.

I said earlier it was not critical which of the fairly good readings was target. This is because if one matches the symbols in Tables

4.1 and 4.2 *down* the vertical columns rather than along the horizontal, the result is comparable. This is to measure agreement about the intonation of each quasi-syllabic section rather than to score individual performances, and the figures obtained should be approximately the same. Leaving out the A1 reading but including the target, the scores are:

know	*then*	*thy*	*self*	*pre*	*sume*	*not*	*God*	*to*	*scan*
100	57.1	50	92.8	96.4	85.7	50	78.6	100	75

The	*pro*	*per*	*stu*	*dy*	*of*	*man*	*kind*	*is*	*man*
78.6	100	92.8	82.1	53.6	53.6	57.1	35.7	64.3	60.7

Table 4.1

Reader	Trace no.	1	2	3	4	5	6	7	8	9	10	Match to target %
Line 1		Know	then	thy	self	pre	sume	not	God	to	scan	
A1	1											80
A2	2											Target
B	3											90
C	4											65
D	5											57.5
E	6											82.5
F	7											80
G	8											72.5
Line 2		The	pro	per	stu	dy	of	man	kind	is	man	
A1	9											80
A2	10											Target
B	11											62.5
C	12											72.5
D	13											67.5
E	14											55
F	15											72.5
G	16											50

Plac'd	*on*	*this*	*isth*	*mus*	*of*	*a*	*mi*	*ddle*	*state*
46.4	78.6	67.8	57.1	70	78.6	42.8	39.2	42.8	57.1

A	*be*	*ing*	*dar*	*kly*	*wise*	*and*	*ru*	*dely*	*great*
71.4	75	78.6	64.3	28.6	57.1	64.3	89.3	92.8	78.6

= 68.6 per cent average match for all syllables.

Even though idealisation of the symbols slightly exaggerates the degree of matching and the scores are not supposed to translate directly into 'reality', the closeness of agreement between the intonation contours strikes me as high and is confirmed by visual inspection of the traces. Tables 4.1 and 4.2, therefore, give some security to preliminary assertions such as follow (they are intended as examples, not as an exhaustive list):

Table 4.2

Reader	Trace no.	1	2	3	4	5	6	7	8	9	10	Match to target %
Line 3		Plac'd	on	this	isth	mus	of	a	mi	ddle	state	
A1	17											75
A2	18											Target
B	19											50
C	20											70
D	21											55
E	22											25
F	23											48
G	24											58
Line 4		A	be	ing	dar	kly	wise	and	ru	dely	great	
A1	25											62.5
A2	26											Target
B	27											77.5
C	28											67.5
D	29											78.75
E	30											43.75
F	31											70
G	32											57.5

Typically, from the better readings we have so far studied, in this poem:

(a) Line 1: the intonation will rise and then fall on 'Know', continue falling and either flatten out or fall still further before gliding (scoop symbol) on 'self'; or
(b) Line 1: 'presume not' falls then rises and falls while 'God' and 'to' each fall, and 'scan' glides; or
(c) Line 2: the individual syllables of 'The proper study of' will be given a falling intonation; or
(d) Line 4: the curve for 'A being darkly wise' will be something like: fall–rise–flattening–fall–glide;

and so on.

As for the voicing patterns, we can inspect Figures 4.2 to 4.5 and make assertions such as these:

Typically, from the better readings we have so far studied, in this poem:

(a) Line 1: 'Know then thy' generally forms one voiced segment, whereas 'self' stands on its own; or
(b) Line 1: 'presume not' is one voiced segment while 'God to scan' has a separate segment for each word, spaced out; or
(c) Line 2: the opening voicing pattern is 'The/pro/per/stu-' with options of '-y/of/man'; but basically short opening segments (individual syllables) are followed by drawn-out ones, sometimes of more than one syllable; or
(d) Line 4: there are minor options for 'A being dar-', but with '-kly wise' it forms two, counter-balanced and longish segments, while 'and rudely great', again despite minor options, forms a third, partner-segment with the option of posing 'great' more markedly at the line-ending by a break before it.

The reader may proliferate such observations for himself; although only relatively secure they have more objective demonstration than traditional literary judgements about a line's pitch, pace and movement. They could be further refined by comparison with traces from some recognised master of verse reading, although we might find that he would depart from the norm to create dramatic emphasis, and this would not be the same as the unmarked (neutral) readings we are studying.

One may proceed, therefore, to the non-scientific language of literary criticism, although I should not normally expect such a hobbledehoy treatment as follows; I am obliged to illustrate the duller stages of method. In more lively use our techniques would promise two particular benefits for full-scale criticism: they provide a *resource* for supporting remarks about a poet's versification, his employment of pitch, pause, and so forth; and, in conjunction with tape recording of readings and glottal buzzes (which make the tune evident and which provide the signal for the F_0 contour), they could be a means for training students to learn the music of verse.

In a carthorse way, therefore, I could say it is well to read Line 1 with continuous voicing, before breaking slightly before 'self' which should glide (the break is obligatory). The result gives a sonorous, authoritative tone followed by a subtly more-meditative emphasis, coupled with maintenance of tension over the heroic line's middle pause. If we know about these middle pauses, presumably we are helped to experience this tension – there is an influence from our knowledge of the abstract metric on how we stress and pace the line. 'Presume not' is continuously voiced and rises in pitch to prepare for an equivalent and balancing authoritative descent, while 'God to scan' is voiced separately and drawn out for gravity, with glide on 'scan' to balance that on 'self' before the middle pause and to preserve tension for the answering line of the couplet.

The sharply segmented, syllabic voicing patterns of 'The proper study' in Line 2 contrast both with the multi-syllable and drawn-out single syllable segments of the previous line to provide short bursts of sound that always make me think of a finger wagging in admonition. Then long, voiced segments in 'of mankind is man' echo the measured pacing of Line 1's conclusion. Readers F and G in Figure 4.3 emphasised 'is man' or 'man' by introducing voicing gaps, and G also altered pitch on 'is' to accentuate this.

In Line 4, the three main voicing divisions respect the three main points made. 'A being dar-' prepares us for an irony and the long segment gives us time to appreciate it, while the insignificant '-kly' can join up with the 'wise' segment to create a similar voicing unit to the preceding one, thus emphasising the ironic contrast through balance. 'Rudely great' can simply match the other two segments in length and the three main semantic movements are posed against each other. Or, if the final irony is to be rammed home, 'great' can be isolated slightly on the line ending.

The traces show that both Pope and Wyatt are very 'busy' with their voicing patterns, and Pope's special mastery of them is part of his expertise with the heroic couplet. Pope's management of a wide repertoire of these patterns, tightly compressed within his strict forms, gives his lines extremely varied pace. By contrast, the readers' traces (not included here) of these four lines by William Blake

> I'll shade him from the heat till he can bear
> To lean in joy upon our Father's knee;
> And then I'll stand and stroke his silver hair,
> And be like him and he will then love me.
> ('The Little Black Boy')

show that while the voicing patterns are important there is less variation and so they are less busily employed for varying the pace. This befits a childlike song; however, I believe Blake is generally less able to confine his voicing patterns quite so tightly as Pope: the marvellous pacing of certain passages in the prophetic poems disturbs and energises the versification rather than so exactly forming concord with it, and leads in the direction of free verse. (It is partly the management of voicing patterns that organises free verse, as indeed it does ordinary conversation.)

Durations of consonants and vowels, and allied syllabic factors, obviously contribute to verse pace; and they are also the building blocks for voicing patterns. To show that these latter patterns play a role of their own in pacing, it would help us to find some way of isolating this role. I have long known that Neville Coghill's translation of Chaucer's *The Canterbury Tales* manages in some mysterious way not fully shared by other translations to suggest the 'feel' and 'movement' of Chaucer's original lines as Coghill himself and other scholars have taught us to pronounce them. Coghill states his aims in the preface to his Penguin edition. He refers to other translators who wreck Chaucer's 'verse *movement*' (my italics) (Coghill, 1951, p. 17):

> I have therefore treated his poem . . . with fidelity not to the

form of a word but to the idiom and the wealth of meaning in a word, and also to the tone of voice or manner in which the meaning is conveyed.

Usefully, there is another translation of Chaucer which has many virtues but gives me less a sense of Chaucerian verse movement. It is by Theodore Morrison (1977) and the translator is equally explicit – and modest – about his aims (p. 47):

> But the lightness and charm of Chaucer's easy *motion* [my italics] is, I am afraid, almost impossible to approximate in English today . . . I have reproduced Chaucer's verse forms in my versions, but I cannot pretend to have caught the quality of his rhyming or of the motion of his lines.

Now, if both Coghill and Morrison are right in their estimations of their own achievements, if my judgement of their labours is also correct, and if I am also right in linking voicing patterns closely with verse movement, we should find that Coghill more closely respects the patterns of voicing in the Chaucer original, read according to modern notions of Middle English pronunciation.

I read the following fifty lines from Chaucer's original in Robinson's edition (1957) into the machinery: *General Prologue*, 1–18, *The Miller's Tale*, 3730–3741, and *The Pardoner's Tale*, 739–759. The only motive in selecting passages was that I liked them.

A system was needed for disclosing any similarities in voicing pattern between either translation and Chaucer's original:

(a) Each line was divided in half at a convenient pause in the original.
(b) Matching segments of voicing were sought in each half of the line between a translation and the original. No account was taken of whether the translator was keeping pace, line by line, with the actual meaning of Chaucer's words, although in fact departures from this were rare for both translators.
(c) A match was said to be made wherever a continuous pattern of voicing comprising three or more syllables was found both in the appropriate half of the Middle English trace and in the translator's version of that line.[2]
(d) If a 3-syllable group or longer, sharing the same segmentation pattern, was found in the correct half of the line both in Chaucer and the translation, it scored one point to the translation for

each syllable included within the pattern. A 3-or-more-syllable group straddling the centre line was only allowed to match a corresponding straddling pattern or one extending at least three syllables on one side of the centre line.

(e) Decisions had to be made sometimes to ignore minor voicing gaps where, otherwise, an obvious similarity would be missed. Usually the decision had to be supported by another recording of the lines, but under special conditions other minor gaps might be ignored.

(f) A total possible line score was arrived at by adding up the number of syllables in the original. The total was usually 10 but a notable voicing feature in Chaucer, such as a very marked pause or significant enjambement would be added to the syllable count, giving a total of eleven matchable features occasionally.

(g) For a given translation, a score per line was then arrived at by adding up the number of syllables involved in the matching groups found.

Two examples of matching in progress, chosen to illustrate the difficulties, are given in Figure 4.6. For example, in the line 'And bathed every veyne . . .', two voicing gaps are ignored in the Chaucer original, shown by asterisks; this is a highly unusual permission and occurs because the gaps do not appear in an alternative reading with which I was happier; so they are not obligatory. Effectively, the translations were matched with this line's alternative reading, shown marked 'comparison'. This is especially favourable to Coghill and therefore needs admitting. Another admission comes with *The Miller's Tale* line, 'Derk was the nyght . . .', which shows Coghill's respect for the original words. Here, to capture flow and similarity, I had to decide that the centre line should be after 'pich' and this is only justice to Coghill, who unluckily loses potential points for 'Dark was' because the Modern English 'k' is not so forcefully pronounced as the Middle English (which obscures devoicing in the Middle English). Morrison is perhaps lucky to score six for this line, mostly with a run of monosyllabic segments not very like the original. The results were as follows:

No. of lines: 50. Maximum number of syllables and special prosodic features possible to match: 510.

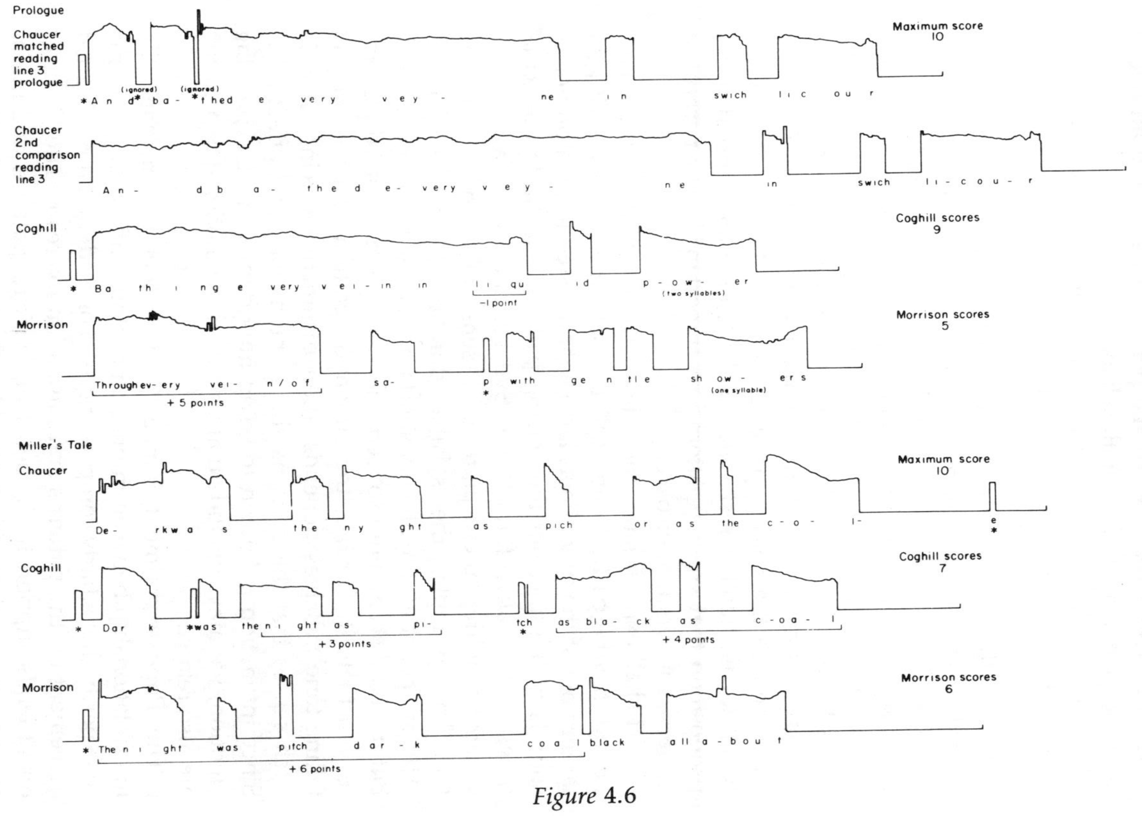
Prologue
Chaucer matched reading line 3 prologue
Maximum score 10
* A n d* ba - * t hed e ve r y v e y - ne i n swich l i c ou r
(ignored) (ignored)
Chaucer 2nd comparison reading line 3
A n - d b a - t h e d e - v e r y v e y - n e in swich l i - c o u - r
Coghill
Coghill scores 9
* Ba th i ng e very v e i - in in l i - qu i d p - o w - e r
(two syllables)
-1 point
Morrison
Morrison scores 5
Through ev- ery vei- n / o f sa- p with ge n tle sh ow - er s
(one syllable)
+ 5 points
Miller's Tale
Chaucer
Maximum score 10
De - rkw a s the n y ght as pich or a s the c - o - l- e *
Coghill
Coghill scores 7
* Dar k *was the n i ght as pi- tch * as bla - ck as c - oa - l
+ 3 points
+ 4 points
Morrison
Morrison scores 6
* The n i ght was pitch d ar - k c o a l black a ll a - b o u t
+ 6 points

Figure 4.6

Coghill matched 232, an average per line of 4.64 and an overall percentage match of 45.5 for all syllables.
Morrison matched 157, an average per line of 3.14 and an overall percentage match of 30.9 for all syllables.

The method is admittedly arbitrary but nevertheless firmly accords with one's intuitions when lines are considered individually. Care was taken to be impartial between Coghill and Morrison. However, Coghill's clearly superior match cannot be explained, I think, just by vagaries in the matching process. No doubt it partly arises because he sticks closer to Chaucer's actual words, but we are only studying the fact that he more exactly catches Chaucer's pace through the voicing patterns, not how he does it or which translator is the cleverest. The results lend some support to the proposition that voicing patterns are important in our perception of verse's movement or pace.

As I shall explain later, the role of overall duration of a voiced period may be partly to link syllables and their stresses with the larger flow of the tune. Poets are also interested in the non-voiced sounds in the line, but the voicing patterns constitute the actual flows and breaks of the tune. Syllabic and other factors may construct, within these patterns, a sense of hurry or slowness too. For example, the syllabic durations in Pope, Line 2, 'The/pro/per/stu-', are all very short and it all seems quite hurried, but it would seem more so were the voicing not to introduce gaps to punctuate it. Further, the intonation pattern of a *succession* of falling-tone syllables depends upon disjunctive voicing. It is in such senses that the patterns shape the melody and affect pace. Since intonation is known to be an important way of expressing emotion, we may conclude that voicing and emotional expression are also related.

The Pope experiment implies that a poet can manage the interrelationship between intonation contour and voicing patterns so expertly that a fairly competent group of readers can reach good agreement on the patterns and intonation to create. The Chaucer result lends support to the belief that voicing patterns and intonation can be worth examining together for their literary significance.

Unfortunately, the Chaucer example is of a rare kind because to match voicing patterns effectively we require an approximate equivalence of syllables between original and translation. We can use a simplified version of the same basic analysis to compare closeness to the original Anglo-Saxon 'Seafarer' of translations by Ezra Pound (1959) and Michael Alexander (1966). I had judged by ear that Pound more than Alexander had sought to express the original's movement and Alexander is generous enough to acknowledge Pound's skill, though its cost was a certain archaism (Alexander, 1966, p. 21). This time, because neither translator always respects the syllable counts of the Anglo-Saxon lines – and alliterative verse was variable in syllables – a total matching score is impossible. But many local examples can be shown where Pound keeps closer to both the intonation contour and the voicing patterns of the original.

I have recorded myself some twenty-five lines at the beginning of the original and of both translations, but only include here, in Figure 4.7, the first line, just to show what Pound tried to do:

> Maeg ic be me sylfum   soðgied wrecan,
> . . .
> ('Seafarer')
>
> May I for my own self song's truth reckon . . .
> (Pound)
>
> The tale I frame shall be found to tally: . . .
> (Alexander)

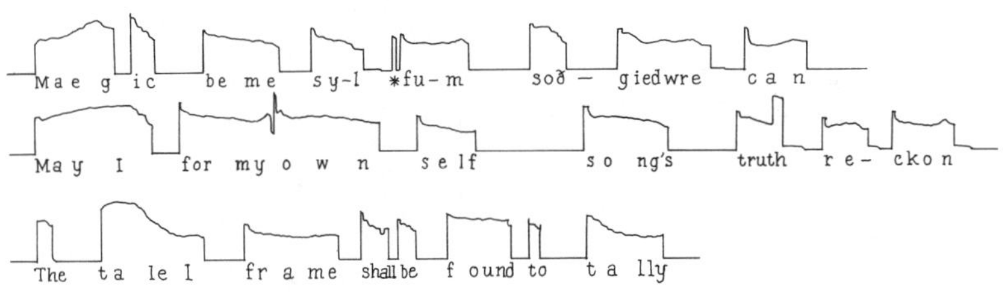

Figure 4.7

The reader may agree from inspecting the closeness of Pound's trace to the original that something like the sounds I uttered was probably inside Pound's head when translating this line, in view of the improbability of chance matching. An inspection of the traces confirms that Pound has frequent success in capturing something of the pace and movement of his original. An unexpected result was that Pound had managed to capture much of the rise and fall of the original's pitch: as I wasn't concentrating upon this I probably had no conscious intention of reproducing the Anglo-Saxon pitch patterns when reading Pound.

Expert translators also have some sense of the intonation contour and voicing patterns of their original. This can now be explored further.

5

The Music of Translation

Owing to the dominance of abstract theories of prosody over acoustic studies of actual poetic performance, no really adequate way of comparing the music of French and English poetry has yet been developed. Of course, traditional French poetry is measured by syllable and English poetry timed by stress. As described in Chapter 1, most recent prosodic studies in English have been by linguists trying to create abstract rules which will determine whether a line of verse is or is not metrical; their basis has been stress analysis and, as a result, the rules have either been specific to English or to a particular metre; they have little to say about the different abstract counting procedures of French metrics. Sometimes these studies do not take much account of intonation and are uninterested in different performances of verse.[1] Where intonation is brought into abstract notation systems, as in the valuable work of Chatman (1965), it is usually considered that a line may be given various patterns of intonation, depending on the reader's interpretation. This must naturally be acknowledged.

If we refrain from rule-creation and simply see what happens when we read French and English verse into the linguistic machinery we can find some of the ways in which both poetries do the same job.

Four female native speakers of French – two teachers of French literature and two linguistic students – were asked to read a Ronsard sonnet into the machinery. They were instructed to read with a modern pronunciation (for example, 'voudroy' was read as 'voudrais'):

> Quand en songeant ma follastre j'accole,
> Laissant mes flancs sus les siens allonger,
> Et que d'un branle habilement leger
> En sa moitié ma moitié je recole,
> Amour adonq si follement m'affole,
> Qu'un tel abus je ne voudroy changer,
> Non au butin d'un rivage estranger,
> Non au sablon qui jaunoye en Pactole.

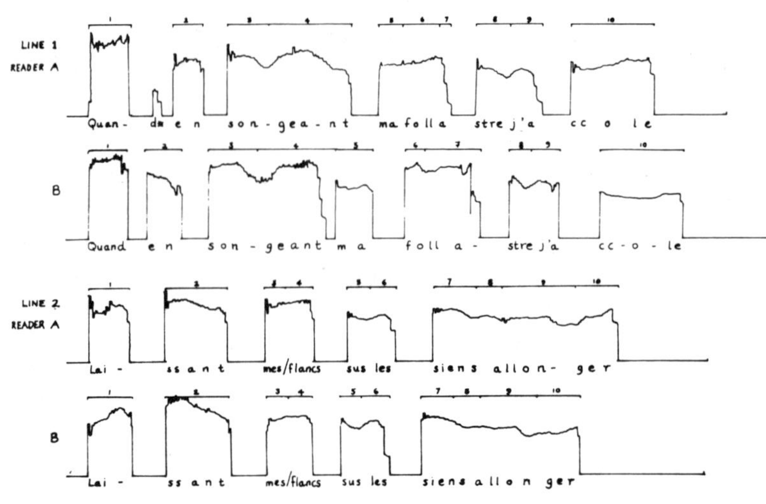
LINE 1
READER A
Quan- d en son-gea-nt ma folla stre j'a cc o le
B
Quand en son-geant ma foll a- stre j'a cc-o-le
LINE 2
READER A
Lai- ss ant mes/flancs sus les siens allon- ger
B
Lai- ss ant mes/flancs sus les siens allon ger

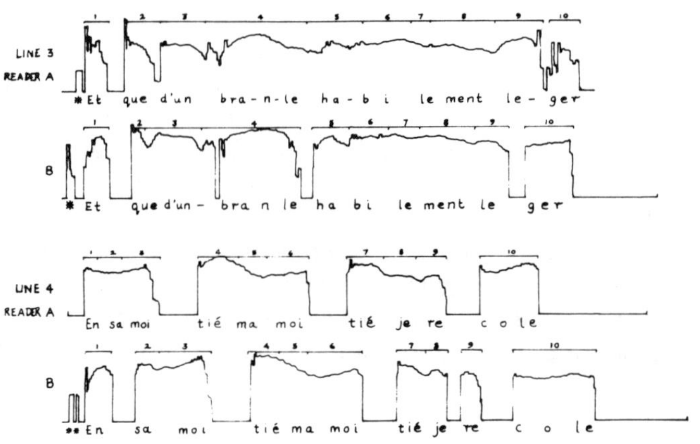
LINE 3
READER A
* Et que d'un bra-n-le ha-b i le ment le- ger
B
* Et que d'un- bra n le ha bi le ment le ger
LINE 4
READER A
En sa moi tié ma moi tié je re c o le
B
** En sa moi tié ma moi tié je re c o le

Figure 5.1

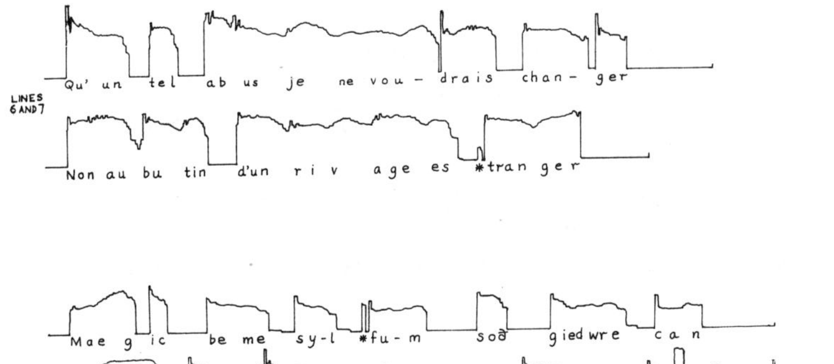
LINES 6 AND 7
Qu' un tel ab us je ne vou - drais chan - ger
Non au bu tin d'un ri v age es *tran ger
Mae g ic be me sy-l *fu - m soð giedwre ca n
May I for my o w n se lf so ng's truth re- ck on
The ta le I fr a me shall be f ound to ta lly

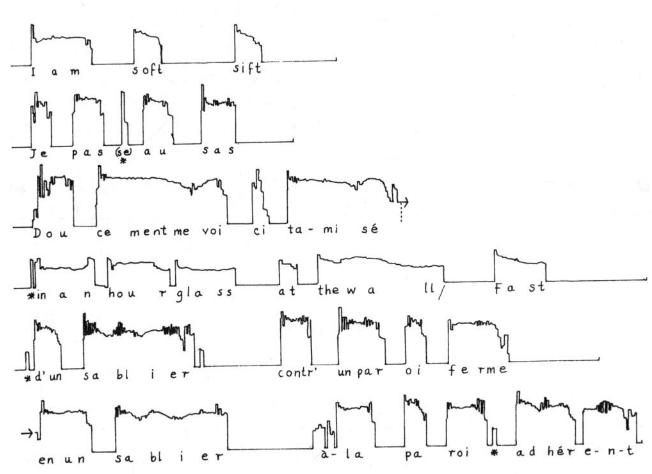
I a m soft sift
Je pas (se) au sas
Dou ce ment me voi ci ta - mi sé
*in a n hou r gla ss at the w a ll / Fa st
*d' un sa bl i er contr' un par oi fe rme
en u n sa bl i er à - la pa roi * a d hér e - n - t

Figure 5.2

Mon Dieu! quel heur et quel contentement
M'a fait sentir ce faux recolement,
Changeant ma vie en cent metamorphoses
Combien de fois, doucement agité,
Suis-je ore mort, ore resuscité
Entre cent liz et cent merveilles roses!
(Pléiade edition)

For brevity, I shall deal only with lines 1–4 and 6–8 and, though I have analysed below all four readings, I am only displaying in the figures the two best, A and B, as selected by opinion poll, because

Table 5.1

RONSARD: MATCHING INTONATION SEGMENTS

Line One:

Reader	1 Quand	2 en	3 son	4 geant	5 ma	6 fol	7 la	8 stre	9 j'a	10 ccole	*Match to Target %*
A	/	∧	‾\	/‾\	—	/	\	\	/‾	⌣	Target = 100%
B	/	\	∧	∧	—	/	∧	‾\	/‾	⌣	73%
C	‾\	∧	‾\	—	\	∧	—	—	\	/‾\	28%
D	‾\	—	‾\	/	\	/	\	—	—	/	38%

Line Two:

Reader	1 Lai	2 ssant	3 mes	4 flancs	5 sus	6 les	7 siens	8 al	9 lon	10 ger	*Match to Target %*
A	∧	‾\	/	∧	\	∧	‾\	∧	‾\	/	Target = 100%
B	∧	‾\	/	∧	\	∧	\	\	‾\	/	89%
C	/‾	—	_/	\	‾\	\	‾\	‾\	\	—	38%
D	∧	—	—	/	—	\	‾\	\	‾\	/	56%

Table 5.2

Line Three:

Reader	1 Et	2 que	3 d'un	4 branle	5 ha	6 bil	7 e	8 ment	9 le	10 ger	*Match to Target %*
A	\	\	¬	⌒	¬	/‾	\	‾_	∧	\	Target=100%
B	∧	\	¬	⌒	∧	—	\	‾\	∧	/	68%
C	∧	\	\	¬	∧	\	/‾	—	\	¬	40%
D	∧	∧	⌒	⌒	/‾	—	/	\	\	/	39%

No. of Segment

Line Four:

Reader	1 En	2 sa	3 moi	4 tie	5 ma	6 moi	7 tie	8 je	9 re	10 cole	*Match to Target %*
A	\	‿	∧	⌒	\	/	¬	‾\	⌒	‿	Target=100%
B	∧	¬	∧	⌒	\	∧	¬	∧	\	⌢	65%
C	∧	\	∧	¬	/‾	¬	¬	¬	¬	—	39%
D	¬	—	¬	/	\	/	¬	¬	\	‿	56%

No. of Segment

the main points have already been made in earlier chapters. (See Figure 5.1 for lines 1–4 and Figure 5.2 for lines 6–7.)

If we want to find out what is the most suitable melody with which to read the poem, it would be helpful if the reading judged second best should prove more like the best one than the two poorer readings were.

The best set of traces, A, was taken as target against which to match the other three readings, dividing the lines into ten sections of the intonation trace, as before. Symbols were chosen for each fragment of intonation curve analysed, with slight modifications to method as necessary.

The results, which are displayed in Tables 5.1 and 5.2, indicate that the second best reader, B, matched the best on average by 73.75 per cent of her symbols. Reader C matched 36.25 per cent and reader D 47.25 per cent. Again, the scores of reader A and B are very close if one thinks that the same reader of Pope, trying to repeat his earlier intonation of four lines after some months' interval, only matched 74.4 per cent of the previous reading's contour (see Chapter 4). The closeness of this matching once more suggests that we can achieve relative, not absolute, security about the pitch contours given to many syllables of a poem read according to a neutral interpretation of it.

I compared the voicing patterns of all four readers rather as before with the following results:

Reader	Percentage of syllables in all four lines taking part in the same voicing patterns as in the target reading
A (target)	100%
B (second best)	87.5%
C	45%
D	65%

We see that the better readers have a clearer sense of how to group the voicing patterns to best effect: not surprising if intonation and voicing are intimately connected, rather as horse and rider, and if a reader's grasping their connection also means pacing the reading properly.

We now have an instrument for half-scientific comparison of the melody created by different readings, a method applicable to most conceivable kinds of poetry. For example, it can even be applied to verse written in tone-conscious languages such as Thai, since the basic work is done on the intonation contour (see List, 1961). However, in all literary judgements about the semantic/emotional/artistic effect of poetry's music we are, as always, talking intuitively. The scientific measurement merely provides a map of what has happened to voicing and intonation in a performance of a line, so that we may point to the part of the machine trace to which our literary judgement refers. Once again a literary analysis allowing full rein to intuition and using the data more selectively would be more sparkling than what follows, but I'll take the four first lines one by one.

Line 1: here the voicing patterns are spaced out, slowing the pace and helping us to attend to the separate pieces of information contained in Ronsard's opening statement. The fall in intonation on the 'son' of 'songeant' aids the nasalisation which creates a standard, sleep-like noise, but generally the intonation rises and falls fairly evenly, no doubt because the line has several information foci of almost equal importance: 'songeant', 'follastre', and 'j'accole'. However, '-cole' rises slightly to maintain tension for the next line's intonation.

Line 2: The measured pacing of voicing patterns continues but we note the joined syllables of 'mes flancs' and 'sus les', a double pulse which then changes into the continuous voicing of 'siens allonger', which by its prolonged nasalisation emphasises the important emotional conclusion of the line, an effect on stress of 'quality' (see Glossary). It also creates continuous voicing patterns which often accompany continuous emotional sensitivity.

Line 3: The balanced tone of the first two lines had been exactly mimed in the regular spacing of most of their voicing patterns. Through such moderation, Ronsard has been preparing for the surprise of a well-nigh sexual spasm on 'branle'. There is a long stretch of continuous voicing as the syllables join together in the tension of 'branle' which is contrasted by the lighter tonality of 'habilement le-'. 'Branle' itself is an unusually long, nasalised syllable and has a rise–level–fall intonation to increase its emphasis. Furthermore, this has been prepared for by the rise then fall through 'Et que d'un . . .'. The intonation levels off through 'habilement', contributing to the lightness of emphasis in the word, and rises to stress the important final word 'leger' in contrast with the heavy fall at the conclusion of 'branle'.

Line 4: This line shows Ronsard's ability to use voicing patterns to create rhythmic effects: 'En sa moi/tié ma moi/tié je re/cole.' The word 'moitié' is literally split in half, and there are three rhythmic voicing groups of three syllables each. The contrast between 'sa moi-' and 'ma moi-' is slightly more emphasised than it would be were there not a voicing gap after 'moi-'. The intonation rises on 'moi-' and falls on '-tié' in the two instances of this word, adding to the patterning. Ronsard's conscious intentions as a poet, by the way, are not at issue: we are simply talking about what happens in the sounds, not trying to 'explain the poetry away'.

I have included also two traces for lines 6 and 7 (Figure 5.2) to show how Ronsard can use voicing patterns to manage pace. Consider these lines:

6. Qu'un tel abus je ne voudroy changer,
7. Non au butin d'un rivage estranger,
8. Non au sablon qui jaunoye en Pactole.

We should naturally judge that, owing to their parallelism, lines 7 and 8 form a rhythmic pair slightly separated from line 6. This is true; but Ronsard has linked this pair on to line 6 by creating a similarity of voicing pattern not between lines 7 and 8 but between lines 6 and 7. This enables the cadence and pace to run smoothly through the three lines while retaining the pairing of 7 and 8. The reader may need to rehearse the three lines several times before he hears how there is similarity in the pulses of continuous sounding of the voice in 6 and 7; this is because we are not used to attending consciously to these effects.

We may now extend earlier remarks about translating from Old or Middle English to translating between languages. I will be helped by Fónagy (1976). He reminds us that there is an original flaw in every translation, in that the notions which form the bases of words in Language A do not correspond precisely to the base notions in the B language into which A is being translated. This is well known in translation theory; it should imply that it is very difficult to create a translation of a poem which will ape the intonation contours of the original, owing to the link between semantic interpretation and intonation. Nevertheless, ways may be found of narrowing the gap between the music and pace of the original poem and the music and pace of its translation to achieve the kind of success Coghill and Pound achieved with their originals.

Pierre Leyris (1980) has a remarkable version of Gerard Manley Hopkins's 'The Wreck of the Deutschland' in which, at the cost perhaps of some strangeness in the French, the idiosyncratic movement of the Hopkins original is often successfully suggested. By contrast, there is another translation, by Jean-Georges Ritz (1980), in which Hopkins's verse pace, to my British ear, is less markedly copied, even though the greater smoothness of Ritz's versions may be preferred by some French readers. I shall show this from a single example, since the point about intonation should now be adequately proved by intuitive grasp. The lines are these:

I am soft sift
In an hourglass – at the wall
Fast . . .
(Hopkins, 'The Wreck of the Deutschland', stanza 4)

Je passe au sas
D'un sablier – contre la paroi, ferme . . .
(Leyris)

Doucement me voici tamisé
en un sablier – a la paroi
Adherent
(Ritz)

There is no need to tabulate results: the reader may trust his ear in pronouncing the verses and his eye in looking at Figure 5.2; and he will, I hope, conclude that Leyris keeps much more closely than Ritz in these lines to *both* the voicing pattern and (consequently) the pace of Hopkins, despite laying the verse out differently on the page. One may say this is just a question of syllable matching, but that won't entirely do: syllables form into the groups of voicing that are the main key to pacing. The fact that the 's's in Leyris are unvoiced is the decisive factor in matching Hopkins's pacing which depends on the same unvoiced sibilance. In the first line, he suggests the intonation of the English too.

The next step is to create a unified description of how a poem unifies rhythm and intonation into an artistic whole. Then we can look at how a variety of poets, ancient and modern, employ the factors we have been studying to create interaction between sound, meaning and emotional significance.

6

The Poet's Finesse

The relationship must now be made clear between (a) the abstract assignment of the position of a heavy stress within the line and (b) those factors which give us our 'exact' sense of how heavy the stress is, or where exactly in the syllable it 'occurs'. The first is a question of rule – word-stress, syntax and metrical system. (This is only one role of syntax. Various levels of syntactical groupings interact with the actual music of performance, as we shall see in Chapter 8.) The second is related to a performance by poet or reader and involves the formation of a mental concept: a plausible conceptual relationship between the assignment of a given stress position at a particular moment of the line and its performance-role in the more overall music. One might build up a hierarchy of description:

By rule, the *stress* is assigned to a notional instant within a syllable. In performance, the exact position of this instant can be tapped and yet the position is *also* mysterious in exact location conceptually, because it depends upon durations of sound. Metrical and grammatical word stress do not always coincide, but in a performance some informational content is always given to us by how heavy or light a stress is compared with its theoretical place in the abstract metrical pattern. So a performance definition of stress (see Chapter 8) must include expectations aroused by rule-governed assignment – an iambic pentameter, for example. In addition, a line of poetry will usually have at least one main informational focus and its 'dominant accent' (see below) takes perceptual precedence over the more minor play of stresses and weaker syllables elsewhere in the line. It makes nonsense, poetically, to talk of any degree of stress on an isolated syllable without recreating the music of its surrounding cadence each time.

The *syllable* is the site where the stress is supposed by us to 'occur'; the syllabic borders partly isolate for us durations of pitch, loudness and voice quality which contribute to our notion of stress. In this sense, the syllable is the smallest unit of rhythm, but what happens during the syllable is not the sole determinant of degree of stress; partly, stress and duration exist in the paradoxical relationship I have described; partly, more overall determinations come into play from intonation, voicing pattern, pause, tempo, longer cadence, syntactic grouping and so on.

The *voicing patterns* unite the syllable with the overall flow of the melody and thus they not only constitute units of melodic flow but also affect the degree of perceived stress at syllable level. Voicing patterns affect our sense of a line's pace because the melody cannot proceed without voicing. (For the role of unvoiced consonants, see below.) In addition, the dominant *accent* at the main informational focus is a moment when a slightly larger-scale artistic unity of sound, meaning and emotional potential is realised than at other stresses. The lines then join into cadences and stanzas and so on. Ideally considered, the point-like incidence of stress is therefore related continuously to the overall musical form of the poem.

Awareness of this hierarchy might affect our reading of a poem in various ways, a few of which are shown below. I believe in the notion of unconscious awareness. To save the reader from having to pore over too many graphs, oblique strokes and spaces show voicing gaps in performances. In the rest of the poetic examples in this book, I am performing the lines myself so as to illustrate as accurately as possible my own intuitive reading of the poem. (For the distinction between these two roles of machine analysis, see the Preface.) I find that machine traces normally do support my expectations but also throw up subtler patterns of which I had only been half-conscious when performing. We are no longer using the machinery quasi-scientifically to distinguish elements of a neutral tune but are firmly in the domain of critical intuition. I have reintroduced into the following examples some now familiar lines, so as to link previous discussions with this section.

LONG STRETCHES OF CONTINUOUS VOICING

(a) /So unwarely was never no man/ /caught
(Wyatt)

The continuous voicing up to 'man', linked with an easy undulation of pitch, keeps us 'unaware' but sensitive and allows an informational accent to be thrown on to 'caught'.

(b) /Love that/ /doth/ /reign and live within my/ /thought
(Surrey)

A similar effect is gained through continuous voicing by Surrey. When the concentration is upon the continuity of feeling, love reigning, the voicing patterns join together; the thought of love, as opposed to the continuous feeling of it, is isolated on the line ending, like 'caught'.

(c) /The long love that/ /in my/ /thoughts/ /doth/ /harbour/
(Wyatt)

Wyatt creates the same effect of continuity, on a slightly smaller scale, with 'The long love' in the above translation from the same Petrarchan sonnet.

(d) The droght of March hath perced to the rote
/And bathed every veyne/ /in/ /swich/ /licour/
(Chaucer, 'Prologue' to *The Canterbury Tales*)

The joined voicing pattern in the second line, very long in the machine trace (see Figure 4.6, 2nd comparison), seems to express continuous, sensuous awareness, and as may happen in continuous stretches of voicing the intonation holds fairly level.

(e) /The young in one another's arms/ /birds in the/ /trees/
(Yeats, 'Sailing to Byzantium')

Rapturous attention expressed through a level intonation contour for the first five words and joined voicing pattern.

(f) /My/ /poor reason thy words/ /moved/
(Sidney, 'All my sense')

The intonation falls from 'poor' onwards but the voicing pattern isolates the word 'moved', those two factors in some way increasing the sensed movement because it emphasises the previous continuity and throws more accent on to 'moved'.

(g) I'll shade him from the heat till he can bear
/To lean in joy/ /upon our/ /Father's knee/
. . .
And/he will then love/ /me/
(Blake, 'The Little Black Boy')

Again passages expressing intense feeling are sometimes effectively accompanied by continuous voicing and a level or gradually falling intonation ('to lean in joy', 'he will then love'), with a slightly plaintive effect wrought by isolating the final 'me' of the Little Black Boy.

These examples could easily be multiplied and we should often find stretches of continuous voicing accompanying phrases about continuous awareness or unawareness or rapt attention or sensuous perception or feeling states – in short, states not broken up by sudden thoughts. At such times the intonation may hold level or undulate smoothly. The continuity may be broken to throw emphasis upon a key word – this is an effect of pace. We must beware the trap of attempting to assign precise meaning to any suprasegmental factor in speech; certain elements of speech have a potential for various kinds of emotional expression, just as one can 'coo' with delight or, somewhat differently, to express surprise. Certain poets use continuous voicing patterns as very important elements in the interaction of their rhythm, music, meaning and emotional tone.

(h) Henry Vaughan is a prime example and voicing patterns are one key to his verse technique.

When shall that cry
'The bridegroom's coming' fill the sky
/Shall it in the evening run when our words/ /and works/ /are/ /done/
/Or will thy all/ /sur/ /prising light/
/Break/ /at/ /mid/ /night/
(Vaughan, 'The Dawning', with altered line break to show continuity)

Here the poet's rapturous attention to the great cry, its 'running', is expressed in the long segment of continuous voicing, which breaks up to express the finality of the 'words and works' being done. The continuity resumes for 'Or will thy all', with just two breaks, emphasising the natural one which makes the word '/sur/ /prise/' expressive. But then the last line, which is most effective if read slowly with emphasised pauses as shown, gives the whole thought dramatic emphasis. Vaughan, this is to say, is above all a poet who works with variations of pace, often to express rapture: stretches of continuous voicing are commoner than usual in such poems.

BROKEN-UP VOICING PATTERNS

Of course, it is just as much a use of voicing patterns to use them disjointedly, limiting them mostly to the length of a single syllable.

(i) Sometimes the effect is unemotional or meditative, as in Larkin's well-known lines:

> Once I am sure there's nothing going on
> /I/ /step/ /in/ /side/ /le/ /tting/ /the/ /door/ /thud/ /shut/
>
> (Larkin, 'Church Going')

To say that the miming of the door shutting is partly an effect of syllabic pace is the same as saying it comes from breaking up the voicing pattern into individual syllables. (Of course, there is onomatopoeia too.) And, along with the modest, unrapturous tone of the poem, the intonation sets up staccato falling rhythms. In fact, if Vaughan in his poem can be described as the poet of rapturous, continuous voicing, Larkin might be described at least in this poem as the poet of modest, broken-up voicing patterns; this well suggests not only the difference between the two poets but also the difference in potential expressivity between the two kinds of pattern:

> /Ano/ /ther/ /church/ /ma/ /tting/ /seats/ /and/ /stone/
> /And/ /li/ /ttle/ /books/
>
> (Larkin, ibid)

The littleness can be emphasised by a quicker tempo in the second line, which is a further syllable-voicing pattern interaction with pace. And the most celebrated lines from this poem:

/Hat/ /less/ /I/ /take/ /off/ /my/ /cy/ /cle/ /clips/ /in/ /aw/ /kward/ /reverence/

(line endings altered)

where it is exactly on the word 'reverence' that the formerly broken pattern is allowed briefly to flow into miniscule enthusiasm.

(j) Coleridge, like Vaughan, another master of continuous voicing – used often in 'The Ancient Mariner' to express anguish – breaks up his patterns to create a meditative effect:

/The/ /frost/ /per/ /forms/ /its/ /se/ /cret/ /mini/ /stry/
/Un/ /helped/ /by/ /any wind./

('Frost at Midnight')

(k) A parallel can again be drawn between Wyatt and Surrey and it will teach us not to ascribe our meanings too positively. We have seen Wyatt reconcentrating his attention in the second line here:

So unwarely was never no man caught
/With/ /stead/ /fast/ /look/ /upon a/ /goodly/ /face/

and should not forget that the second line is in contrast with the continuity of the first: the rhythmic management of variety increasing the reader's awareness.

(l) Surrey has:

/With/ /shame/ /fast/ /cloak/ /to/ /shadow and re/ /frain/

where I do not feel able to describe the expressive effect of the broken patterns except to say that it is contrasted dramatically with the more continuous patterns at the end of the line.

(m) Another potential expressivity in broken patterns will remind us that the range of effects from voicing patterns is, in fact, extremely broad. Very often broken patterns make us think individually about the syllables; they are therefore useful when describing quick movements or a series of quick perceptions. Marvell's fawn is an apt example:

/With/ /what/ /a/ /pre/ /tty/ /ski/ /pping grace/
/It/ /oft/ /would/ /challenge/ /me/ /the race/
/And when/ /it had/ /left/ /me far away/
/'Twould/ /stay/ /and run again/ /and/ /stay/

where I have spaced the last line so that it can be seen how the effect upon pace of syllables and voicing patterns can be used in a reading of the poem to mime the contrary movements of the fawn. It will be noticed that the third line returns to a slightly more continuous pattern when we see the deer no longer frisking about but receding. To underline how voicing pattern and intonation are linked, the performance also shows similar rise-fall intonation cadences in the first two lines and so have ''Twould stay' and 'and stay', for the slowness of these two phrases on either side of the quicker, running phrase is mirrored in their intonation too.

MIXED VOICING PATTERNS

More usually, a poet will alternate between continuous and broken voicing patterns as part of the range of musical effects he has at his disposal. If the data is examined with sensitive eyes and ears, it will be seen that a near-infinity of effects can be gained, most far too psychologically subtle to be described convincingly.

Rather than strive for this vast range of effects I will just give a pair of examples, not without a special interest, because they show that the nonsense poetry of Edward Lear sometimes creates musical effects remarkably like those in the serious poetry of his friend, Tennyson. Davidson writes (1968, pp. 200, 214) that Lear was a popular after-dinner singer, when he would generally perform some of his own settings of Tennyson's songs. He illustrated his poems, which became the chief occupation of his old age, and was influenced by him more than merely to the extent of using his metres, Davidson adds. Sometimes the music is so close that a parody seems in question:

O my aged Uncle Arly!
Sitting on a heap of Barley
Through the silent hours of night, –
Lear ('Incidents in the Life of
My Uncle Arly')

Only reapers, reaping early
In among the bearded barley,
Hear a song that echoes cheerly
Tennyson ('The Lady of Shalott')

Figure 6.1 shows how close these are in voicing pattern and in intonation. Sparing the reader the exact calculations, the voicing patterns matched by an average of 70.8 per cent for all three lines, and the intonation contours an average of 72.1 per cent. If these percentages are compared with those for different readings of the same poem's lines, it will be seen what a close match these lines from different poems are, as indeed an examination of the text could also show us. The example is so clear that it confirms that these methods can add an examination of how the parodist works to the examination of translation, because intonation and voicing patterns are involved there too.

If what has been said above is true, then surely two poems of evidently similar movement and music should show the same voicing patterns? Yet there is little similarity of voicing pattern between the following two lines and even the intonation contours do not very closely match, although the rhythm and pacing are evidently very similar:

On the/ /Coast/ /of/ /Coromandel where/ /the/ /early/ /pum/ /pkins/ /grow/
(Lear)

Row/ /us/ /out/ /from Desen/ /zano/ /to your/ /Sirmione row/
(Tennyson)

The main effect of similarity of pacing in the above lines comes from the fact that words of similar syllabic count are placed in an almost identical order. The number of syllables in successive words is as follows:

Lear:	1, 1, 1, 1, 4, 1, 1, 2, 2, 1
Tennyson:	1, 1, 1, 1, 4, 1, 1, 4, 1

However, a good reader performing these two lines will also notice a *difference* in their pacing and in their manner of carrying their music. Especially in the last half of the line, Tennyson's poem

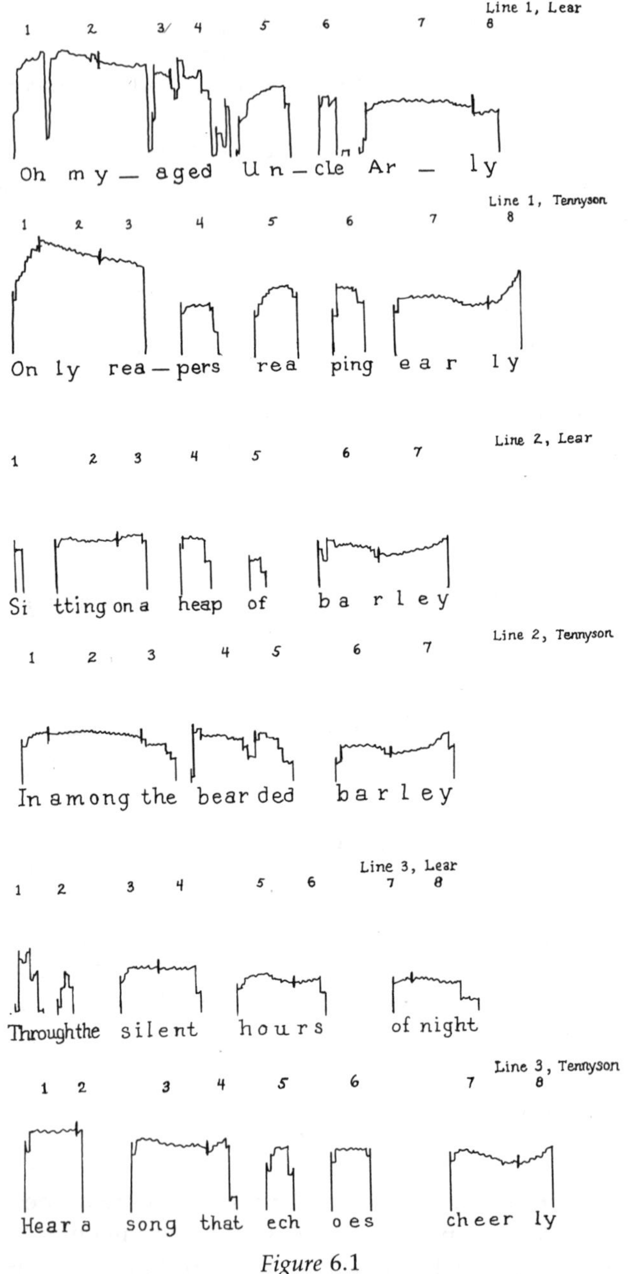
Line 1, Lear
1 2 3 4 5 6 7 8
Oh my — aged Un — cle Ar — ly
Line 1, Tennyson
1 2 3 4 5 6 7 8
On ly rea — pers rea ping ear ly
Line 2, Lear
1 2 3 4 5 6 7
Si tting on a heap of barley
Line 2, Tennyson
1 2 3 4 5 6 7
In among the bear ded barley
Line 3, Lear
1 2 3 4 5 6 7 8
Through the silent hours of night
Line 3, Tennyson
1 2 3 4 5 6 7 8
Hear a song that ech oes cheer ly

Figure 6.1

seems more fulsome of emotion and more serious in implication, while its pacing flows more mellifluously. Lear's 'pumpkins' on the other hand make the line jerky and a little ridiculous, fit for the absurdity of his meaning. It is precisely the voicing pattern which creates these differences: it interferes with the rather beautiful, flowing melody of the beginning of Lear's line and makes it jerkily absurd. Tennyson's more continuous voicing keeps the throat open and the music flowing throughout the line. So these lines afford a delicate demonstration of the difference between the effect of syllabic rhythmic similarity and that of dissimilarity of voicing patterns.

VOWELS, VOICED AND UNVOICED CONSONANTS

We began with the notion of poetic stress. However, aspects of a line's sound smaller than syllable length, such as a consonant's or vowel's sonic characteristics, probably affect our only half-conscious awareness of 'infinite' gradations of stress. Most particularly, since voiced consonants take part in the intonation contours along with the vowels, what about the role of unvoiced consonants which do not even appear on the machine traces so far studied?

Unvoiced sounds may be described as the whispered parts of an utterance, as in 'whisper' itself, where only the 'i' and the 'e' are sounded in the glottis. Meyer-Eppler (1972) has shown that whispered (i.e. devoiced) speech has its own substitute for changes of pitch in ordinary speech: there are shifts of some formant regions accompanied by added noise between the higher formants (for 'formant', see Glossary). His work implies that changes to the unvoiced but spoken parts of ordinary speech, and of poetry too, are important to the ear. Such sounds create a *substitute* for music with changes to the higher formants and further effects from the *contrast* between voicing and non-voicing. Each consonant has its own frequency pattern, makes different demands on the mouth and tongue with consequent emotional significance, and is long or short to say. Of course, consonants interact with vowels too. I shall content myself with just a few examples whose main import is to illuminate my later topic of emotion. For this we shall need a different kind of machinery.

In Figures 6.2–5 I have included photographs from a remarkable real-time speech intonation spectrometer, developed

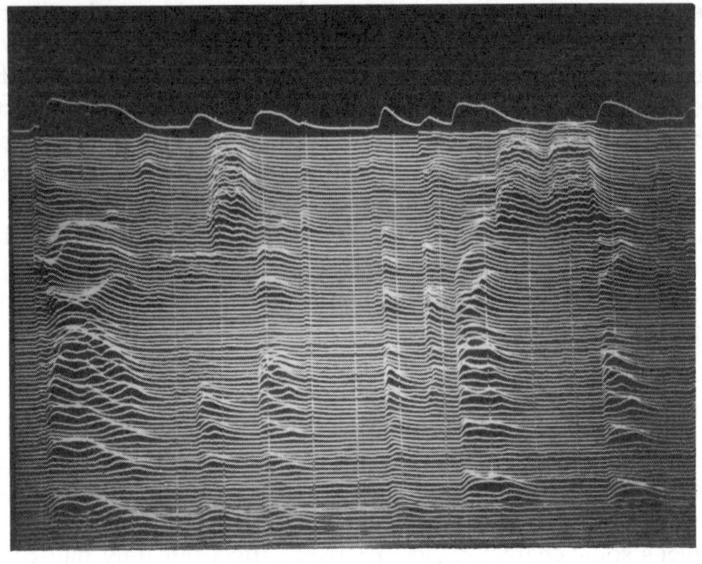

D r i – v e h e s d for Chr i – s t’s s a k e

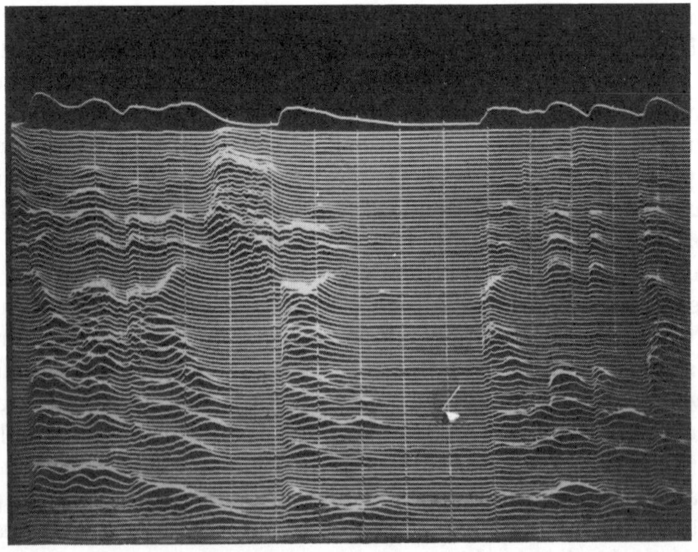

T i llher e y – e s s h i – n e l l – i ve/ in ...

Figure 6.2

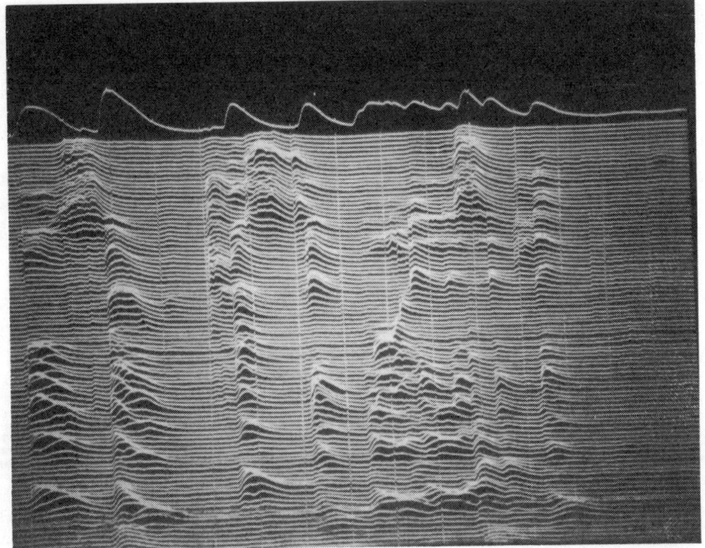

Figure 6.3

by D. C. Jeffrey, Department of Mechanical Engineering, University of Edinburgh, and H. C. Longuet-Higgins, of the Centre for Research on Perception and Cognition, Laboratory of Experimental Psychology, University of Sussex. The machine traces lines of light across a screen, each line indicating a frequency filtered out from the overall sound waves of the voice as the performer reads. There are 12 filters per octave and 96 in all, spaced at intervals of a keyboard semitone. The fundamental frequency contour (whose traces we have been previously studying) can generally be seen as the path followed by the cluster or band of frequencies (formant) at the bottom of the screen. One of the many virtues of this display is that it clearly identifies the role of fricatives such as 's', whose high, sibilant frequencies group at the top of the overall 'contour map' created by the 96 lines. An unvoiced sound can be distinguished from a voiced one because if there is no voicing the band of frequencies at the bottom of the photographs falls to zero, leaving only disturbance at the higher frequency bands. The sharp onset of gutturals, such as 'k', and the merging into vowel sounds of liquids, such as 'l', can also be seen, while vowels or other

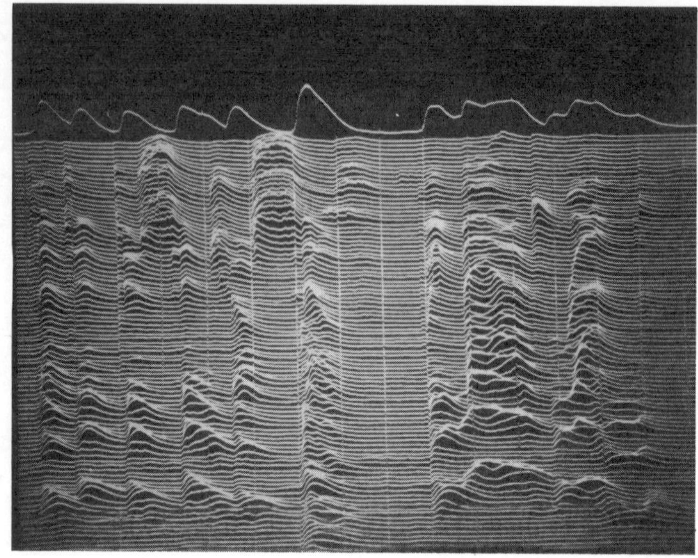
That it do singe yours elf We may outrun

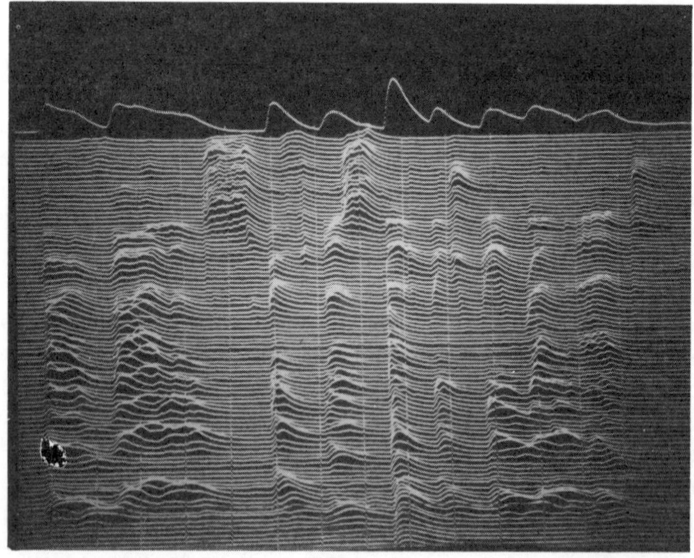
By v iolent sw ift ness that which we run at

Figure 6.4

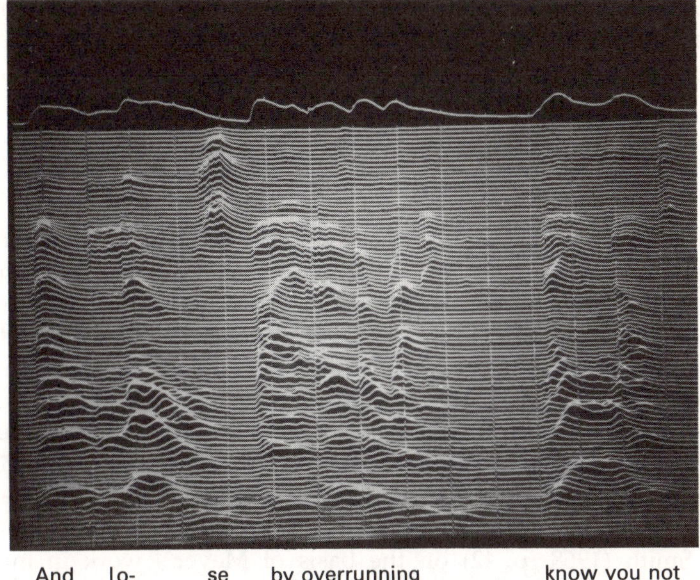

Figure 6.5

sounds which activate wide bands of frequencies across the whole voice can be distinguished from the much 'lighter' sounds such as 't'. The line at the very top of the photographs shows intensity, which correlates with our sense of loudness and indicates the basic rhythm.

CONSONANTS AND VOWELS

From examples mentioned in other chapters we have already been studying details of consonants. The minute air explosions in Pope's 'The proper study of mankind is man' break up the voicing so that we attend to the admonition. As will be seen from the photograph in Figure 6.2, the devoiced 'z' in Sidney's 'Till her eyes shine I live in darkest night' could be extended (upper band of down-sloping frequencies between 'eyes' and 'shine'); and a reader could accentuate this to create emotional tension.

Sibilant consonants, or fricatives, such as 's' and 'z', enable us to be more precise about the relation between continuity of sound in poetry and emotion. Since I have deliberately employed sibilance in a poem of my own and there is necessarily no other case of which I have inside knowledge, I hope to be forgiven the unforgivable in quoting the lines:

> His darkening litter trail is of gratitude also
> harm follows steeply. He distrusts literacy and also
> trusts it more illicitly.

This concerns a poet's literal descent into a cave to conduct a moral inquiry, and the intention, as far as it was conscious, was to use 't's and 's's to prevent the reader's voice sounding; the result breaks up the melody so as to interrupt that emotional outlet of voicing. This also makes for fast pace. The result, I would claim, accentuates our sense of unease and distrust.

I believe, in fact, that any change of sound in poetic music involves a change of emotional tone, even if the sound change is minute and the emotional change not really perceptible. This belief is an extreme version of a Gestaltist psychological principle followed by Smith (1968, p. 42) on the basis of Meyer's work in music (Meyer, 1956). She supposes a poem with eight-syllable lines consisting of random words and continued without variation. A reader would become increasingly irritated, bored or oppressed. Repetition, she adds, stabilises a structure of which it is a part, but the longer it continues the more desperate we become for variation or conclusion. She associates this with the Gestaltist notion of 'saturation'. Meyer says that the reaction of a listener to music will depend upon the degree to which he perceives the signal as meaningful. To extend this, we have noted how even minute sound changes can be interpreted to give clues to a person's emotional state; and we have been examining the effect of slight changes in various kinds of poetry. Because the structure of a syllable is so small, the tolerance limit on how long a vowel continues to make the same sound is very short in duration and boredom quickly sets in when we hear a reciter 'intone' verse, especially by over-lengthening the vowels.

A line by the American poet, Robert Creeley (1966), shows how the unvoiced sibilants in 'for christ's sake' can be employed to maintain tension across a voicing gap.

> drive, he sd, for
> christ's sake, look
> out where yr going

There would be some optimum interval in any one performance of this line for how long the 'hissing' 'for christsssssake' should last across its voicing gap if maximum tension is to be attained. The same is true for the use of this expletive in normal conversation: it can be made more menacing by prolonging the inter-word interval while maintaining the 's' sounds, but only up to a certain duration. Similarly, in the line from Sidney already quoted, 'Till her eyes shine', the two words linked by the sibilance are extremely important semantically. The emotional tension between the eyes (closed at present in sleep) and their future shining can be emphasised by prolonging the devoiced [z̥] until it changes into the unvoiced [ʃ] but, again, this can only be done up to a certain duration.

We may conjecture that the cause of this is a link between poetic stress and emotion. It may be that the unvoiced gap 'sssss' between the voiced parts of 'for Christ's sake' can only be extended up to the point where we may still reasonably back-date its meaning and emotional significance on to 'for Christ' and post-date it on to 'sake'. If the 's' becomes a sound *on its own* it loses its tension, because it loses its tie with the meaning and emotional significance of the two words it contemptuously joins. Of course, it could acquire new meaning (and almost does so) as a simple, aggressive hiss – but that is another question. It would incur new durational limits, for a hiss that is too prolonged loses its tie with the original impulse of aggression that promoted it and would become boring. And so on. The durational limits involved here can be extremely precise – it is the poetic artist's secret of timing, and is similar to the way a comedian times a joke. Good readers of poetry must instinctively know that the durations and timing of consonant, vowel and syllable are governed by the whole sound of the line. This is too subjective to pursue far, but a poet like Sidney gives the impression of immense 'speed of ear' – I can't think of another phrase to describe it – by which I mean that his specification of durations of sound and placement of consonant seems remarkably exact in lines like:

> Come sleep, o sleep, the certain knot of peace,
> The baiting place of wit, the balm of woe

'The certain knot of peace' and 'The baiting place of wit' are similar rhythmic units with similar intonation, and the syllables 'knot', 'bait' and 'wit' are sonically related. A good reader can assess exactly how much to make 'bait' longer than 'knot' so as to increase our sense both of parallelism and difference between the two units. And so too with 'sleep', 'sleep', and 'peace'; and with 'place' and 'peace'; and 'o' and 'woe'; and 'wit' and 'woe'. But, more than that, an even better reader will know how quickly to pronounce the 'sl' of 'sleep' each time and the 'pl' and 'c' of 'place'; and how much to prolong the 'alm' of 'balm' so that 'the balm of woe' may form an equivalent but *not* identical rhythmic unit to 'The certain knot of peace' and 'The baiting place of wit'. The exactness is, therefore, not just a question of vowel length but also of consonant management; and exact timing is governed by the lines' whole form. I have always supposed that it is because of this exactness that Sidney has often been called 'a poet's poet'.

In these well-known lines from *The Merchant of Venice*, so much is going on in the sounds and there is such exact specification of durations that the ear can hardly contain it all:

> How sweet the moonlight sleeps upon this bank!
> Here will we sit and let the sounds of music
> Creep in our ears; soft stillness and the night
> Become the touches of sweet harmony.
> Sit, Jessica. Look how the floor of heaven
> Is thick inlaid with patens of bright gold.

Once or twice in my life, I have read these lines to myself and discovered a strange sliding sensation in my consciousness. At each stress, there is a temporal glide in my mind, as if I had extra time to choose when to pronounce a vowel or consonant or decide a duration. It makes me feel how immensely gifted and versatile poetically I *could* be, although it is really Shakespeare who has placed that potential in me. Unfortunately, not being Shakespeare, I can never be sure of repeating the experience and feel chary of trying to persuade the reader that it happens. This is more than just seeing how 'sweet', 'sleep' and 'creep' have durations that can be mutually adjusted, how the 'ch' of 'touches' modulates into the 'J' of 'Jessica', or how the 'i's and 'k's work in the extraordinary last two lines. I can only suppose that all those post-datings and back-datings of durations on to points of stress have such formal excellence that the notional instants and the durations of sounds are brought into almost complete interdependence; once an initial duration has been decided (the durations of 'How sweet'), every other duration seems decided at the same time. The notional instants become impregnated, so to speak, with their ambiguous opposite, duration, until time itself seems to slide.

We may escape a little from such subjectivity of reaction by looking at photographs (Figures 6.4–5) of the following three lines from *Henry VIII*, the lines in brackets being included for context:

> (Heat not a furnace for your foe so hot)
>
> That it do singe yourself. We may outrun
> By violent swiftness that which we run at
> And lose by overrunning.
>
> (Know you not
> The fire that mounts the liquor till't run o'er
> In seeming to augment it wastes it . . .)

Prosodic mastery here makes extraordinary a fairly commonplace thought – that in hunting, perhaps, or in a tourney, one should moderate the speed of attack to the quarry's speed. The word 'violent' has a heavy stress which we think of as sited either on the 'i' or between the 'v' and 'i'. But it will be seen from the photograph that the 'io' diphthong and the liquid 'l' share a voicing duration in which the vocal frequencies do not much change, the sounds merging into each other: although the stress on the first vowel of 'violent' must be point-like, it simultaneously seems to spread out across the prolonged sound so that its location is precise but also not precise. The effect holds us in suspense and makes the verse seem to stand still while also moving, as Olson (1967, p. 85) rather colourfully suggests. The sibilance at the beginning of the word 'swiftness' has been prepared for by that on 'singe yourself'. We can increase the ambiguity of stress on 'violent' by prolonging slightly the 'sw' of 'swiftness'; the vowels of the second word are very short and there is renewed devoicing and sibilance throughout it; this means that the emotional suspense in the word 'violent' is not resolved by more-steady, voiced syllables until 'that which we run at', where the voicing goes in measured pulses. Often in poetry, during devoicing, emotional resolution is held up because there is no pitch; and intonation and emotion are tightly linked, as we have seen.

With the word 'overrunning', on the other hand, there should be a heavy stress on '-run-', but the stress is almost lost in a steadily declining pitch and unemphatic union of vowels and nasal consonants. That is, the ear marks a heavy stress because that is what the abstract metric requires, but the actual sounds are very weak and so are fit to express 'lack of success', as the semantics require. Because abstract metric contradicts actual sound we gain a finer appreciation of how weak the syllables, '-running', are. The effect is a reminder that we must include abstract metric as an influence upon how heavy a stress seems, as we shall see in Chapter 8.

7

Eve in the Garden

Describing the qualities of Milton's versification has never been easy. Back in the fiery days of Dr Leavis, he wrote of 'Milton's habit of exploiting language as a kind of musical medium outside himself, as it were. There is no pressure in his verse of any complex and varying current of feeling and sensation; the words have little substance or muscular quality: Milton is using only a small part of the resources of the English language' (Leavis, 1963, p. 71). We must allow a great critic his blind side and old disputes can be left aside; but the comments provide a sounding-board by which to judge Milton's practice. A passage of *Paradise Lost*, examined by machine, can show that the music is by no metaphorical stretch 'outside' Milton, nor lacking in the most subtle currents of feeling and sensation. This time again, the machinery is being used only as objective evidence of my personal interpretation of the verse music.

One profitable approach to the music of Milton's poetry is to combine analyses of: his care in syntactical placement of key words; his management of syllabic pace; the incorporation of this movement and syntax into longer cadences organised into paragraphs of the sonorous measure; and the interaction of this with the poem as a whole. A study which includes the patterns of voicing and pitch according to the principles established in this book will reveal, however, kinds of pattern in Milton's poetry often inadequately considered. For brevity, I shall not discuss patterns of stress, as the essential points about the role of this in prosody have already been made and I shall return to some philosophical aspects of the subject in Chapter 8.

Many of the voicing patterns in this passage are so broken up that each syllable is isolated in the sound continuum and it is at syllable level that many of the complex effects of pacing, rhythm and melody are achieved. We shall see that this is not always so, and in any case voicing patterns and syllables are, as previously argued, in necessary conjunction. This time, only parts of the overall trace patterns will be displayed where necessary. (Figures 7.1 to 7.5.)

Much of the beauty is obtained through a Latinate syntactical management and placing of key words. This is a good moment to mention the role of syntax in all these studies, although in the final definition of stress in Chapter 8 the role will be included. Syntax always plays an important part in prosody; but it should be related to more overriding concerns, for I imagine that most poets, like musicians, *compose* essentially through the flow of their music. Syntax that is too orthodox can result in dullness. My concentration has been upon a-grammatical, non-linguistic, often neglected aspects of prosody, referring to syntactical aspects only when they seemed specially of note. To repair this partial omission and to suggest how syntactical study might combine with the methods so far explored, it is convenient to treat of it in Milton who, of all English poets, most expertly adjusts his syntax to interact with his cadences.

A single passage, with a selection of internal patterns distinguished, is enough to show his versification most characteristically in action.

> By fountain or by shady rivulet
> He sought them both, but wished his hap might find
> Eve separate; he wished, but not with hope
> Of what so seldom chanced, when to his wish,
> Beyond his hope, Eve separate he spies,
> Veiled in a cloud of fragrance, where she stood,
> Half spied, so thick the roses bushing round
> About her glowed, oft stooping to support
> Each flower of slender stalk, whose head though gay
> Carnation, purple, azure, or specked with gold,
> Hung drooping unsustained; them she upstays
> Gently with myrtle band, mindless the while,
> Herself, though fairest unsupported flower,
> From her best prop so far, and storm so nigh.
> (*Paradise Lost*, IX, lines 420–33)

The interpretation of this passage has been illuminated by generations of critics, whom I mostly silently acknowledge.[1] I shall discuss the lines under three headings: (a) interpretation of the passage; (b) the role played by syntax; and (c) what the machine traces show. Each section, *I*(a), (b), (c), etc., treats of a line or two almost chronologically down the passage.

I. (a) Satan, after being defeated in his rebellion, has decided that his only possible revenge against God is to fly down to Paradise and to incite Adam and Eve to an equivalent rebellion. Milton holds a precise version of the traditional Medieval-Renaissance view of woman that she is more easily corruptible than man, owing to her allegedly weaker reasoning powers; so Satan has most chance if he can find Eve separated from her husband. It is almost but not quite the beginning of her sin that she has left Adam; it merely leaves her vulnerable: her sin must be presumed to begin after eating the apple and then only. Satan, who is in serpent form, seeks Eve both by the fountain that in so much late medieval poetry symbolises a source by which to discuss true love, and by shady rivulet. Very conjecturally, the sun in Renaissance poetry usually symbolises divine, regal and masculine reason, justice and order. The rivulet, as opposed to the leaping-yet-fixed form of the fountain, more naturally stands for changeability, a stream which is distanced from the fountain and from which the sun is withdrawn; this may further emphasise Eve's vulnerability (though in fact Satan will find her employed in a flower garden).

(b) In the syntax, we note the initial inversion which places 'both' at the end of a clause to contrast with 'separate' at the end of its clause. Syntactical parallelism makes us notice the possible opposition between fountain and rivulet. Then, too, 'separate' is cadentially positioned so as to augment the following syntactical pause, which makes us notice this key word.

(c) From the traces we see the sonic coupling which immediately strikes our unaided ear:

By fountain or by shady rivulet

Eve separate

He is setting up intonation patterns that he will use later, and the pairing of these words would underline the conjectural association between the changeable and shady rivulet and Eve's vulnerability. On the other hand, the greater weight given rhythmically to the fountain, with its two long syllables, plus the repetition of 'by', points up the difference between the two words and associates the weakness of 'rivulet' with that of 'separate'. A voicing gap within 'separate' plus the weak and falling intonation increases the effect.

II. (a) Milton has from the beginning of his narrative placed Satan's desires into an impossible condition. The only real hope that angels and men can have comes from adoring God and hoping to follow the divine plan, because that is the source of all good. A rebel angel is therefore cast down, hopeless, into despair; and the rebel can only have experience of chance and chaos in his own actions; this is what his 'free will' must come down to, since nothing can withstand God who provides form and justice through his mercy. Satan has created from this very despair, through his fierce desire, the negative counterparts to Christian virtues: a despairing hope that is no hope but is subject to chance – from Satan's point of view. As Augustine wrote in *The City of God*: 'For our very wills are in that order of causes, which God knows so surely and hath in his presience.'[2] In Book II of Milton's poem, for example, Satan is described as:

> by merit raised
> To that bad eminence; and from despair
> Thus high uplifted beyond hope . . . (l. 5)

and so through the despicable windings of the hellish council, where Beelzebub describes their state as strictest bondage while God will

> over hell extend
> His empire, and with iron sceptre rule
> Us here, as with his golden those in heaven . . . (l. 326)

and again Milton writes:

> By false presumptuous hope, the ranged powers
> Disband . . . (l. 522)

Whereas man's relationship to hope is obviously different:

> Devil with devil damned
> Firm concord holds, men only disagree
> Of creatures rational, though under hope
> Of heavenly grace: and God proclaiming peace
> Yet live in hatred . . . (l. 496)

Milton's notion of free will can be explored from his *De Doctrina Christiana*.[3] He says that God perfectly foreknows what will happen from contingent events and out of man's free will, so that such events will happen certainly, but not out of necessity. Thus God foreknew that Adam would fall of his own free will; his fall was therefore certain, but not necessary, since it proceeded from his own free will, which is incompatible with necessity.

(b) Consequently, 'wished', 'hope', 'chanced', 'wish' and 'hope' are key words, emphasising the contradictions in Satanic desire and despair: Satan's wishing for results that cannot finally be hoped for, since they are against God's plan.[4] By renewed syntactical (and therefore rhythmical) patterning, these words are set into ironic compilations. This is emphasised by rhythmically-interrupting devices of parenthesis and/or by placing words at ends of clauses.

(c) So in the traces we find:

but wished his hap

he wished but not with hope

Here, the intonation and voicing patterns are similar from 'but' onwards. The remarks about rhyme at the end of Chapter 8 are appropriate here, for the half-rhyme takes a longer syllable on 'hope' than on 'hap' and the quality of the vowel is more breathy. It is the difference between two apparently similar sounds that makes us reflect and respond emotionally to the contrast between the triviality of 'hap' compared with Christian 'hope'. As we have said, Satan's emotional medium is despair ('not with hope'), desire ('wish') and chance ('hap'). There is a variation on this:

when to his wish

Beyond his hope

make similar intonation patterns, although this is disguised through the voicing gap between 'his' and 'hope'. However, the similarity, plus the prepositional contrast with its effect upon voicing pattern, helps us to reflect upon the antithesis in the prepositions.

We can take up the theme of separateness:

Eve separate; he wished . . .

Eve separate he spies

Again the difference is as important as the similarity. The shorter syllables of the first line's 'Eve separate' emphasise her weakness through the light, unvoiced sounds of 'separate' and its syntactical position at the end of the clause. And the pause here is quite the opposite to that following Wyatt's word 'late' in Chapter 3: it makes us reflect back upon Eve's frailty and so makes the light stresses of '-arate' seem even weaker, not stronger; it is an example of how our semantic–emotional apprehension plays effects into our sense of how heavy or light a stress is – lightening here, whereas in Wyatt's case the result was to make the stress seem heavier. Further, in the second line the syllables of 'Eve separate' lengthen out because they are syntactically linked to the movement of Satan's desire. 'He spies' is a little sinister semantically and a reader can lengthen it in the normal conversational device of uneasy suspense employing sibilance. (See my remarks on sibilance in Chapter 6.)

III. (a) Satan now sees Eve in the paradisaical garden, surrounded by the roses that symbolise permanent love: love of God, and of his creation, Adam.

(b) Syntactically, by another parenthetical device, Milton emphasises that the roses get in between Eve and Satan's 'half-spying', so that at first glance she seems surrounded by these symbols of love before we see her stooping as though premonitory of her own, unpropped fraility and propensity to fall.

(c) Similar intonation and syllabic length can create congeries of words that interact in significance:

his hap might find

Eve separate he spies

half spied

where she stood

where 'find', 'spies' and 'spied' are linked by intonation and duration and contrasted in duration with 'stood'.

IV. (a) She is binding and strengthening the roses with bands of myrtle. Fowler points out that the two flowers were associated in the Renaissance iconography of the festival of Venus, following an incident described by Ovid, where Venus, bathing, hid behind a tree to escape satyrs. The head of the rose symbolised, of course, the frailty of human happiness and love, as in the *carpe diem* theme, and binding the rose with myrtle 'should be read as an emblem of the dependence of unfallen bliss upon conjugal virtue'. Panofsky (1972, p. 161) notes that in the iconography of Renaissance painting myrtle symbolises faithful, everlasting love and was called *myrtus coniugalis* in classical literature.

(b) The adverbial clauses that follow 'he spies' mean that Milton does not need to repeat 'she' as subject for 'oft stooping', but this lack of subject associates Eve all the more closely with the 'glowing' and adds slightly to our notion of her, too, as a rose.

(c) With more continuity of attention upon the beauty of the scene the voicing patterns characteristically stretch out:

> So thick the roses bushing round about her glowed

whereas when we are to attend to her separate movements these patterns break up:

> oft stooping to support Each flower

and so our concentration is thrown upon the prolepsis, further emphasised by the parallel, 'oft stooping', 'hung drooping'. (See Chapter 6 for continuous and broken voicing effects.)

V. (a) The purple, azure and gold colours of these flowers are those of Minerva, the virgin goddess, as Fowler notes.

(b) In the syntax these colours are given to us through parenthesis, and the syntactically unnecessary word 'them' is inserted to emphasise the strength that the binding power of the emblematic myrtle lends to them.

(c) In the traces the music works through modulation and variation of voicing pattern, syllabic length and intonation to bring out the contrast in the different colours of flowers:

> whose head, though gay
> Carnation, purple, azure, or specked with gold

with intonational parallellism between 'gay' and 'gold'.

VI. (a) Eve's lack of rational strength is underlined by the word 'mindless', or heedless, as dreamily she binds the flowers, herself more at risk than any of them since her own prop, Adam, is far from her. Fowler helpfully reminds us of Proserpina earlier in the poem, described as 'Herself a fairer flower' when carried off by the king of hell in IV, l. 270.

(b) Syntactically, this important word 'mindless', which might otherwise be little noticed, is set in relief by inversion and by the way its meaning is thus so oddly thrown on to 'herself'.

(c) Because 'the while' and 'herself' create parallel intonation and rhythmic patterns, 'the while' makes us notice 'herself' and associate it more strongly with 'mindless'. The shorter fall on 'self' places the emphasis on this last word.

We have to be cautious about pushing the machine traces too far into interpretation, but there are other patterns of intonation, unifying the music though with less obvious play-off on meaning:

specked with gold

unsustained

myrtle band

These are all syncopated, short–short long; but 'specked with gold' breaks the voicing pattern, as happens often with a meaning where attention is visually divided (see Chapter 6); 'unsustained' has an extremely weak intonation fall, in keeping with its meaning; whereas 'myrtle band' is generally longer throughout, as the voice stays on these two words of marital value.

How such detail binds part of the poem together can be shown from a last pair of examples:

VII. (a) With Eve's and, later, Adam's fall the whole harmony of nature, man and God will be broken: the storm, in which nature's elements are thrown out of order and into chaos and chance collision, is about to break.

(b) The connection between her frailty and the coming chaos is brought out by syntactial parallelism: 'prop so far', 'storm so nigh', which again leaves its marks upon the intonational trace.

(c) We look first at the pairing:

unsupported flower

(From her) best prop so far

Both lines contain allied meanings and provide similar voicing patterns and rhythms, with the half-rhyme on 'flower'/'far' echoed in similar intonation. The 'farness' is mimed, however, by greater durations of vowel and voicing interval in the second line.

This sonic pairing is then drawn tighter in the last line, where the syntactic parallel already noticed under (b) binds together:

prop so far

storm so nigh

The similarity in the trace is mainly one of voicing pattern: the intonation is not copied. One difference is a voicing gap before 'far', perhaps emphasising distance compared to the lack of gap in 'so nigh', which increases, through extra pace, our sense of the storm's threatening nearness. This contrast in meaning is brought out by a contrast in intonation, rising on 'far' for suspense and falling very low on 'storm so nigh' to bring out the sombreness of the threat. 'Unsupported flower', 'prop so far' and 'storm so nigh' are thus linked by two sequential bondings into musical similarity.

I have emphasised that I am here using the machine traces for deliberate pedagogic purposes; in many ways I have put into the reading what I thought ought to be there. Nevertheless, much of the patterning discovered above was put in unconsciously on my part; and in the fine detail of the traces more yet can be found. So many of the stresses and durations are bound into longer patterns extending across the cadence. The passage is lively evidence that we cannot know what stress to give any one syllable without a sense of its interaction with the flow and pauses of the music, both in the syllable's past and in its future.

Of course, in all poetry there is this necessary tie between syntax, music, rhythm, meaning and emotional significance, and I hope the foregoing, read in conjunction with the analysis of intonation and voicing, is enough to show how one might create a unified prosodic description. This short passage yields a host of Milton's musical mirroring devices, some semantically and emotionally significant, some just elements in a musical unity. I do not say that a sensitive ear could not spot these details; but the machine traces become a useful adjunct to our normal critical intuition as well as being an aid where the ear is not sensitive.

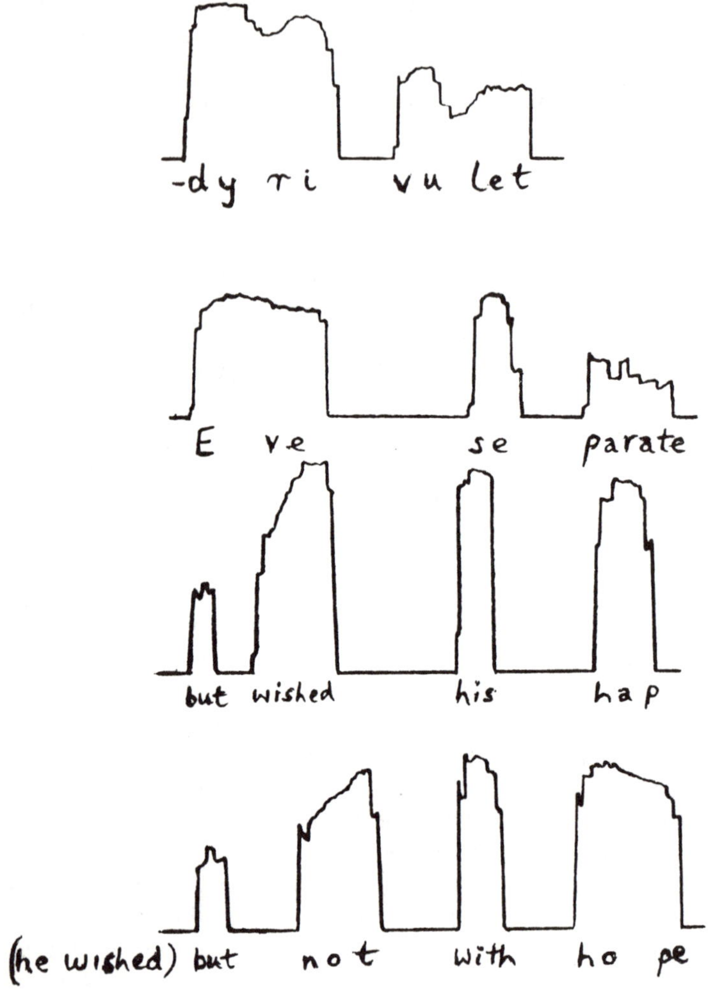
-dy ri vu let
E ve se parate
but wished his hap
(he wished) but not with ho pe

Figure 7.1

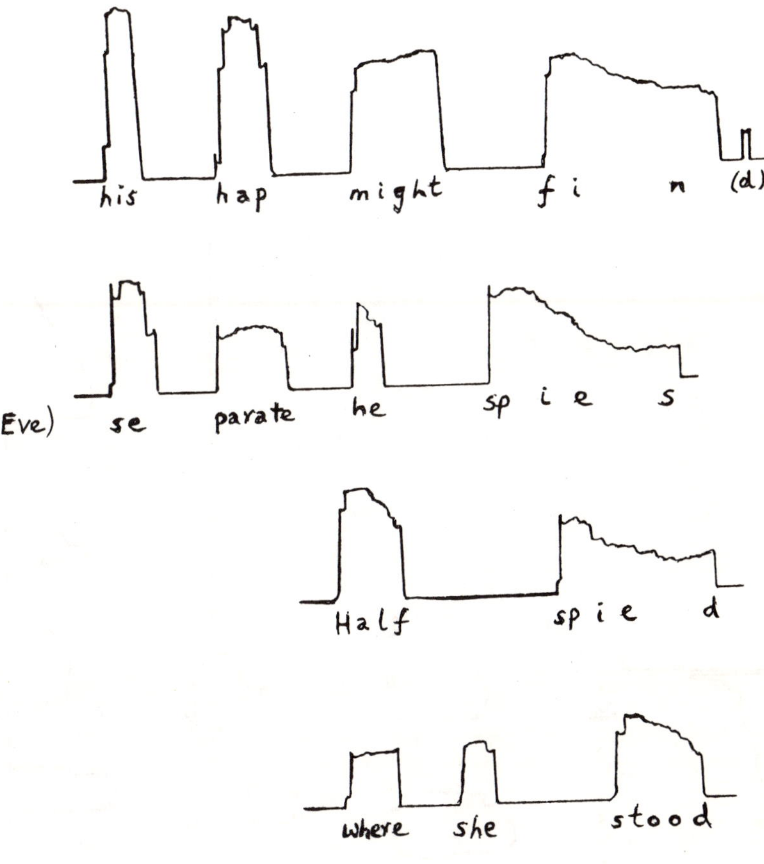

his hap might f i n (d)
Eve) se parate he sp i e s
Half sp i e d
where she stood

Figure 7.2

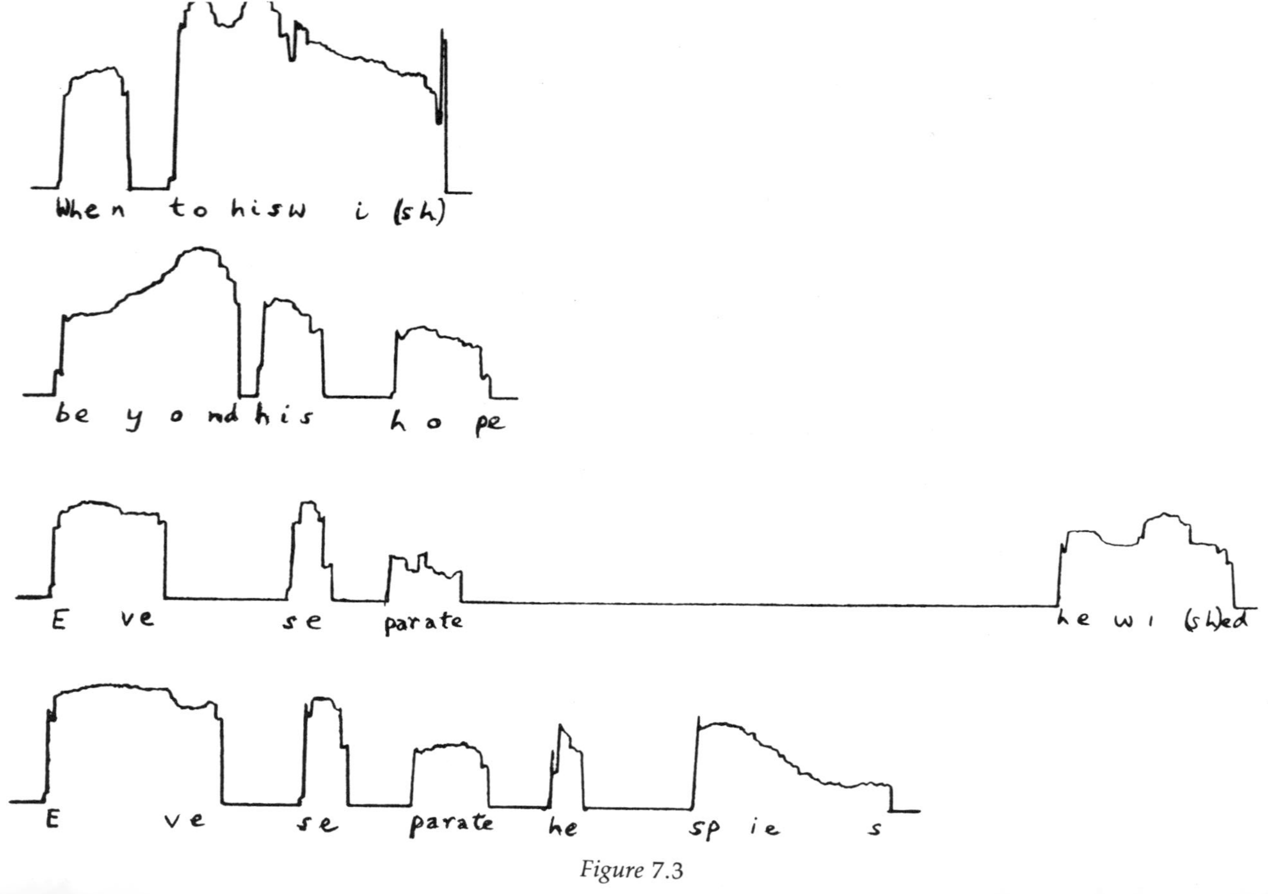
When to hisw i (sh)
be y o nd his h o pe
E ve se parate he wi (sh)ed
E ve se parate he sp ie s

Figure 7.3

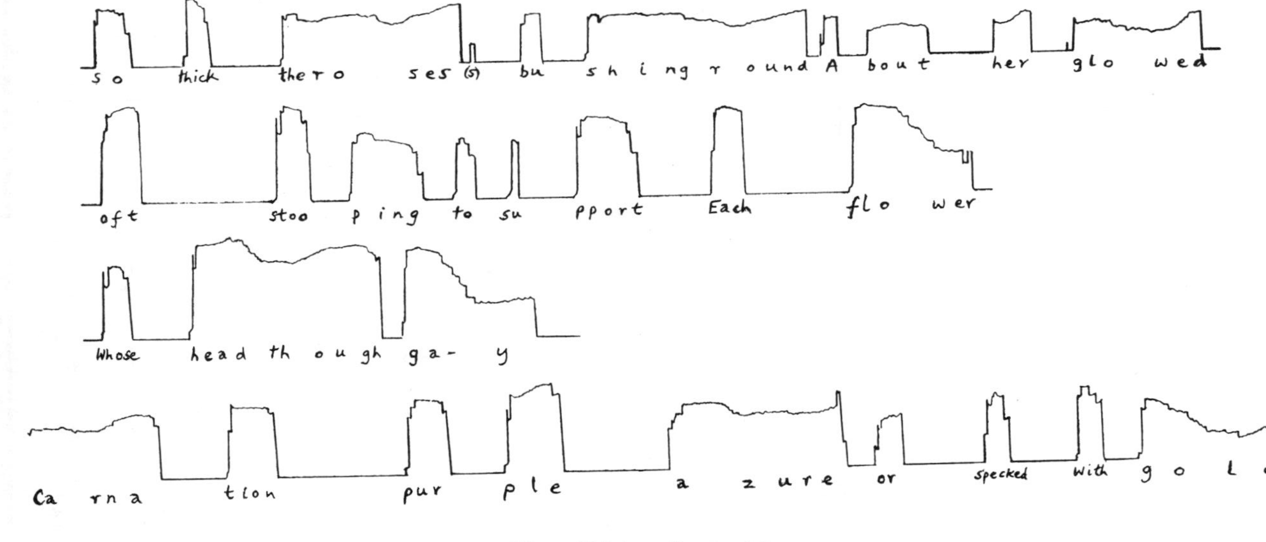

Figure 7.4 (smaller scale)

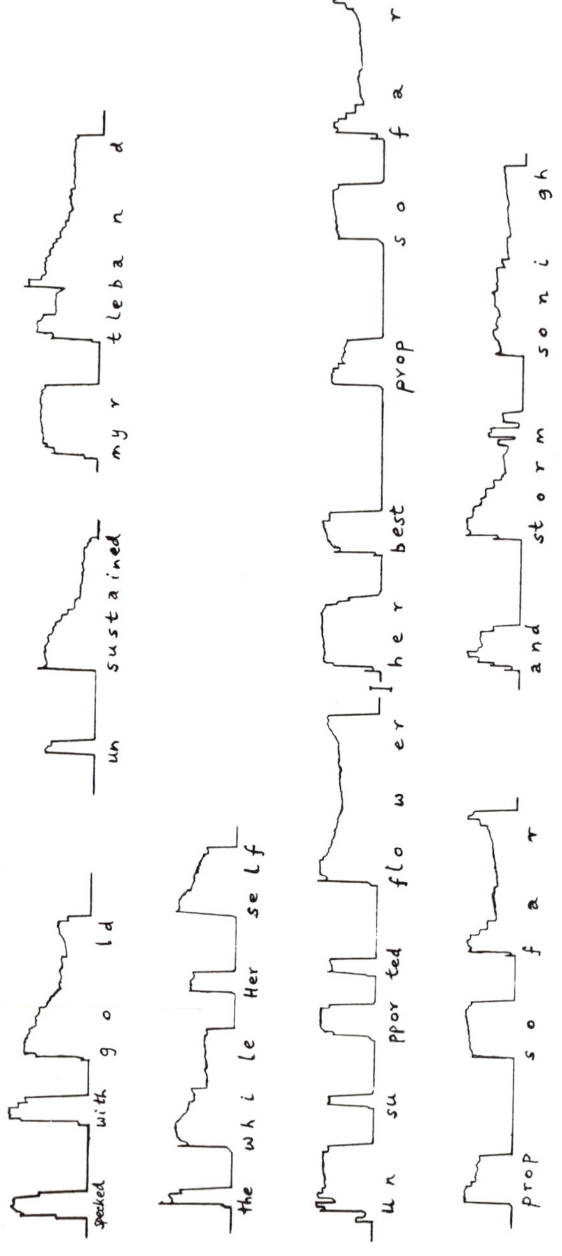

Figures 7.5 (smaller scale)

8

Tunes and Instants

In a couple of genial essays, the English poet Roy Fuller argues that the main determining metrical factor in the stress pattern of English verse is syllabic length, rather than variations of pitch or loudness (Fuller, 1976, 1977). I think this belief of Fuller's comes out of his own expert handling of traditional metres, and I mention it to emphasise how selective the listening process is. It should now be clear that none of the four factors, pitch, loudness, duration, or quality is by itself determinant. As I have remarked, the position of stress may be determined by rules but its actual degree in performance, being a complex concept unique to that performance, cannot easily be assessed. Given assignment of a stressed position by, for example, abstract metrics, we should still have to judge what combination of the four sonic factors, plus semantic, emotional and syntactic contributions, create the exact degree of stress. For ordinary speech, Ladd (1980) notes that listeners' judgements of degree of stress change according to context. Barry (1981) concludes: 'We therefore have to recognise that speaker attitude, as interpreted by the hearer, is a complex interaction between situation, prosody and the semantic content of an utterance.' Why should we think poetry more simple? To bring more subtlety into our description requires an excursion into philosophy.

In any case, pitch and loudness cannot be understood without duration. Rather than duration's being the principal indicator of stress, as the linguists Liberman and Prince (1977) would join the poet, Fuller, in arguing, duration is the fundamental antithesis to stress, as a stroke and a line are antithetical; yet duration is what contains all the features that give us our sense of stress, including, very paradoxically, duration itself. We need a notional moment at which all the forces of change concentrate, or otherwise we have no way of relating musical flow to musical change; it may be a stress, as in English verse, or a unified realisation of syllabic measure, as in French. Change of sound, meaning and emotional significance create durations whose centre is, like the two aspects of 'time as changing' and 'time as still', double-faced. Intellectual modesty, a genial classical scepticism about grandiose or obscure statements, a refusal to be blown far beyond the stuff of ordinary life, have often been modern English critical preoccupations since the 1950s. These Larkinesque approaches have many virtues – and one drawback. They can make the ancient aspirations of poets in many cultures and many languages seem but a deviation from English modesty.

To rediscover the excitement of prosody is also to rediscover primitive aspects of mind: the birth moments of its language. In our intonation we are well-nigh as primitive as babies. 'Poetry is the voice of a poet at its birth', as Guy Davenport (1984) remarks. The excitement lies in the apparent points of origin of melody, the stresses and their necessary unity with duration, in seeing what a nexus all of it is in the sophisticated discourse of poetry. So far, in Chapter 1, I have given only a preliminary definition of stress; the definition must now be modified.

If it is a semantic, emotional and sonic unity, an instant with content, it is obviously a tricky question whether an instant can be said to have content. We run against a problem which also arises in the medieval notion of eternity.

Instants. . . eternity. . . it is a pity that such traps have to be set into our discussion. To see the precise relation of form to content it will be helpful to see how analytical philosophy tackles the medieval notion. Let us return to two of the key sources, Augustinian and Thomist, which influence the tradition of Christian mysticism that Eliot was following in 'Burnt Norton' (see Chapter 2). Both St Augustine and St Thomas Aquinas subscribe, of course, to the eternal simultaneity of God's standpoint in time. St Augustine says in the celebrated Book XI of his *Confessions*:

> Thou precedest all things past, by the sublimity of an ever-present eternity; and surpassest all future because they are future, and when they come they shall be past; but Thou art the Same, and Thy years fail not.[1]

whereas St Thomas says:

> Only things which are moved are measured by time: because *time is the measure of movement*, as stated. Now God is absolutely without movement, as we have already proved. Therefore we cannot mark *before* and *after* in Him. Therefore in Him there is not being after non-being, nor can He have non-being after being, nor is it possible to find any succession in His being,

because these things cannot be understood apart from time. Therefore He is without beginning and end, and has all His being simultaneously; and in this consists the notion of eternity.[2]

In the Augustinian and Thomist view, eternity is present, simultaneous, and outside finite time. Before we get to an attack on this conception, we have to go further into the question of instants apparently containing content. St Thomas was interested in Aristotelian paradoxes concerning the reality of time. He reports[3] that Aristotle has two arguments to show either that time does not exist or that it is hard to perceive. The first argument is that anything composed of things that do not exist cannot itself exist or have any substance. However, time is composed as infinite and perpetual from past and future, which do not exist (that is, do not exist *now*. The *now*, having no duration, cannot exist in time – see next argument.) The second argument is that no divisible part of time exists in act. The 'now' that exists in act is not a part of time.

We might solve these problems if (a) there could be a continuum of identical instants and all would be one, unending instant which might therefore be real, if it had any meaning at all; or (b) there could be single instants with a content whose various elements coexisted in the instant's simultaneity. If (a), the moments of existence would entirely link up. If (b), the 'now' which exists in act might, even if it had no real existence, at least be a part of mental time, if we could show that its contents were memories of the past and anticipations of the future and that these form a conceptual unity. It will be seen that this relates to my definition of stress. However, we are once more thrown into paradox.

Aristotle, St Thomas adds, has two ways of regarding the 'now'. (To make this clearer, I shall interpret these arguments somewhat.) On the one hand, time is composed of infinitesimally divisible instants which must be each the same as each other but which do not coexist. This is needed to explain the continuum of time: otherwise there would be moments which were 'not time'. On the other hand, the instants cannot be the same because all finite things, such as stretches of time, have at least a beginning and an end, at instants which are evidently not the same. Another proof of the difference between these instants is that simultaneity may be defined as existence within the same instant; so if the same 'now' remained in the whole of time it would follow that things which existed a thousand years ago are simultaneous with things which exist today. This is obviously an argument against the simultaneity of real events which happened at different linear times, but its application to the mental creation of conceptions of time is uncertain.

Anthony Kenny's (1979) attack upon the Thomist notion of eternity will be useful because it employs one of Aristotle's own moves:

> The whole concept of a timeless eternity, the whole of which is simultaneous with every part of time, seems to be radically incoherent. For simultaneity as ordinarily understood is a transitive relation. If A happens at the same time as B, and B happens at the same time as C, then A happens at the same time as C. If the BBC programme and the ITV programme both start when Big Ben strikes ten, then they both start at the same time. But, on St Thomas's view, my typing of this paper is simultaneous with the whole of eternity. Again, on this view, the great fire of Rome is simultaneous with the whole of eternity. Therefore, while I type these words, Nero fiddles heartlessly on.

This is a *reductio ad absurdum* of a fundamentally mystical point of view and in those terms is unanswerable. From a finite viewpoint, it makes no sense to say God has simultaneous knowledge of real-world events unless this somehow includes knowledge of them in the sequence of their changes, that is, unless we suppose that sequence coexists with non-sequential simultaneity, which seems ridiculous.

A Christian poet like T. S. Eliot can deal with Kenny's argument through a supernaturalist refuge, claiming, along with St Augustine and St Thomas, that eternity transcends the notion of finite time and that therefore the incarnation is necessary: this is the intersection of the timeless with time. My own view of stress is, so far, a small reflection of Eliot's position but is without his recourse to supernatural solutions; I am talking about form, not about God. So if Kenny is allowed to win his attack upon St Thomas's notion of eternity my doctrine fails or will need modification.

Kenny notes that the sixteenth-century Jesuit, Suarez, in his *De Scientia Dei Futurorum Contingentium*, saw the difficulty in proposing that God has knowledge of timeless things; he insisted that though temporal things coexist with the whole of eternity, because eternity coexists with all times, past, present and future, yet these times do not coexist with each other. God is 'like a tree standing in a river which is successively present or adjacent to different masses of flowing water' and the only sense in which things are eternally present to God is as objects of His knowledge.

If what we are talking about is the simultaneous presence of objects of knowledge in the divine mind and not the simultaneous presence of real events in the eternal awareness, the question arises, as Kenny points out, whether a timeless being can have any knowledge of finite events. Further, if God is unchanging, won't knowledge of real, changing events change Him?

Kenny convincingly argues that God cannot know the passing of time without changing Himself (at least in respect of what we normally think of as time, constituted by past, present and future relationships). He gives a bizarre example to show that we cannot get out of this difficulty through the argument of Aquinas, that is, by supposing that God has some special kind of knowledge which is not dependent on propositional or linguistic expression. Kenny allows that animals may have non-verbal language but thinks an analogy between this and divine awareness problematic. But even supposing that divine awareness does pre-exist language: what happens immediately it is put into language?

> We could perhaps conceive of a cosmic timekeeper on the model of the GPO speaking clock: a voice from the clouds that said, with unfailing regularity, sentences of the form, 'Thus saith the Lord: at the third stroke it will be 12.52 precisely' followed by three crashes of thunder.

His argument is that this would not give substance to the idea that a changeless being might know the time:

> Merely creating, at the beginning of the world, a cosmic apparatus of the appropriate kind, would not by itself constitute knowledge of the time; the GPO engineers and the voice who recorded the speaking clock are not, by virtue of that very fact, apprised of the correct time at every moment of the day. Whereas if we attribute to God in addition awareness of what the cosmic clock is saying at any given moment, we merely reawaken in fantastic

form all the difficulties about changing awareness of a changing world.

The point here is that the time pronouncements of the divine speaking clock now become the changing events that we are considering. Even if we suppose that there is a divine awareness which is prior to them, as soon as the divine awareness is *applied* to the sequential items of language (the spoken times, that is, time as changing) we have again to accept that the awareness changes. Therefore, we cannot in the same breath propose that the divine knowledge is both omniscient, knowing all times, and unchangeable.

How does this relate to my definition of poetic stress? Let's concentrate on sounds for the moment and set aside meaning, emotional significance and other factors. In a poetic line, our conception of stress is composed of content from a past stretch of sound, content from a future stretch of sound, both post- and back-reported on to an 'instant'. Let's suppose that in this instant the performer is not only aware of the point-like co-presence or simultaneity of these sounds but also of their duration and temporal sequence. Now we are forced to admit that the human mind 'cannot do this'. It cannot put duration and sequence into the 'durationless' instant; it cannot have awareness of simultaneity of two different things without that awareness also changing, presumably through time. It cannot logically reconcile (a) the instant when time stands still and the elements of sound are simultaneous – the moment when the beat is marked as though it were a fixed point in time; and (b) the experience of the sounds as extended durations occurring in a particular sequence. But how can the awareness change during an instant? To put it another way, it is as though during the instant we have a passive aspect of mind (the stress is still and all the durations are static) and an active (all the elements of sound that compose the stress are moving). Whether the paradox is between stress as instantaneous and as durational, as still and as moving, or as passive and as active, does not perhaps matter. The whole dynamic is ambiguous at root. I am in fact quite happy with this ambiguity, for on it the notion of artistic form depends.

If stress is an example of artistic form and if we *could* have an unambiguously 'eternal' awareness of that form in an instant, along with all the past and future movements of sound that created it, then the awareness would lack the ambiguity of real spatio-temporal dynamic. Although the movement of sounds would be within the conception, the movement would be trapped within the instant. The passive stillness of such a formal conception would stand right outside the poetry. Each beat in the poem would bring us to a dead stop while we contemplated our eternal awareness of the simultaneity of past and future movements. Although we have apparently given the beat dynamism by supposing that the movements of sound are continuing within the instant, we have seen that this is impossible. When we stop considering stress in its passive aspect and consider it *also* actively in a real performance of a poetic line, we shall revive the true temporal dynamics of it even if describing these dynamics analytically leads to ambiguities similar to those in Kenny's analysis.[4]

There is a stronger version of the mystical idea that the description of eternity transcends ordinary language. It is that language itself embodies the very paradoxes of simultaneity that Kenny is discussing. Thus, a sentence has its flow of change from one sound or word to another and has its 'static' forms too, such as the meanings of individual words or phrases that differentiate one part of an utterance from another, along with the internal forms within words which build them up. We have to experience the sentence as movement but also retain the relative positions of words in the syntax, and we have to understand the whole through its form. The form of the sentence unites change and stasis just as the unity of a poetic line's sound does. It is to be questioned, therefore, whether the analytical use of language is a sufficient instrument to fathom paradoxes inherent in the instrument itself.

We can illustrate grandiosely that there is a space–time paradox that language is powerless to investigate too far by appealing to modern astrophysical mathematics. Early mathematical models for 'Black Holes' demonstrated that time would become symmetrical (that is, reversible) within the singularity of a massive star collapsing under a given idealised set of conditions (Hawking and Ellis, 1974). When amateurs consider the implications of modern space–time mathematics in relation to the human mind, pretentiousness is an immediate risk. I merely want to point out that the mathematical description of the universe breaks down when confronted with hypothetical astrophysical singularities; so, therefore, would any language we could use to describe what goes on inside the singularity, except an entirely contradictory language which would say 'Time A is also Time B'. I am describing stress as a sort of tiny, postulated mental 'singularity'; I do not propose that we should talk about it in the terms of astrophysical mathematics. In considering poetic performance we are safer trusting to our normal beliefs, acknowledging when our language breaks down in talking about them, shelving any final ontological judgement, glad that our beliefs entail values and emotions and hints of unity.

We have been restricting the notion of stress to its sound correlates. If a stress also unites 'instantaneously' ('simultaneously') meaning and emotional significance with sound, a further problem arises if we think of meaning as a set of mental 'concepts'. Cassirer (1957, p. 307) says that simple phenomenological reflection tells us that if we take the 'concept' as immediately given, it appears as something totally different from the mnemonic image:

> We must go behind the sphere of consciousness, we must pass from pure logic and phenomenology to physiology if we wish to maintain an equivalence between concept and remembered image. The concept then becomes a product of unconscious traces and residues that have been left behind in the brain by earlier sense perceptions. But aside from the fact that this notion distorts the simple meaning of the logical question, transforming logic into a brain metaphysics, the concept would be very inadequate to its task if this *were* its actual task. Here, we should have a true application of Bacon's quip that anyone who supposed he could grasp reality through conceptual thought seemed to him like a man who, to gain better knowledge of a distant object, climbed a high tower and looked out from it even though he was perfectly free to approach the object itself and observe it close at hand. Here one thing is seen correctly: that the concept, in accordance with its characteristic attitude must, unlike direct perception, move its object off into a kind of ideal distance, in order to bring it within its horizon. The concept must annul 'presence' in order to arrive at representation.[5]

Cassirer goes on to emphasise that formation of concepts does not represent a break in the totality of knowledge extending forward (in time presumably) from the first stages of sensory, perceptual knowledge. Nevertheless, as I have called a stress a concept – and shall in my final chapter argue, too, that aesthetic emotion is conceptualised – this seems to produce more problems for a definition of stress in which past and future contents are considered to 'occur' at a present instant held in memory. For the contents are composed of such elements as sound, conceptual meaning, and emotional significance. If Cassirer is right, and I believe he is, how can concepts like meaning and aesthetic emotion unite with sense impressions from our direct perception of sound?

One answer is that it is the precise role of the formal ordering of poetic rhythm and music to make the beat coincide with moments when we grasp semantic and emotional concepts. Such concepts are not so linked to the time-scale of physiological processes as real emotions, such as fear, are. We shall see in the final chapter (when I shall also go into my reservations) that real emotion is cognitive, but that the origins of the cognition are more direct than normal conceptual thought, like the cognition in direct perception. In poetry, on the other hand, the emotions are not real but conceptualised; like all concepts they are therefore viewed from an ideal distance. This allows them to be accorded in time with the conceptual meanings of the words of a poetic line. But the fictitious emotions are also mimed in an intonation pattern almost perfectly suitable for their expression; and the link between emotion and intonation pattern, even when mimed, *is extremely direct*, like that link between sight and cognitive awareness in perception, for it is sensuous once we begin the performance of a poem. What we do when we read a poem well is modulate our speed and emphasis of reading, so as to bring the conceptualised emotion into temporal consonance with the semantic field and to let emotion's necessary sensuous conjunction with sound create a unity between all three factors. It is almost as if the emotional and temporally accorded semantic concepts drag the sound directly and sensuously along with them: when we recite well we have almost to wait for the right instant to speak each syllable, delaying very minutely durations of vowels to make the tempo perfect.

Another answer to the philosophers, therefore, is to make appeal to our beliefs about what happens when we read a line – when we cease to view language and concepts abstractly and consider what happens in performance.

If unity of sound, meaning and emotional significance is to be regarded as only an ambiguous concept (and it is partly ambiguous), two things have to be explained: first that we try at all to tap a poetic stress, as if some sound 'happened' at an instant of time, an instant which forms part of the continuum of sound which influences our intellectual and emotional response to the poem;

second, there is a surprising confidence in our belief that this moment could be tapped absolutely exactly, if we were only sharp enough to do so. The confidence is private and, in that common application of Wittgenstein, not accessible, you may say, for public discussion; but it is also international and deeply historical, for it is cardinal to musical drumming from the most primitive tribes to the most highly paid pop-music performer. How can we presume to judge, for example, the incredibly minute, extra-exactness of beat that a top-class drummer can tap, as against a lesser performer? Of course, even this drummer, let alone ourselves, is always slightly too late or too early: the closest approach to unity of beat and melody always escapes our grasp. The tap that we make shows, none the less, that we have a belief about its being instantaneous; and in performance, but not in analysis, this seems to be a belief that can be shared, since we can express that by tapping together, just as a singalong Wembley Stadium audience claps fairly exactly on time. It is a public awareness in that sense.

What this complex instant is actually like spatio-temporally we cannot know. In my discussion of St Augustine below, greater sophistication might be available from the most refined modern models of space–time, if we could only know their applicability to the events inside our head. Ricoeur (1985, p. 19 *et seq.*, p. 351) has drawn attention to the temporal paradox that pits St Augustine against Aristotle: the former's (not quite pure) phenomenological perspective upon time and the latter's cosmological perspective are mutually exclusive. We might say that in the performance of a poem the external temporal relations and the internal phenomenological temporal relations come into consonance. But for a more developed philosophy on these questions I refer readers to chapter I of Ricoeur (1985).

We have said that perfect formal unity is impossible. To widen the discussion from poetry to narrative fiction in general for a moment, this impossibility is easy to see; the forms we use are impregnated with all the past encoding of literary language: the encoded linguistic procedures that make up meaning, the genres of what we say, the intertextual field of genre, and the social, environmental, political and historical production in the midst of which the author tries to write and to create a new movement in this vast process. In poetry, as in the novel, artistic form exhibits great variety of disunities within its attempt at ever-imperfect unity; there are always what Ingarden (1973, p. 251) calls in regard to the novel, 'spots of indeterminacy'. Yet in narrative fiction, too, as I shall show in Chapters 10 to 12, it is the nature of form to suggest a unity that can be captured in an instant, whether this actually happens or not.

Returning to poetry, I am in any case going to play it cautiously. I am not saying that poetic stress is a literal instant with simultaneous, varied content, which is perceived in conscious reflection. Instead, I am calling this instant notional only: bearing its sundry poetic contents as a structure in memory, as described in Chapter 2. This is partly an Augustinian solution, because for him we only know the duration of time by comparing expanses of memory of different durations. Interestingly, the question was placed by St Augustine into the same context: in both his *De Musica* and *The Confessions* he discusses how we measure the durations of syllables in Latin prosody.

In Book XI of *The Confessions,* St Augustine agonises over the nature of time and brings in just the issues of verse that we have been discussing. A line from an Ambrosian hymn, *Deus creator omnium,* fascinated him, perhaps because, apart from its meaning, the long '-ea-' vowels in the middle make the centre-point of the phrase extend, while the past and future of it are relatively short and it is as though we concentrate on the present moment lying within. He considers its being recited (i.e. in performance). How is it, he asks, that we can measure the duration of the short and long syllables, since while they exist, in each present moment of their sounding, we have no knowledge of their duration, and after they have finished they no longer exist and it is only in memory that we can know for how long they have sounded? His answer is that it is in the mind that we measure times, by the establishment of a triple present – the past-as-present (memory), the present (attention), and the future-as-present (expectation). This runs counter to the Derridean trace, which is an attack upon logos-centred views. But providing we exercise the caution of my last paragraph and call the present 'notional', emphasise that the triple present is itself held in memory, and acknowledge that logical difficulties will arise if we consider these questions abstracted from performance, St Augustine's is an appropriate formulation to apply to the performance of poetic stresses.

Ricoeur (1983, p. 39; and 1984) links this view of temporality with a theory of narrative in ways which relate to the approach taken later in this book. He distinguishes the active and passive facets of Augustine's triple present. It is a double-facing triple present, triple in activity, triple in passivity. Augustine has a passive description of the present as an attentiveness along with impression-images in memory and sign-images in expectation. These are spatial expressions and therefore need another spatial expression in which they can remain, a space which may be thought of as distended, yet present. For Augustine this is the soul, considered under Ricoeur's passive aspect.

Ricoeur says that in the active aspect of the act of reciting, the present changes sense: it is no longer a point, not even a point of passage, it is a present expectation. He calls this 'intention' in so far as the transition through the present has become an active transition. Augustine talks of the past increasing and the future emptying; but there would be no spatial representation of a future which diminishes and of a past which fills without a spirit to perform the action. Combining the active and passive: 'The mind expects and remembers, and yet expectation and memory are "in" the soul as impression-images and as sign-images', Ricoeur says. The contrast concentres on the present, where there is a passive past and future and an active past and future, which double up the process onto the double present. 'But . . . inasmuch as through the attention that "which is to be passes toward [pergat] the state in which it is to be no more", it must be said that "the mind's attention persists [perdurat attentio]."' This is exactly the paradox I have pointed to in my definition of stress. Ricoeur's own citation is from Augustine's celebrated description of reciting a psalm, which I repeat for the reader's convenience. (I have adapted the English translation that I am using.)

> I am about to repeat a Psalm that I know. Before I begin, my expectation extends itself towards the whole; but when I have begun, however much of it my expectation separates off into the past is extended along my memory; thus the life of this action of mind is stretched between my memory as to what I have repeated, and expectation as to what I am about to repeat; but attention is present with me, that through it what was future may be conveyed over, so as to become past. The more this is done again and again, the more the expectation is shortened and the memory enlarged: till the whole expectation be at length exhausted, by which time that whole action, being ended, shall have passed into memory. And what takes place in the whole

> Psalm, the same takes place in each separate part of it, and each separate syllable; the same holds in that longer action, whereof this Psalm may be a part; the same holds in the whole life of man, whereof all the actions of man are parts; the same holds through the whole age of the sons of men, whereof all the lives of men are parts.[6]

If, for the active and passive aspects of the Augustinian position, as commented upon by Ricoeur, I substitute on the one hand the actively changing durations of the poem's sound and on the other the passive conception of these durations, both grasped through a doubled-up triple present (past–present–future) which is held in the memory as 'a present still and moving', it will be seen that in defining poetic stress I am not replacing the Augustinian description but providing an alternative language for discussing essentially the same experience. And what I am describing is not the whole age of the sons of men but how stress unites with duration to bind the linear experience of a poem to its whole form. My description is limited to the phenomenological realm, our internal sense of stress.

With its active and passive aspects[7] Ricoeur's text has similarities to modern discussions of the two aspects of external, physical time, as fixed and as changing. I'm thinking here of the way that McTaggart raised the Aristotelian question of time's unreality, since it has two apparently contradictory aspects, which he calls the A- and B-series. In the A-series, time seems to change: today becomes yesterday and tomorrow becomes today. The B-series is stative; events never change their position but maintain their relation towards each other: thus the Battle of Waterloo will always be before the Second World War. The contradiction has been much discussed: a possible resolution of it is that we illegitimately give the same content to events in the A-series as to those in the B-series. It may not be legitimate to say 'Yesterday, the day I went to the pictures' and 'Today, the day I went to the pictures' if I then go on to argue that these are two different days, unless we say that 'Yesterday' and 'Today' are being used abstractly, without content of their own, rather like plus and minus signs being added to the content.[8] Or we can treat the question rather like poetic stress and say that it is the nature of time as changing and time as stative or formal to exist in a contradictory relationship, since the changing of events fills the stative conception with a content which both conceptions impossibly seem to share.[9]

I am now going to revise my preliminary definition of stress (Chapter 1, p. 5), separating it into three sections: stress in relation to verbal sound; stress as abstract and rule-governed; and stress as an element appearing in poetic performance in the way I have just analysed.

Revised definition of stress:

(a) In the sound of a poem, the correlates of stress are pitch, loudness, duration and quality, although duration is, in other respects, its paradoxical opposite. Duration is that period which gives content to the stress, whether this be the duration of a syllable or some wider (suprasegmental) duration.

(b) The major assignment of the position of a heavy poetic stress within the line is from abstract metrical pattern, word-stress and syntax. These positions may well be describable adequately by abstract linguistic rule structures or by traditional abstract norms, such as the iambic pentameter, which permit exceptions. Metrical rule must, as Cureton (1986) reminds us, be distinguished from the actual rhythm of a line. Metrical pattern, word-stress and syntax also play a role in our judgement of exact degrees of stress in actual performances, though this is irrelevant as far as the rule-governing of stress position is concerned.

(c) Our assessment of degree of stress, weak or strong, in actual performance may be speculatively defined as follows:

(a) and (b), above, are combined in performance with semantic and emotional considerations because the formation of a mental concept of stress in sonic or positional terms is never pure, but is influenced by our sense of how important a word/syllable is.

Our sense of poetic stress arises from our conscious belief that we have, just recently, in a notional instant, unified some of our experience of a poem's developing sounds (including any metrical, grammatical, or syntactic conditions under (b)) with some of its developing intellectual–semantic and emotional significance, attaining that unification through the medium of the sound and bringing into the unity at least some of the poem's past and future by anticipation and retrospection. By 'unity' is meant a working model of it in memory to which we attend and which includes our sense of expectation.

Under (c) we should note the following points:

(1) By 'unification' I imply some version of the simple structures of unification of past and anticipated future into a notional present that I have modelled in Chapter 2 and have further discussed here.

(2) By 'just recently' I mean that these structures are accessible to consciousness only through memory or, in renewed performance, through this repetition.

(3) By 'notional' I mean that we are not stating that an experience of a content-filled temporal instant is possible; only that the structures held in memory give us a confident notion (cf. 'belief') of what such an experience would be like.

(4) The above definition deliberately creates a confusion about durational aspects of sounds and the instants in which those durations are conceived as 'happening'.

(5) By 'any metrical conditions' I specify that the imposition of a pre-existent, abstract metrical pattern can make a difference to how we hear the rhythm of a poetic line in performance. The word 'any' also allows the definition to apply to freer verse forms. Cureton (1986), for example, concentrating mainly on syntactical groupings, has developed an interesting 'hierarchical phrasal scansion'. These levels are worth mentioning here. First comes a system of metrical scansion, although he distinguishes metrics from actual rhythm. Second comes a level where individual words group syllables into rhythmic groups. Third comes the rhythmic effect of clitic phrases, a clitic phrase being determined by basic grammatical dependencies such as the fact that articles group with following adjectives or nouns (for example, 'to darkness' is a clitic group). Fourth come phonological phrases which group usually one to three clitic phrases. Fifth comes the organisation of phonological phrases into intonational phrases which are the main units of information. Intonational phrases are grouped into utterance units, which are the maximal sequences between overt structural pauses, when speaking ceases temporarily. This links with the broader organisation of verse into paragraphs and so on. I do not deny the interest of this method of scansion, some of whose techniques are borrowed from musical notation: all these elements are acknowledged (with less subtlety) in my definition, which would therefore make room for such further refinements. The difficulty is that Cureton's hierarchy does not seamlessly unite musical flow with the point-like occurrence of rhythmic beat, as I have suggested we should. This is because the distinction between voiced and un-

voiced elements is not made. With that, we have problems in defining stress. Including intonational phrases though it may, Cureton's useful system mainly tells us about the rhythmic grouping of the poetic line into rational and informational units. But there would be too much emphasis upon *reason* in poetry and not enough upon its emotional musicality were we to lose our essential concentration upon pitch.

The definition has become very complicated because any sense by us that a moment of stress is important in some way influences how we hear it. Since I have been talking all along about how the mind forms this concept, the definition would easily be misunderstood as an attempt to explain 'how the mind works'. Whether the human mind's temporal operations are relativistic or whether it sniffs along like a bloodhound I have, of course, no idea, and it is quite irrelevant whether or not we can create mechanistic simulations of its operations. Here, and when I come to narrative, I am just talking in a normative way about what our beliefs about mental activity seem to be like. I must re-emphasise that very many of the above influences upon our sense of stress may either not be in play for any one stress or be quite unconscious because of the fleeting passage of the rhythm: we are talking about possible influences only.

The definition, plus the detailed analyses of poems earlier in the book and the proposed hierarchy by which stress is bound to overall music (see Chapter 6, from which I shall borrow all the examples below), have implications for other aspects of versification, as follows.

Poetic feet. If a metric involving poetic feet is imposed on the verse, then such feet may be considered as entities to the extent which, consciously or unconsciously, they are brought into mental play. In performing verse, our conscious perception of feet would be slight at best; it is hard to hold a complicated abstract pattern in consciousness when we are concentrating on so much else. Begging the question of what happens unconsciously, the problem is how the abstract metrics are actually realised in the sound of our voice. More often, it is the stresses themselves which seem to become our *conscious* structuring principle – with the post-dating and back-dating of sounds on to instants that that implies, an apparent time-bending operation that partly destroys the delimitation into poetic feet even while perhaps affirming it. The feet reappear, however, if we apply our abstracting intellect to their rediscovery. Even so, the necessity of checking such an analysis against our mental performance of a line will revive uncertainties about the foot structure at any moment of irregularity – a necessarily circular argument.

This is allied to the problems that arise when we try to use linguistic machinery to show what, in a poetic line's sound, marks the borders of poetic feet. We cannot come up with any one calculation that will account for the following factors, all of which affect our sense of stress: changes to pitch (up or down), duration (long or short), loudness (loud or quiet – even sudden whispering can be used to mark stress), and voice quality. And we have to add intellectual, syntactical and emotional factors as outlined above. One or a combination of the more evident factors may be used to create rules for stress placement, as in some synthesised speech, and this can be accompanied by a musically influenced structure of feet,[10] but this takes us out of the human mind and into practical application.

Line endings. As with poetic feet, there is no such thing as a sure poetic line, definable in advance, unless an abstract metric imposes it. Even then, the question is not simple, owing to possibilities of enjambement and of continuing a voicing duration across a line break, so that the point where one line ends and another begins becomes an elusive instant. A related problem is that of delimiting one syllable from another within a word which, because of consonant durations and the modulation of vowels almost imperceptibly into consonants ('violent swiftness' was an earlier example), is almost impossible to attain with precision. Another example comes with continued voicing over a line break, as in Vaughan's

/Shall it in the evening run when our words/

discussed on p. 69, where the natural line break is on 'run' but the full emotional effect of the verse is lost if the voicing is not continued over the break. A sense of the missing break can be suggested in a good reading by minute intonation changes during the interim sound, but the actual moment when the line ends will remain unlocatable. I remember an obtuse review of the poetry of the American, Robert Creeley, which refused to see how he plays exactly with the ineffability of line endings. We looked at his

Drive, he sd, for
christ's sake look. . .

'For' is so syntactically and sonically weak that the enjambement is fast and makes both line-ending and the duration of the sibilance inside 'christ'ssssake' mysteriously adjustable in timing. (Creeley's own hesitant, rich voice creates further ambiguities of duration when he reads the words.) Consequently, whether a line ending be imposed metrically or played with by a poet like Creeley, it will always be an unlocatable point which is nevertheless hit exactly right in any one good performance of a line, each performance setting up its own parameters in this respect.

Rhyme. As the notion of a merely 'flat' (= boring) rhyme can tell us, rhyme sets up the expectation of absolute sameness, and then, by minute *variations* of sound, suggests the semantic–emotional development between one rhyme and a nearby rhyme. The semantic–emotional development must be sensed by us through the operations of post- and back-dating that I have described in relation to stress, now at work over a whole cadence. For example, Marvell, one of the great employers of rhyme, lets a need for enjambement make the word 'fleet' very quick, and then stops temporarily on "'Twas" to mime the deer's movements in the poem we looked at in Chapter 6. Machine evidence confirms that the vowel in the rhyme word, 'feet', is not nearly so quick, and so the meaning of 'fleet' is emphasised and the movement of spirit in watching the pet fawn is expressed in the pacing through the enjambement and through the contrast with the end-stopping after 'feet':

It is a wondrous thing how fleet
'Twas on its little slender feet. . .

9

Narrative in Performance

In the three chapters that follow I am going to talk of what happens to time, space and the 'I' pronoun in fictional narrative. This discussion will exclude many aspects of prose and poetic writing: for example, I shall not consider genre, intertextuality, or metaphor (unless we take this widely to mean imaginative reconstruction of space and time). My argument continues from my previous analyses of poetic stress and musical form, where I have described the way in which the point-like moment of stress is bound into the overall flow of a poem's music and therefore into its meaning and emotional significance. I now want to show how our perception of form in narrative fiction has essentially the same spatio-temporal dynamic: it, too, involves emotion and meaning and it, too, creates spatio-temporal paradoxes.

The reader will recall that any incorporation of duration into the point-like moment incurs ambiguities of space and time – space because a duration of mental time is necessarily also a spatial extension. In a poem, verbal music is what most immediately binds stress as a tiny artistic form into the overall form of a poem. What plays a similar role in a novel? What is the point-like moment and what is the binding power? The point-like moment is *any* moment when the reader suddenly grasps a formal achievement of whatever size in the novel: it may be an evanescent realisation of part of an event's significance in the plot; it may be a grasp of elements of a character's personality, or of the relationship of that personality to the overall 'poem' of the novel; it could be a host of things, from a formal conception that yields a sudden moral awareness or even a sudden erotic feeling, all the way up to an 'instant-like' appreciation of a novel's whole form. As for the power that binds instant to form, it is a broader concept than 'plot': 'plot', 'character', 'action', 'setting' or 'point of view' can be logically distinguished, but their mental effects upon us are harder to distinguish each from the other. I am calling the binding element narrative 'movement', understanding by that a portmanteau term in which the mental dynamic created by character, setting, action, plot and so on may all play a part. If we can isolate for study a point-like moment when the ambiguity of narrative form is revealed, we shall find comparable ambiguities of space and time to those noticed with the poetic stress. This is simpler to show than might be supposed, because some comic writers, such as Chaucer and Rabelais, have burlesqued the formal processes underlying their own narrative construction; the burlesque therefore exposes exactly what we want to look at: there will be no need to search for more complicated examples.

But before reaching that point I have to interpolate the present chapter so as to acknowledge certain trends in modern literary criticism. I shall only very selectively use any findings of the new 'science' of narratology or of Derridean–Yale 'deconstruction', and shall prefer an ordinary way of talking. It is a necessary difference of procedure, comparable to my distinction in Chapter 1 between rule-governed poetic metrics and poetry conceived as performance: I am to consider narrative as a mental performance of its movement, just as I considered poetry as a mental performance of its musical flow.

But narratology is not a study of performance. As one of the most self-aware critics in that field, Genette, has pointed out (1983, p. 12), two narratologies have developed, one thematic and concerned with analysing the story or the narrative contents, the other formal, or modal, an analysis of the narrative text itself as a mode of representation of stories. Story here usually means the chronological events abstracted from the text's organisation of them. (To illustrate the former, the work of Northrop Frye in categorising story genre is an excellent representative.) Genette reserves the title of 'narratology' proper for the second, modal analysis, and adds: 'The only specificity that a narrative has resides in its mode, and not in its content, which could equally well conform itself to a dramatic, graphic or other representation.' In fact, we have to add that narrative is also specific in its mode of performance *each time it is performed*, which necessarily involves

content and extra-linguistic factors such as emotion. The idea that an isolated, individual occasion may have absolutely necessary laws to itself alone is unscientific but required for a full discussion of art in action.

Story can be studied in isolation from the narrative text, but when considering performance it is not clear we can be so purist, because then we are considering real acts of mind which might both respond to the narrative directly as text and mentally rearrange it chronologically as story. There is a theoretical narrative movement and also what actually happens inside our heads. The reader's reaction has been well described by Wilbur Sanders (1985):

> Just as the author, word by word, sentence by sentence rears *his* structure, so, in the reader's mind, a parallel construction is proceeding – experience and intuition racing ahead here in anticipation, pausing to look back there in disapprobation, checking, confirming, collating, dissenting and (most importantly) bringing to bear whatever in our own life seems relevant and responsive to the life the writer is creating.

The rather ill-defined categories of traditional literary criticism reflect this impurity – that something happens between reader and text which is not just responding to the text, straight. Traditional criticism takes the text as a starting-point for a human reaction towards the work, including many extra-linguistic elements such as evaluations of the fictional world in terms of the real world, the critic's emotional response to what he reads, and so on. It is an intuitive art, open to pressures from the social and political position of the critic, which will necessarily be different from that of the author. Then there is the newer study, 'narratology'. It is distinguished by considering the structures of the text or of its relationships to other texts in an abstract way, sometimes by applying methodology drawn from linguistics, analytic logic, mathematics or aid from other disciplines, such as structural anthropology or psychoanalysis. Meanwhile, the Derridean–Yale schools have often concentrated upon the way that all structures seem to disappear in a basic ambiguity when you look closely enough at their points of origin, but then reappear in necessary conjunction with their deconstruction. This essentially mathematical conception has been applied to the study of narrative forms. I do not borrow the complicated language of the deconstructionists because it is too abstract for my purposes and because it is not apt for describing the mental performance by a reader of narrative movement; but ambiguity of structure is certainly supposed in what I write.

One starting-point for narratology, a branch of semiology, was to try to find for the structure of fictional texts a grammar-like set of rules equivalent to those which govern the structure of individual phrases. Narrative was to be treated as a special case of an extended phrase – not that it was to be dealt with as a structure composed of individual phrases (that would be an absurd task) but that the logical structure of its composition was to be found in grammar-like rules (see Barthes, 1977, p. 10). The new 'science' began to expand at a time when Chomskyan linguistics had shown that a phrase grammar which dealt only with the surface appearance of language – the normal succession of words – could not explain all the ways that sentences were constructed. Transformational grammar created a deep level of abstract rules and then an intermediate set of rules which, with the realisation into actual words, would transform the deep-level structures into possible sentences.

Some of the narratological methods work in a similar way in this sense: underlying structural principles are sought for narratives, usually by making abstract entities out of the literal surface entities, such as actual characters, events, temporal relations, ways of representing speech, framing and embedding of stories, levels of narrative, different points of view and so forth. Once these features have lost their particularity in a given text – say, Pinkie, his point of view, his level of narrative, his role in *Brighton Rock* – and once they have been assimilated to more general formal entities (x-factor, y-factor, etc.), the underlying structure of the novel can be brought out. To give only one example, one of the clearest and best known: in the extremely abstract early work of Greimas, at the deep level an *actant* is a structural entity to which both human characters and inanimate objects (a magic ring) or abstract forces (destiny) may be reduced.[1] Consequently, the rules of their interaction at the deep level of text may be given a wider generality, and so become capable of specifying a greater variety of possible realisations of characters, objects or abstract forces in actual narratives.

If one were to build up these rules from the smallest detail, one would have to find some minimal unit that could be called a narrative. As Genette has shown (1983, p. 14), it is not easy to consider what a minimal phrase, and therefore a minimal narrative, might be: 'I walk' immediately prompts the questions 'Where from?' 'Where to?' He refers to Forster's distinction between story (event in time sequence), 'The king died and then the queen died', and plot (emphasis on causality), (' . . . of grief'); but it seems to me that even 'The king died' obliges us to think of the resulting change to a nation and raises all sorts of causative considerations about what happens next. Also, there are in story already emotional reverberations which plot will mould. In his development of the story, Forster has, interestingly enough, added in more evidently this emotional significance which was, anyway, there in germ. When we read (perform) the actual content even of this simple plot the question of impurity of response immediately arises. This poses the opposition of extra-linguistic factors, such as emotional resonance and moral or other evaluation; and these are extremely important in distinguishing the study of narratology from that of narrative performance. Emotion, when referred to in narratological analysis, usually seems such an abstract factor, for example, an 'axis of desire' linking the deep structures to the surface of the actual text; and it therefore lacks fully realised application to the complexity and ambiguity of everyday desire. Rimmon-Kenan (1983, p. 28) says that she as yet knows no real method of crossing from deep abstract narrative structure to the concrete text. It will be argued that activating the temporal relations of the surface text is what makes fictionalised emotion important to us. Activation, I shall show from Ricoeur's work, can best be studied in the light of the Aristotelian Mimesis, or imitation of the characteristic, permanent or universal modes of human thought, feeling and action.

A quotation from Todorov (1978, p. 175), another influential early figure in narrative poetics, will help us. Like some of the new theorists he heralded a new age in the study of literary texts by the decline of old categories: in this case the doomed categories are 'imitation' and 'representation' (presumably in the sense of representation of a 'fictionalised' reality). For the novelist, Ricardou (1978, p. 15), concerned to develop a left-wing theory of literary production rather than of creation in the traditional sense, the doomed categories are the 'expression' of aspects of the Self and the 'representation' of aspects of the World as novelistic programme. Todorov writes:

> Although we may have stopped considering art and literature as an imitation, we have difficulty in ridding ourselves of a manner of seeing, written into our linguistic habits, which consists in seeing the novel in terms of representation, of transposition of a reality – which would prexist it. Even if it only seeks to describe the process of creation, this vision already presents a problem; it is straightforwardly deforming if it relates

> itself to the text itself. What exists, first of all, is the text, and nothing but that; it is only by submitting it to a particular type of reading that we construct an imaginary universe from it. The novel does not imitate reality, it creates it: this formula of the pre-romantics is not a simple terminological innovation. Only the perspective of construction allows us to understand correctly the textual function called representative.

On this I have four comments, which I shall summarise and then discuss. It will be seen that often I am not disagreeing with Todorov but merely insisting on a different kind of discussion of the same points:

(1) We cannot so easily do without the notion of imitation because taken in conjunction with plot it permits a necessary temporal dynamism in narrative performance.
(2) Something exists before the text or it would imply creation *ex nihilo*. To experience this 'something' we must respond to the text as Todorov suggests with 'a particular kind of reading', not as a textual entity isolated from the circumstances of its creation and of its being read; instead with an active performance.
(3) To recreate the spatio-temporal world of the fiction, non-linguistic entities must be brought into consideration (I do not suppose that Todorov would necessarily disagree).
(4) 'Expression', 'Mimesis', and 'Representation' in the traditional senses re-enter the discussion whenever we set out to consider the narrative as a performance and not as a text. This is because the novel, as Todorov himself goes on to argue, exists in a relationship between author, text and reader. I should add here that in the recent reader-response strain in criticism, the concentration is often upon text–reader, and not so much on author–text–reader, so that the study is mainly of communication, as in the so-called 'hermeneutic' study of information gaps in the text. The variety and riches of the reader's response require to be linked more directly to the authorial input of dynamism.

To discuss these points:

(1) Many people have not stopped seeing art and literature as

imitative; only some semiologists have. What is mimed in fictional narrative is not just the referential capacity of words to represent reality (or the fantastic), but also their capacity to reawaken, to mime, the temporal movement of thought, along with an imagined emotional movement. Aspects of all this can be redefined into abstract entities, and temporality itself can be reduced to an operator function in a diagram of narrative structure or to a topology in some diagrammatic representation of novelistic structure, whereupon their dynamism becomes potential or immanent and their extra-linguistic, performance aspects are neutralised for the sake of the analytical science. With the neutralism of their dynamic, their true temporality, which has the extra-linguistic, let us say spiritual, effect upon us, retreats also into immanence. This is partly Ricoeur's point (1984, p. 50), for, talking of extracting codes from language, he says that a systematic organisation of linguistic structures can be mastered if the simultaneous (synchronic) aspects of language can be isolated from its successive and historical (diachronic) aspects, providing a finite number of different base units (such as Greimas's *actants*) can be established and combined under rules which generate all the internal relations. Under those conditions, he defines a structure as a closed group of internal relations between a finite number of units. 'The immanence of these relations – that is the system's indifference to any extra-linguistic reality – is an important corollary of this closure rule which characterises a structure.' A result of this isolation of the synchronic axis is the 'achronic' aspect of the deep structures postulated (1984, p. 54). I should only add that if the time relations between author, text, and reader have become achronic, then, although we may draw out the spatial aspects of a text into elegant models, the true nature of spatiality (that it exists in a paradoxical relationship with time which a performance sets in motion) is also held in immanence. (This is true even if operator functions are included in the formal model of narrative structure which, *if put into action*, would generate the spatio-temporal experience.)

Of course, I do not imply that the narratologists cannot see this: it is a question of critical intention. Genette (1983, p. 105), in his lively way, refers to a criticism by Booth of the former's reading of Proust, in which Booth complains that Genette is too centred on notions of narrative information, of signification, and, as far as the reader is concerned, on the single feeling of intellectual curiosity to the exclusion of all moral and affective solidarity with the characters and especially with the narrator. Genette explains that he does not think the procedures of analysing narrative discourse greatly contribute to determining these affective moments, since sympathy or antipathy for a character essentially depends on the psychological, moral or indeed physical characteristics, and the conduct and discourse which the author attributes to him; they depend very little on the techniques of the *Récit* in which he figures. He adds that his earlier work, *Discours du Récit* (1972), has to do with the *Récit* and narration, not story; and the qualities or faults, the graces or disgraces of heroes do not essentially arise from the *Récit* or from the narration but from the story, in other words from the content or from the *diegesis* – that is the universe of things signified to which the story comes. He adds:

> To reproach it for having neglected these things is to reproach its choice of object. I otherwise conceive of such a critique very well: why do you talk to me about forms when I am only interested in content? But if the question is legitimate the response is only evident: each one concerns himself with what interests him.

The precision is welcome and makes evident that to consider the effect of content upon us we have to study performance.

(2) What exists first, linguistically considered, is the text: agreed. But the linguist comes to the text after it has been finished. In the author's performance what exists first is *not* the text but the mental tension that creates it. I leave this word 'tension' deliberately inchoate at that phase of the creative process, because although there is much order already in the tension, it will more fully become this order as it elaborates into text and, finally, into achieved form. From a performance point of view the creation of text is teleological and filled with intention, even if the intention changes as the creation proceeds.

At stake, then, is the familiar linguistic distinction between rule and performance, which comes in various guises: competence–performance (Chomsky); *langue–parole* (Saussure); rule–realisation; or virtual–actual. Temporary forgetfulness of this continues to bedevil interchanges between literary critics and linguists, as the exchange between Booth and Genette illustrates. To study the living art requires a value-laden, extra-linguistic, intuitive criticism; to appreciate its formal relationships one can be aided by narratology. For a fuller philosophical discussion of the issues involved, I refer the reader to a volume edited by Lerner (1983) and to the work of Ricoeur (1983, 1984, 1985).

To make the difference between rule and performance as clear as possible to readers not wholly familiar with the distinction in linguistics, let us make as non-referential a statement as possible: 3 + 7 = 10. Then we imply an extra-linguistic context for the sum such as (unspoken) ('Dammit, why ask me such a stupid question?'): '3 + 7 = *10!*'

It has become a conversation, open to extra-linguistic considerations, such as impatience. Whatever structural rules we may create to describe the statement, we still cannot decide when performing this conversation exactly what extra, impatient force to give to the '10'. We need some way of judging the mental field of the speaker in relation to context and in relation to his listener (say, 'ourselves'). In art, we judge such things through the performance of form. This is also the favourite sum of St Augustine,[2] presumably since it puts the Trinity in relation with '10', the number of divine perfection in medieval numerology, via the number of weeks of creation. (It is also the cosmically important sum that governs Boccaccio's *Decameron*, where three men and seven women tell stories for 10 days.) The number '10' could therefore be spoken with utmost reverence if we consider it, intertextually, in relation to St Augustine's other works. But if we try to perform the equation not impatiently but slowly and meaningfully as we guess someone like St Augustine might have pronounced it, we may have to call on our knowledge of the world or of cultural history in order to decide how to emphasise it. The task would be rather absurd. Suppose St Augustine had set the sum in a poem or into one of his formal rhapsodies to divine creativity, that is into some artistic expression which itself would be a working formal model of St Augustine's own reverence. We should then have better guidance (because repeatable through form) about what emotional emphasis to give it. What semiology does not recreate for us is the drive towards perfection, resolution of tension, or 'truth' of response that creates form. It can only be appreciated in performance.

(3) Non-linguistic entities. Temporal relationships are complex in the average novel and as I have said are only taken out of immanence through performance. For example, there is a play-off between length of narrative passages (number of lines of text, etc.)

and the speed of events in the fiction; another between speed of events and descriptive passages; description has its own dynamic; the variety of forms, voices and registers in complex prose has temporal effects, and so on. Despite all this, providing there is a reader to perform the narrative, all the different aspects of temporal experience (ideally) unite into an overall and activated experience of temporal form. Along with this experience necessarily goes a host of extra-linguistic experiences: time passes slowly or quickly according to the reader's aesthetic–emotional response and to his sense of a passage's semantic significance in terms of his own life. Through this experience, the reader brings the fictional text into his own world, where he experiences a tension that answers to the artist's tension that pre-existed the text, changed as it developed, and can be considered as its cause. Here again, Ricoeur is helpful (1984, p. 150). He has been analysing the temporal structure common in semiology between the utterance (*l'énonciation*) and statement (*l'énoncé*) in the *Récit*, and studying the doubling-up, parallel to this distinction, between the time taken in recounting a narrative and the time-scale relating the things recounted. His argument basically continues that only the confrontation between the world of the text and the world of the reader's life will create the true relations of temporality that the text has to offer. This will be more fully understood in terms of Ricoeur's three phases of Mimesis, as described below. (I shall reserve my main analysis to my final chapter.)

(4) The novel, then, does not only create reality: it is born in prospective relationships between the artist and his imaginary world and the reader and his imaginary world. Todorov (1978) has a diagram to show this, that the author's *Récit* conducts us to the imaginative world evoked by the author which conducts to the imaginative world constructed by the reader which conducts to the reader's *Récit*. 'These two *Récits* bearing on the same text are never identical', he adds (p. 179). He explains this variation by the fact that these *Récits* describe not the universe of the book itself but this universe transformed, as it exists in the psyche of each individual. This is accurate. But, as he evidently realises, it remains to bring this relationship alive through a living experience of the text – arrows in diagrams will not do it.

The conjunction author–text–reader creates an active intersubjectivity, relating to the real as well as to the imaginary world. The imaginary only preoccupies part of our minds; we are enabled to grasp form through the difference between the imaginary and the real. Form cannot be fully grasped just from inside the text. If both writer and reader fully entered the imaginary world they would be mentally ill – supposing, which I really do not, that mental illness itself occupied the whole of conscious and unconscious mental life during its apparent empire. (There would be little point to mental illness if it did.)

In Ricoeur's model,[3] this interaction between author, text, and reader depends upon three phases of the Aristotelian imitation. Mimesis 1 exists before the actual act of configuration of the textual world. It has, however, pre-existing 'narrative' characteristics – an action about to be described, for example, may have traditional or situational symbolic significance. Leaving aside (since it belongs to a different method of analysis) many of the hermeneutical aspects of Ricoeur's thinking here, I shall for my own purposes talk throughout this book of a primary tension, meaning by that simply whatever pre-narrative characteristics one might imagine in it for a given work – symbolic, semantic tension, emotional tension, melodic tension, all of various kinds, and so on. Ricoeur's Mimesis II is the configuring activity by which the text itself is created. Mimesis III is the reader's activity in re-configuring the text and therefore carrying into his own world the dynamic effect of the text: it is not quite the same as the first phase of Mimesis (not least because the reader's real life differs from that of the author and readers differ from each other), and Ricoeur compares the two phases as the counter-moving currents that bring the second phase to life. (There is no real English equivalent of the French *amont et aval*, which literally means upstream and downstream.) By such an image Ricoeur no doubt expects us to visualise Mimesis I and III as in a continuously active relationship with the creation (and performance) of the text.

By constructing the interdependence of all the three mimetic modes Ricoeur explains the relationship between time and the *Récit*. Unlike Todorov, he starts from a phase preceding the creation of text; and that is very important. He suggests that an Aristotelian activating of the plot (*mise en intrigue*) mediates between a stage of practical experience (Mimesis I) which precedes it and a reader-activity stage which succeeds it (Mimesis III). This presentation of the three phases adds temporality to the Aristotelian model of plot. Talking of the interaction between Mimesis I (the prenarrative phase), Mimesis II (the configuring of the temporal world in the text) and Mimesis III (the reader's own recreation of that configuration), he says: *'We are following therefore the destiny of a prefigured time that becomes a refigured time through the mediation of a configured time.'* In my own view, plot in the novel arises from that drive which shapes the semantic and emotional significance of characters and incident into form: it results from the drive to make things move in time and resolve into unity. 'Movement' (the *'mise'* in the *'mise en intrigue'*) in narrative fiction therefore corresponds to music in poetry (though, of course, many poems also have plots, even if very disguised ones, and are also narratives). I have described poetic stress as unifying into a notional point a content from past and future; and I have compared this with St Augustine's 'triple present'. A moment of formal conception in a novel likewise unifies a content into a point-like awareness and it is the narrative movement which permits this. This may appear odd, but 'setting the plot to work' and 'making the sound flow' are both the moving elements, the media, through which creative tension is resolved, part is related to whole, and the true temporality of the reader's response is awakened. The performance of a fiction by writing or reading it creates a repeatable experience of the Augustinian triple present in which the soul is distended with temporality, discussed in my previous chapter, through a *mise en intrigue*. If I do not specify the Aristotelian *mise en intrigue*, as developed by Ricoeur, but prefer the general conception of 'movement' it is because if we are considering plot in poetry too, it does not do to be too specific. My closing chapter will show that, although I may use a less philosophical language for this process, I am much of Ricoeur's party.

The writer's original creative tension (modifying itself as it goes) exists at every phase of creation if form is to result; and the presumed reader's response is thereby necessarily entrained at every phase too in the creation of the text. All the minor examples of formal achievement along the length of a work also depend upon this mutual presence of all three phases of Mimesis in Ricoeur's theory. Author is already in contact with an ideal reader as he writes; reader recreates author at each stage of reading; the intersubjective temporality is alive at all times of vivid creativity or creative response. It must now be shown how the point-like moment in narrative response exhibits the kinds of spatio-temporal ambiguity we should expect if we compare it with the paradoxes of poetic stress.

10

Poles Apart and Together

The term 'Implied Author' was given wider currency by Booth in a 1961 essay[1] to express the sense that, even where there is no explicit narrator in a fiction, an author whose presence arises from the text alone seems to be behind the scenes. It is not the same as the 'Real Author', but a version of him experienced through the text. The theory comes in various versions, according to critic concerned. Often, the notions of narrative level are placed into a linguistic embedding structure, somewhat on lines originally suggested by Chatman:[2]

> (Real Author (Implied Author (Narrator (Récit) Narratee) Implied Reader) Real Reader)

The Real Author writes a text which implies a second-level author who has written it. There may be a narrator figure inside the text who apparently 'speaks' all or most of the *Récit*, for example Marlow in 'The Heart of Darkness'. The *Récit* is the place where all the levels of embedding meet. The story may be told to one of the other characters by the narrator or to the reader; so we need a Narratee figure, defined by Rimmon-Kenan (1983, p. 89) as an agent at least implicitly addressed by the text. If this figure is directly addressed, the reader may enter the text himself, fictionally, as a counterpart to the narrator, perhaps a figure of fun, like the 'candid reader' whom Sterne addresses in *Tristram Shandy*. Next, the text implies an ideal reader who will read it perfectly and be the sum of possible responses, just as it has implied an author. Such a reader cannot be made fun of because he is already on the border of the text: Implied Author and Implied Reader frame the text. Finally, the Real Reader conducts the whole activity of reading and comparing the fictional experience with his real life, reconstructing for himself the various levels of embedding.

Genette (1983), who believes that the Implied Author and the Real Author are usually the same, would admit two exceptions to his identification of the two, both 'fraudulent'. The first would be where a writer deliberately constructs a false view of himself in the text and gives no counter-indication; and the second is ghost-writing autobiographies of famous people.

Booth must be right, because the Implied Author (and therefore the Implied Reader too) is a textual construction fundamentally different from that of the real novelist, even where this figure is very hard to discern. An amusing example would be Norman Mailer's *Ancient Evenings*, where the hero-narrator undergoes several reincarnations while remaining the same, essential spirit. The Implied Author, therefore, would have to believe in reincarnation if we are to take the novel seriously; otherwise our poor hero becomes dismembered and scattered into the mists of time. If the real Mailer does not believe in the doctrine this would construct a 'fraudulent' presentation of the author's own views. But the question goes deeper, because what the Real Author says he believes, through the textual medium, is always the operating belief of the text; and on the coherence and profundity of this, not on the author's real-life beliefs, the authority of the text depends. Furthermore, in real life an author is rarely so concentrated in his thinking as in his texts, where the words take over and create their own density, so that he can be surprised how superior he is to his normal self and how much clearer the fictional structure is than that of real life. Proust commented that a book was a product of a 'second self'. In Fielding's *Tom Jones*, the language is graded downwards from high-rational (upper-middle-class, Allworthy at his best), down through booby squires (Squire Western), through the confused rationality and warm-heartedness of the worthy lower classes (Partridge), down to the unjust language of the mob. There is a second grading, to one side, of those who employ rational language for cruel (Thwackum) and cold-hearted, hypocritical purposes (Blifil). Within these grades lies a multitude of subtle distinctions between personality. The pervasive irony employs these linguistic levels. In Fielding's text, a eulogy of his real wife, Charlotte, cannot be ascribed to the real Fielding, whatever his love for her, because its high rhetoric is identified as one of the Implied Author's possible tones. And this author, who was to be in real life such a compassionate magistrate, presumably did not imagine that real society was so neatly stratified into dialogue levels; the Implied Author's beliefs are a satirical instrument. Yet the text implies that there has to be a 'something' where these levels of irony and rhetoric concentre. Rimmon-Kenan (1983, p. 87) is right to suppose the Implied Author an impersonal construct, since he 'is' only what emerges from the text. But we cannot imagine that nothing wider than the text created it; otherwise there would be no wider authorial consciousness in which Fielding's narrative levels are unified and the irony would not be made evident. There is an irony specific to the Implied Author and we must imagine that he knows more than he tells us because irony depends upon such extra knowledge: he is very like a person. But Fielding's construction of his Implied Author is itself tongue in cheek and impregnated with irony; so we must *suspect* a yet wider consciousness, the 'real' author, by whom these higher-level ironies are created, but who cannot be known to us through the text.

The 'I' in fiction can now be linked with the 'I' who writes a poem. Here, we have to consider the music of the poem and what kind of 'I' created it along with the meanings and emotional significance.

Supposing Dylan Thomas represents to us his feelings at the death of his father:

> Do not go gentle into that good night,
> Old age should burn and rave at close of day;
> Rage, rage against the dying of the light.

He talks as if a Real Poet were speaking at the deathbed; and he expresses a combination of brave outrage at the fact of death along with graver dying cadences.

In the poem's music, one way this is done is through management of assonance, pace and voicing. I shall give two examples. The first line is similar to the Welsh prosodic device called 'cynghanedd', where consonants are repeated in crossed-over patterns: d n g g g n, with extra internal patternings of 'n's and 't's, linked with assonance to accentuate the effect. In the second and third lines the voicing goes like this:

> /Old age/ /should burn and rave at/ /close of/ /day/
> /Rage/ /rage/ . . .

The continuous passion indicated by burning and raving takes part in continuous voicing in contrast with the 'close of day' phrase, rather as I should expect from my previous examination of voicing patterns in Chapter 6. 'Rage, rage' are separated for dramatic and imperative emphasis. As before, our sense of what force and pace each syllable has is affected by the post- and back-dating operations I have described in Chapter 2. Depending on the sound, and on how we pace the emotional movement in our performance, our perception of the courage of the 'I' who speaks this poem is subtly affected. Again, the 'I' cannot be assimilated to the real Thomas, who had to resort to literature to create it. He has mimed what the deathbed feelings are like in the music, which creates through form a repeatable experience in which this 'I', the Implied Poet (the word 'persona' would be confusing), is permanently accessible to us. That is why we can so confidently identify our own, Implied Reader's, 'I' with it. We can say, 'If I were that "I" expressing those thoughts and emotions I would, ideally, have made that verbal music when I gave my optimum performance (whatever that may actually be).' The 'I' has semantic, emotional and musical elements which give us its ideational form.

In so far as we respond to this specifically as a poem, how does the mind grasp the weight of this 'I'? Not quite in a normal rational way but through the music, because in poetic response it is the music which unites sound, meaning and emotional significance into form. How do we respond to form in the music? I have claimed it is through uniting tiny perceptions of form (stresses) with the larger forms of the music.

This should mean that at many or all tiny moments of perceiving Thomas's musical form, at many or all stresses, something should be added to our grasp of the 'I' or Implied Author that writes the poem. In another way of talking, there should be an intersubjective transfer between us as reader and Thomas as Implied Author. The reader's imagination can assimilate and identify with this partly musical form, the 'I', since a form, like an image, is immaterial, whereas actual sounds, words, and people are not. Since in these stresses we have discovered the spatio-temporal ambiguity of all moments of formal perception, it should logically follow that moments (stresses) when our minds grasp something of the 'I' are ambiguous in that way: our mental construction of the 'I' is implicated in spatio-temporal paradox, in other words. This may seem a highly speculative extension of the logic. But we can find in narrative fiction further evidence that the author, in constructing the authorial 'I' through artistic formal procedures, incurs a similar spatio-temporal ambiguity.

I am reminded of the most familiar account by a major modern writer of what experiencing fiction is like. It is Proust's description of Marcel, near the beginning of the novel, discussing how he used to read in his garden. Marcel says that when he saw an external object in the real (not the fictional) world, his consciousness of it remained between himself and it, bordering it with a thin spiritual layer which prevented him from ever touching it directly. There were, as he read, constant movements taking place in him from the internal to the external, real world, an interplay which created the consciousness.

Marcel then seeks to explain how we experience emotions in encounter with fictional events. In real life, all the feelings which the joys or misfortunes of a person arouse in us do so by an image of the joy or misfortune. But however profoundly we sympathise with a real person we perceive him partly through the senses (as an external object), and this means that a part of that person always remains opaque to us, as described above. If some sorrow happens to him we can only be moved by a small part of the whole idea we have of him. By substituting unreal for real people, the novelist gets over this drawback; he replaces these impenetrable parts of the soul by equivalent immaterial parts that our souls can assimilate. (All – that is, the character and his sorrow – is transformed into fiction, into image.) We have made the fictional characters our own, since it is in ourselves that they produce themselves, and in ourselves that they persist in their relationships. Through this, the novelist can activate in us all possible joys and sorrows, some of which might take many years to experience.

So, too, with Marcel's sense of place: an imagined countryside would seem to him a truer kind of Nature (presumably because completely image) than even the real garden in which he sat reading. As space, so fictional time, which achieves flexible imaginative dimensions.

To adapt Marcel's proposition, literary art requires that the whole of a character, or a narrator, or an Implied Author should be imaginary in order to be 'assimilable' and for the artistic experience to become general. For what is meant by 'assimilable' here, I refer the reader to my final chapter.

I shall now look at Chaucer's *The Canterbury Tales* to see how a simple logic (far from the complications of modern structuralism) might be constructed. It is the logic of how the Real Author's consciousness splits into the characters he creates on the one hand, and on the other into an 'I' that does the narration.

Even at its most scatological, Chaucer's humour is never simple, always multi-layered. This is particularly clear in the 'Miller's Tale', where the Oxford scholar and astrologer, Handy Nicholas, and Alison, the carpenter's wife, play one of literature's more unpleasant tricks upon another clerk, the amorous Absolon, who for the sake of a kiss has promised to leave Alison in peace:

> Derk was the nyght as pich, or as the cole
> And at the wyndow out she putte hir hole.[3]

We do not know how to take the episode properly unless we have read far enough into the *Tales* to see the jokes and ironies that play all along its narrative levels at such moments.

Irony is usually a touchstone of narrative level. In its derivation it means dissimulation, usually through understatement, such as the ignorance Socrates sometimes feigned to encourage his disciples to progress in their arguments. Our modern notion of dramatic irony suggests that, when we consider narrative levels, irony is a tone imposed upon one level of the narrative from a higher, transcendent level where more knowledge is available. In the simplest terms of Chaucer's jape: Alison, at a higher level of awareness, knows what she's putting out of the window and Absolon does not; and to make it slightly more complex, the episode is a development of a main plot in which Alison's husband, John the carpenter, has the least knowledge of all, since he has been persuaded to take refuge from a coming second flood in a trough in the roof while Alison and Nicholas get on with things down below. And then again we as readers know that the story is told by the Miller among the Canterbury pilgrims as a way of getting at the carpenter, the Reeve. So the Miller knows a purpose for his story hidden from his characters, Handy Nicholas and Alison, and those two know purposes hidden both from her luckless lover, Absolon, who at least knows a little more about Alison's activities than her husband, John. Further, we as readers are able to enjoy the joke, but presumably the Miller is not, when the Reeve tells a subsequent and parallel story about a Miller of Trumpington, as his way of getting back at the pilgrim Miller. From this later standpoint, we carry knowledge of both pilgrims, Reeve and Miller, within us, whereas the Miller carries knowledge only of himself, and we cast this later knowledge back on to the Miller's tale. One could construct hierarchical diagrams to show the different awareness of each character and the resulting irony.

Chaucer's story-frame of the pilgrimage aids in setting up the larger-scale ironies because, in distancing us via the voice of Chaucer the Pilgrim from the more direct and more knowledgeable voice of the Implied Author, it makes the narrative levels more subtle. Chaucer was the inheritor of developments in Medieval narrative framing in which Dante and Boccaccio are key figures. Whether we consider the case histories told to Dante as he passes through the circles of the afterlife or the more earthy stories related by Boccaccio's narrators in *The Decameron*, they are set into divine and cosmological significance by the authors' framing devices and by the numerology which governs not just the number of cantos or stories but other aspects of form too. This cosmic framework sets up narrative levels according to a character's moral worth. Auerbach (1968) sees that even in Dante the great cosmological model – of human souls set into the *Comedy's* trinitarian divisions and sets of 10 circles – is disrupted by the sheer earthly vividness of the characters and by the poet's sympathetic reaction to them. It is an inevitable consequence of filling a form, supposedly infinite, with finite human characters or other finite material, including words themselves, for I have already said no artistic form is perfect. The same applies to the shortest lyric poem.

Chaucer has been supposed to have had an analogous frame in mind, substituting for the divine numbers 9 (for completed earthly perfection) and 10 (divine perfection), which overall govern Dante's *Comedia*, and 3 (men), 7 (women), and 10 times 10 stories which govern Boccaccio's, the number 120 (perhaps the zodiacal 12 signs multiplied by 10), the total stories that would have been told had the Host's original plan been carried out. Chaucer actually finished 20. Their order cannot be clearly determined because the manuscripts have come down to us in fragments, usually lettered A to I, with each of those fragments grouping one or two tales together. We do have a sure beginning, a *reverdie* or chant of welcome to spring, and a sure progression to the 'Knight's Tale'. The ending of the whole series may have been intended to be the 'Parson's Tale', but it is merely the tale told as they approach Canterbury and has an uncertain role, relating perhaps to Chaucer's changed intentions as he realised he was not going to finish the full number of stories.

Chaucer as pilgrim tells two stories: the comically ridiculous 'Tale of Sir Thopas' – whose headlink is important to what I want to say – and also, when this tale is shouted down, a sober piece of prose moralism, the 'Tale of Melibeus' – so sober that he forgets he is supposed to be a pilgrim telling a tale and admits that he is just writing it. A consequence of that admission is instant loss of some ironic possibility.

Near the end, an extra character, the Canon's Yeoman, joins the pilgrims and himself tells a tale. And the sequence we have, whatever its proper order, rounds off naturally with the 'Parson's Tale' giving a Christian exposition of the deadly sins and remedies against them, which, considering some of the sins disclosed during the series, might have struck Chaucer as a necessary admonition.

Baldwin (1955), whom I have partly depended on in my above account, claimed that Chaucer planned a progression from the highest social eminence among the pilgrims, the Knight, to the pinnacle of saintliness, the Parson. This is quite convincing, but a more recent critic, Helen Cooper, who has carefully inspected the structural evidence, concluded that all attempts to impose a rigid scheme 'recoil before the multifariousness of the work' (1983, p. 2). Even more than with Dante and Boccaccio, the sheer secular vitality and variety of his stories resist a modern recreation of late Medieval schema. Had there been a secure framework of divine redemption as in Dante, the drunken Miller and his vulgar story would have been cast yet deeper into irony and our sense of the overall Implied Author of *The Canterbury Tales* would have been markedly changed.

There is a scholar's task: to reconstruct what Chaucer the Real Author may have intended to write; this entails manuscript, textual and inter-textual study. There is a reader's more natural response: to be content with the order of stories as they have conventionally come down to us. The problem will recur in the next chapter with Rabelais, where scrupulous modern scholars often refuse to discuss the last of the five books in *Gargantua and Pantagruel* because of its doubtful authenticity. This is correct procedure, but we have alternative Chaucers and alternative Rabelaises, one a scholars' creation and the other our more naïve reaction to the Implied Author arising from a given text as handed down.

Finally, Chaucer tagged a retraction on to his masterpiece, just as Boccaccio had tagged a less repentant but defensive tailpiece on to his. Chaucer prays for forgiveness for anything offensive to God in *all* his work, not just in *The Canterbury Tales*. This is in direct contradiction to the 'General Prologue' where Chaucer the pilgrim disclaims responsibility for any salacious matter, since he is reporting faithfully the words of others.

Minnis (1984) has recently linked the evasion of responsibility with the difference between 'compilator' and 'auctor' in Medieval narrative tradition. An auctor was regarded as someone whose works had considerable authority and who bore full responsibility, whereas the compilator firmly denied any personal authority and accepted responsibility only for the manner in which he had arranged the statements of other men. Chaucer seems to have exploited the compilator's typical justification, he remarks. Partly, he has done this by creating a lower-level version of himself within the text. He can, by pretending to be the pilgrim, off-load on to him this evasion of responsibility for any risky element: whereas at the end – perhaps the repentance of an old man – he has felt obliged to apologise, as it were out of his own mouth – at a higher narrative level – for that evasion. (This is, incidentally, a reminder that responsibility in real life depends upon degree of awareness.)

We have just been looking at two 'I's in the narrative. One is a figure of reduced vision, Chaucer the pilgrim, who is only responsible for his own two tales, 'Sir Thopas' and 'Melibeus'. A second 'I' is a graver figure, one who accepts responsibility, who repents his sins, and who has a vision which encompasses not only *The Canterbury Tales* but also other productions in Chaucer's long writing career. This second 'I' is almost the direct voice of the real-life Chaucer himself, speaking from his fearful heart, and only slightly hidden from us at this rare moment by the ornaments of literary style. He is the widest possible version of the Implied Author, able to look beyond the present text to others.

Narrative levels in Chaucer have been a theme of much modern criticism, but I should set out a hierarchy of 'I's that will prove more complicated than the representation of implied author/reader etc. with which I began this chapter.

Chaucer 1. We begin with the real-life Chaucer, the figure in history. We shall always lack sufficient awareness to know him directly. This would still be true, for the Proustian reasons mentioned above, even if he were standing beside me as I write; a 'spiritual layer' masks the concrete person from us. So between this and '2' there is an unbridgeable gap in our knowledge.

Chaucer 2. The 'Historical Chaucer'. However, through his surviving works and through historical scholarship, we may construct a version of him which, though partly a work of our imaginations, is serviceable. We may study literary conventions, the books he read, the social circumstances, even what he looked like in an illustration, and we may act as scholars to reconstruct the tales' structure. But Chaucer 1 had a creative mind and we cannot know this mind merely from historical investigation. No work of source-tracking, 'sociology of literature' or historical insight can do more than slightly reduce the gap between Chaucer 2 and Chaucer 3.

Chaucer 3. The Implied Author. After we have read *The Canterbury Tales* and reflect upon it, we sense the Implied Author, source of all forms, 'radiating outwards from a single point', in that phrase of Frye's I quoted earlier. It would be a confused perception, given the inchoate length of it all, were it not that, as I have said, the Implied Author seems 'almost a person'. Chaucer 3 stands at the top of the structure of *The Canterbury Tales* as its implied author who wrote only *The Canterbury Tales*, including its retraction, and nothing else.

For three main reasons, we cannot stabilise in our minds this ghostly Implied Author. The first, linked with the problem of stabilising a notion of poetic stress, stems from the impossibility of imagining a single point at all, especially out of such sprawling complexity. It is the problem of imagining events that have duration as packed into a notional instant. The second is that we cannot purify this figure from other knowledge extraneous to the *Tales* – he keeps getting infected by Chaucer 2 and by everything else we know and cannot keep out of our mind as we read – the fact that the Miller reminds us of someone we once knew and so on. The third reason is that the *Tales* could not have been written without a wider vision than the text, as I have remarked. The Implied Author can only be regarded as the sum of every word in the text if it is just the text we take, not our reaction to it in re-performing it. Once we do that, our notion of him widens beyond the text. Perhaps if perfect form were possible to achieve, we should not think it necessary to widen our conception, since perfect form implies an infinite aspect anyway; but in impure, finite existence Chaucer 3 is at all times an unseen master, hidden like Jove, and with some unused thunderbolts up his sleeve. In glimpses, we can almost widen our notion of him to think we share consciousness with the *real* author (Chaucer 1), even if we are unable ever to be sure.

Constantly the Implied Author has to divide his creative energy at a lower narrative level than himself, between, on the one hand, a subjective pole, an 'I' of some description, a vantage point, and on the other hand, an objective pole, a world of characters and incidents 'over there' which is viewed. (I'm talking of fairly traditional narrative.) So much is commonplace. When we apply it to the *Tales* we find a pattern as follows.

The Implied Author (Chaucer 3) first utters that reverdie to Spring and then creates a reduced version of himself, Chaucer the Pilgrim (Chaucer 4). At every stage, Chaucer the Pilgrim, elegantly discussed by Donaldson (1954), appears as less knowing than Chaucer 3 must be. Donaldson cites the pilgrim's statement after the Monk has implied that he did not keep to his cloister: 'And I seyde his opinion was good.' The best reading of this is surely that the pilgrim is being either sincere or respectful to the holy cloth, but Chaucer 3, the Implied Author, is making fun both of the Monk and of Chaucer the Pilgrim. Innocently, we might wonder how we know what Chaucer 3 means, because at no point would a literal reading tell us. Our historical knowledge is vital here, and so is our perception of the overall narrative voice as a unity of the discordant levels of voices in the text. With those aids, we match the comments of Chaucer the Pilgrim and the Monk together, gain a brief insight into the consciousness of Chaucer 3, and share a rich humour with the Implied Author. This is why we are so content to practise Coleridge's suspension of disbelief; by making the lower-level characters vivid through our belief in them, we acquire access to the hierarchy of narrative levels that yields wider forms of knowing.

Having created himself as pilgrim, through which to keep the subjective pole fairly steady, Chaucer is free to create the world that lies outside it, that world of other pilgrims and other incidents whose controlling figure will be the host, Harry Bailey. The Host's function is to set the plot going, to keep it lively, and to bind together activities of all the characters, including Chaucer himself as pilgrim.

As the tales unfold, there is no end to this splitting process. Logically, when each character starts to tell his story, Chaucer has during the prologues half to abandon his role as pilgrim and step into the shoes of the new story-teller, so that the story-teller may, in turn, become an Implied Author in relation to his own story. If Chaucer is to pretend that the Miller is telling his tale, he has to allow the Miller knowledge and purposes which do not enter the literal text of the story but which nevertheless affect it. Such purposes, for example, as the rivalry with the Reeve. Then, if we believed that it really was the Miller telling his story (that is, if the overall form perfectly imposed on us), we would have to think of the Miller as also dividing his consciousness into a subjective pole of himself as story-teller and an objective pole of all the characters in his story. Within the story itself, he has to create yet finer distinctions. Logically (but ideally), to make the incident between Alison and Absolon come alive he would have to enter the minds in turn of Alison and Handy Nicholas, as they giggle on one side of the window, and then to take the stance of Absolon as he approaches.

On the subjective side, I shall only add that Chaucer the Pilgrim, as teller of two tales of his own, is ruled by the same laws of narrative splitting. He too becomes an Implied Author at this lower level and has to split his consciousness into subjective and objective poles to create his diverse characters. Chaucer the Pilgrim, the Implied Author of 'Sir Thopas' is a brilliantly bad versifier, but we could not add that adjective 'brilliantly' without a sense of the levels. And again finer distinctions could be drawn within the text of the stories. We have a structure like this.

The Real Chaucer (Chaucer 1)
(Proustian gap)
The 'Historical' Chaucer (Chaucer 2)
(gap)
The Implied Author (Chaucer 3)

Subjective pole	*Objective pole*
Chaucer the Pilgrim as author (Chaucer 4)	*The Host* The other characters, including Chaucer the Pilgrim when viewed objectively by Chaucer 4

Subjective

Pilgrim tells story

Subjective	*Objective*
Other pilgrims speak or tell stories	Characters in their stories

Subjective *Objective* *Subjective* *Objective*

•   •

•   •

(finer distinctions, according to who is speaking/seeing in the headlines, prologues, or within the stories themselves.)

•   •

•   •

etc.

This is where a distinction between my approach and that of narratology becomes important. I am talking about the splitting of 'point of view' and, as Genette has shown (1983, p. 48), point of view is insufficiently abstract to explain narrative structure; he prefers 'focalisation'. Rimmon-Kenan (1983, p. 72) also adopts this term, and adds that point of view confuses two separate narrative functions: 'who sees' the action (whose eyes we share), and 'who speaks':

> Obviously, a person (and, by analogy, a narrative agent) is capable of both speaking and seeing, and even of doing both things at the same time . . . Moreover, it is almost impossible to speak without betraying some personal 'point of view', if only through the very language used. But a person (and, by analogy, a narrative agent) is also capable of undertaking to tell what another person sees or has seen. Thus, speaking and seeing, narration and focalisation may, but need not, be attributed to the same agent. The distinction between the two activities is a theoretical necessity, and only on its basis can the interrelations between them be studied with precision.

Were it important to go farther into the detail of the levels of point of view in the *Tales* it would be better, perhaps, to talk of focalisation. For three reasons I do not. First, my points can be made without such detail. I have specified 'finer details of speaking/seeing' to cover focalisation. Second, the more detail we go into the less intuitively obvious the structure tends to become. Third, it is therefore better to avoid new jargon. The appeal of my structure is to our less-technical beliefs about how we respond to the text at any one time.

But there is one moment when by an artistic burlesque all these levels of meaning surge inwards towards each other. It comes in the headlink to Chaucer the Pilgrim's first tale of Sir Thopas. The Host suddenly notices that for ages Chaucer has been keeping in the background:

> Whan seyd was al this miracle, every man
> As sobre was that wonder was to se,
> Til that oure Hooste japen tho bigan,
> And thanne at erst he looked upon me,
> And seyde thus: 'What man artow?' quod he;
> 'Thou lookest as thou woldest fynde an hare;
> For evere upon the ground I se thee stare.
>
> 'Approche neer, and looke up murily.
> Now war yow, sires, and lat this man have place!
> He in the waast is shape as wel as I;
> This were a popet in an arm t'enbrace
> For any womman, smal and fair of face.
> He semeth elvyssh by his countenaunce,
> For unto no wight dooth he daliaunce.
>
> Sey now somwhat, syn oother folk han sayd;
> Telle us a tale of myrthe, and that anon.'
> 'Hooste,' quod I, 'ne beth nat yvele apayd,
> For oother tale certes kan I noon,
> But of a rym I learned longe agoon . . .'

A fairly typical interpretation is in John Speirs's still-useful *Chaucer the Maker* (1951): 'We have had one or two portraits of the artist before – notably in the *Hous of Fame* (by the eagle) and in the *Prologue* to the *Legend of Good Women* – and all the self-portraits accord with each other in disclosing, self-critically, a gentle, elusive, scholarly (but not ascetic) humane personality, humorously aware of himself as seeming to others abstracted.'

In fact I think there's more going on in *The Hous of Fame* and here than a portrait of the artist inserted into the text. The Host remarks that Chaucer the Pilgrim has kept himself almost wholly free of the goings-on so far, not chatting to anyone. His eyes are cast down to the ground. The Host calls him 'elvyssh' – meaning, apart from its modern senses, aloof and other-worldly. And that immediately strikes me not as some real-life scholarly aloofness of Chaucer, but as the author himself aloof from his own tales, his eyes cast down to his writing hand.

So when the Host blurts out, 'What man artow?', it is as though a much more aware figure than Chaucer the Pilgrim, a vague and giant figure, comes near the narrative. The Implied Author has called himself to mind. Simultaneously, because of that, he makes the Host call this little joke across from the objective world of the other characters to this subjective pole where Chaucer has previously had to keep himself as pilgrim apart from the rest of his creation in order to report it. You could almost say Chaucer catches himself by surprise. 'What man artow?' For a second, the pilgrim could have exclaimed: 'I'm your author; I created you.' But then, with the joking about his 'popet' appearance, the giant immediately reduces back down to the comic pilgrim, and the moment passes by. The instant when the two poles collapse back together is so brief that we only glimpse it; and when we look back at the page it is ordinary once more. The logic of the narrative is that this moment bridges the subjective–objective splitting processes.

Were that instant maintained, it would destroy *The Canterbury Tales;* it would unify all the mental splitting processes that must be kept apart if character is to be created and if interplay, jokes, and ironies are to be perceptible. In fact the Implied Author would become the Real Author, and we just about sense that during this brief collapse. When a narrative reflects back on itself like this it suddenly reveals to us its own mechanism. We are left with the instant of creation itself, but now *empty of all its content*. The point of the narrative-splitting may therefore be gauged by the contrary: ideally considered, it is to create an artistic form which, if perfect, would fill an apparent instant with content, the divine paradox that Dante tried to express through his rose of light at the end of his *Paradiso*.

More, it is in the Implied Author that the minds of the real-life author (that unattainable Chaucer 1) and of the modern reader seem almost to meet. The work of art creates a central medium in which, through a mutual performance of the form, minds can be shared. In this case, Chaucer 3 takes an equivalent role in this narrative to that of the fundamental 'I' of a non-narrative poem.

We could set out the poetic structure for comparison as follows:

Real Poet
(Proustian gap)
The 'Historical' Poet
(gap)
Implied Poet
Speaker of the lines (perhaps almost indistinguishable from Implied Poet, perhaps set at a distance for ironic or other purposes)

•
•

Possible narrative-splitting in a poem.[4]

Let me take this to the extreme. If only a narrative form were good enough, if our response were vivid enough and total, if there were no gap between our knowledge and that of Chaucer, then so intense would be our experience of its unity, of its instant packed with content, that the minds of the Implied Author and our own minds as Implied Reader would exactly meet. We would not be here; we would not be sucked into the fourteenth century, since the world of the *Tales* is hyperbolical and therefore undated; we would not be undertaking the fictitious pilgrimage exactly either, for the real-life Chaucer would be meeting us in that ambiguous consciousness of a world whose exact locus we could not site, except to say that it is at all times 'where' the unity of the form takes place and that in entering that world both our own 'I' and Chaucer's had been assimilated into an author–reader 'I'. However, if this were to happen so fully, we should lose all standpoint, all external 'I', by which to judge the story: we should not be aware enough outside the story to exercise a responsible reading; it would, as I have remarked, be a mental illness more severe than human mental illness. Perfect response to perfect form would transcend life itself.

I need hardly say that Chaucer was not trying to exemplify my theses but simply burlesquing his own narrative, although the device of 'author in the text' was not unknown in Medieval times. For instance, in one Medieval illuminated manuscript[5] the artist shows himself in a bubble, turning away in discomfort from an immoral scene he has just depicted, and saying in French, 'I am too upset [to look at this].' A moment from Rabelais' *Gargantua and Pantagruel* that Auerbach (1968) has brought to everyone's attention, will show that what I have just said about our sense of the 'I' also applies to the time and space of events and to descriptive passages. In grasping their form we also fill an instant with content.

11

The Universal Giant

Marcel's account of reading in the garden mentions the ability of the self to lose itself in the story and the incorporation into the self of the world of other, fictional characters. Marcel's account is too extreme. Half the point of literary art is that we do not lose our sense of the real world; half the point is that we do. But he also mentions the flexibility and apparent greater reality of our notions of time and of space (an imagined countryside) in fiction. A celebrated narrative burlesque – of the same essential type as Chaucer's – in Rabelais' *Gargantua and Pantagruel* has already been expertly discussed by Auerbach (1968), whom I only need to extend a little to explore the structural implications of fictional space and time. As I am ranging over different kinds of study fields, I shall not assume all readers know the work well or are at home with Rabelais' French; so I shall first present the whole work in its historical and ideological context.

Rabelais wrote first the book, *Pantagruel*, actually placed second in modern editions because the narrative concerning the son then follows that concerning the father. He next published the story of Pantagruel's father, Gargantua (Book I now), before continuing the rest of Pantagruel's adventures in Books III and IV: Book V, which rounds the story off, is either substantially by Rabelais himself, was assembled from notes of his (perhaps the most likely), or is by another hand. Many modern critics refrain from discussing Book V in the same breath as the others; if I do bring it into consideration it is with that caution.

Pantagruel was probably written and printed in 1532 – written, for in that year an anonymous chapbook, not written by Rabelais, about a miraculous giant, Gargantua, appeared at the Lyon summer fair. The prologue to *Pantagruel* acknowledges that the success of the anonymous author's book had prompted Rabelais to continue the adventures of Gargantua's son.

As we read the five books, the story obviously moves from place to place, beginning with the birth of Gargantua in the Chinon area, Rabelais' own home district in the Loire region. But the setting is a Chinon transformed into a fictional space to suit the gigantesque scale of the episodes, as Gargantua grows to manhood after being born from a mother who has guzzled so much tripe her arsehole falls out during the delivery. Everything is aggrandised: for example, a true incident, a minor quarrel over river rights involving Rabelais' own father, is expanded into a full-scale war between the peaceable, war-hating giants and the grandiose king, Picrochole. The first book ends in contemplation of an abbey founded by Gargantua and the fighting, drinking monk, Frère Jean. In this Abbey of Thélème, men and women live together in perfect harmony, a harmony symbolised in the magical conformation of the building, in the clothes worn by the inhabitants, and in their behaviour.

Book II has a similar structure, describing Pantagruel's equally monstrous birth, his humanistic studies, and a war with the Dipsodes who have invaded his maternal birth city. Two characters are particularly important as well as Frère Jean. They are Pantagruel's humanistic tutor, Epistemon, who shows many signs of the real wisdom possessed, after a suitable humanistic education, by Pantagruel himself. The other chief character is Panurge, the supreme example in the book of a man attractively but immorally swayed by his passions and appetites. Devoted to lechery, irresponsible about money, prey to fear and superstition, ebullient and uncontrollable in his nevertheless learned language, he has no morals or, more exactly, his morals are the reverse of those of reason. The key episode I shall discuss, that of the narrator's taking shelter inside Pantagruel's mouth during a storm, comes near the end of this book.

Book III shows Panurge beginning to learn about himself, as he consults various experts and various oracular sources to decide the questions, should he marry and if he does will he be cuckolded? But the answers, as from all oracles, are ambiguous: the wise Pantagruel interprets them to mean he will be cuckolded; Panurge interprets them wildly and optimistically, since he is in a passion, as they say, to get married. I shall discuss two episodes from this book: Panurge's great praise of debts near the beginning of it, and an exchange with Pantagruel on the nature of language.

They decide to visit a new oracle, that of the Holy Bottle, set in a temple at the distant corners of the earth. In Book IV they undertake this journey by sea, encountering bizarre lands which give Rabelais opportunity to mock political and religious movements he was opposed to. The new world of Renaissance exploration can be sensed behind these journeys cast in the mould of Menippean satire and of Lucianic fantasy. Another episode on the nature of language comes in chapter 55, where the party find some sounds and words that have been frozen into lumps.

In Book V, despite its dubious authorship, we have a fitting conclusion, and despite computer analysis to the contrary I find it hard to believe that we don't have much of Rabelais in it. They reach the oracle temple, which, like the Abbey of the first book, is a magical architectural structure, a harmonic synthesis fit to answer the marriage question, since that involves male–female harmony. This underground temple, its buildings and ornaments, are in their conformation symbolic of the divine universe; especially for our present argument the harmony of flux and form, of passion and reason, and of Renaissance male and female principles as imagined. In its fountain, for example, water is made to flow by the magical formal power of Pythagorean mathematics alone. At the oracle site Panurge does receive his answer from a miraculous crystal bottle, half immersed in a second, elementally pure fountain: and the answer of the bottle is that he should 'trink', some special, magical form of drinking. He does so and then, babbling poetry like a priestess of the Delphic oracle, prophesies that he will be married three times happily. Pantagruel turns on Frère Jean when he protests about Panurge's poetry; the giant declares that the wine has given Panurge poetic *fureur* and made his heart a rhetorician and a lord over all mockery. But Pantagruel has not himself needed the oracle to teach him how to drink in the secret of internal harmony, for he is already scheduled to be married on his return from the quest. As Screech (1958) pointed out some years ago and has well supported in his more-recent extraordinarily meticulous work on Rabelais (Screech, 1979), the lesson is that a virtuous man will make a virtuous marriage but a lecherous man can only expect to be cuckolded.

Before I discuss narrative logic, I should deepen my presentation of the ideas that lie behind the extravaganza. Including Book V, both Gargantua's and Pantagruel's stories end with equivalent visions of male and female harmony as reflective of harmony in the soul and of this soul harmony as reflective of divine harmony. Excluding Book V, Panurge's progress still tends towards some kind of parallel insight.

We're talking about the Medieval world-view as it began to be modified in Renaissance times, with man poised between earth and the heavens and having the possibility of either reaching upwards through his reason (suitably educated by the new humanism) or of being dragged downwards to the bestial through his passions and appetites. The principal Rabelaisian jokes set the body's changeable earthy nature which is fed by appetite into tension with passion, passion into tension with reason, and reason into tension with divine wisdom and love. Flux; digestion; eating disgusting flowing stuff like tripe; urination; defecation; farts; the formlessness of matter in corruption; the messy side of birth; a use of language that we might nowadays call verbal diarrhoea – such themes gather at one extreme of the trinitarian conception of the body and soul conventional in Medieval and Renaissance eras and accepted by Rabelais.

In Book III, Panurge's praise of debts envisages the whole universe as dependent upon flux, translated into the metaphor of money constantly borrowed and lent. As we shall see, it is the Heracleitan vision. He is substituting here the principle of unceasing flow, of unceasing mutability, for the divine love which for the neo-Platonists who followed Marsilio Ficino bound the universe together and harmonised mutability and order. Usefully for our purpose, after describing how 'debts' of influence bind one planet to each other and determine the links between lower world and upper, Panurge travesties the orthodox relation between the macrocosm and the microcosm of the human body and soul in Renaissance medicine and Christian belief (Book III, chapter 4).

According to Panurge, man can create for himself a harmony like that of the heavens in the following way. The purpose of the body is to house the soul and maintain life. Life is composed of blood and blood is the seat of the soul. Therefore the body's only real job is to keep on making blood. The appetite takes in the primary (sacrificial) foods of bread and wine and then, using a little black humour from the spleen, tells the stomach to shut the food in. The excrements are voided and the rest is sent to the liver which turns it into blood. All parts of the body rejoice and prepare to receive and purify this treasure. The kidneys draw off urine and the spleen draws off the earthy part and the lees, called melancholy, while the bile extracts choler. The blood is sent to the heart which in the right ventricle perfects it and sends it through the veins to all parts of the body. In the left ventricle the heart further refines the blood refreshed with air from the lungs and it is sent through the arteries to heat and give air to the blood in the veins. Eventually, the blood passes to the 'miraculous network' (the modern 'circle of Willis', a formation of the internal carotid and vertebral arteries at the base of the brain from which the cerebral arteries are derived), where it becomes the material for the animal spirits which give us imagination, reason, judgement, resolution, deliberation, ratiocination, and memory. To make Rabelais even clearer, the principal stages of this process are: (a) the conversion of food (obtained via appetite) by the liver into natural spirits, associated with the vegetal, mere-growth side of human nature and carried by the humours along the veins; (b) the perfecting and conversion of the blood by the heart with air from the lungs into vital spirits, the heart, of course, being associated with the passions; and (c) the further refinement of the blood at the level of the brain into animal spirits which, as Tillyard (1972) puts it, 'are the executive agents of the brain through the nerves and partake both of the body and of the soul'.

For Panurge, all this is one intricate system of debts as one organ lends or borrows from another. Rabelais, an evidently learned doctor, is parodying here the three-fold nature of the body–vegetal, passional and rational; it corresponds to the three-fold nature of the soul; this corresponds to the three-fold cosmos of the anarchic, hellish underworld mocked in Book II, chapter 30, the sublunar world, and the heavenly; and the three-foldedness is resolved at the transcendent level of the realm of God in the divine wisdom of the Holy Trinity, expressive of divine Mercy. Similarly, Rabelais tries to bring all three levels of the body into his own resolutions, symbolised by male–female harmony. I think this is why Panurge, who starts off in the narrative as prey to changeable passions, ends up in Book V prophesying that he will marry three times: it might be a Panurgian version of divine harmony expressed in the marriage of the three-fold souls – 'thrice-three' was a similar superlative in Elizabethan drama. In the Christian dialectic, flux or mutability is made fixed by form, and flux and form are resolved in divine creativity and charity; the orderly love in the sacrament of a good marriage is expressive of this. What Panurge does is to seize upon one element of this dialectic, flux, and to pretend that it is the whole of the harmony.

What follows is not, as it may seem, a digression. First, it will show that Rabelais portrayed a double foundation for language, one natural and the other conventional, and associated these language functions with lower and higher levels of the interior of the body. Second, it will deepen our sense of the narrative burlesque which I shall shortly discuss. And, third, Rabelais' approach to language has some affinities with the relationship between poetry and prose developed in my final chapter, partly because poetry makes ordered use of more primitive elements of language – intonation, stress, voicing patterns, consonant sounds and other features expressive of emotional states.

Screech has well explained that Rabelais' theory of language is similar to medieval commentaries upon Plato's *Cratylus* and Aristotle's *On Interpretation* which sought to reconcile two apparently discordant classical opinions. Aristotle would say, as Pantagruel asserts in Book III, chapter 19, that there is no natural language but that words are ascribed to things by arbitrary convention. But in Book IV, chapter 37, Pantagruel apparently contradicts himself by asserting that the names of people or places can yield supernatural or prophetic knowledge. He advises one of his Pantagruelians to read the *Cratylus,* and it is certainly true in that dialogue that Socrates goes to considerable pains to derive names from the natural qualities of Gods, people and things. In fact, in Plato's dialogue the issue is left unresolved: one reason is that because Socrates breaks words down into natural etymologies – for example, deriving the word 'demon' from another word meaning 'knowing' or 'wise' – he would have in the end to find elementary words from which the others could be built up. These primitive names would have to express the fundamental nature of the universe which according to Heracleitus was a state of flux and change. To simplify, against this Socrates poses the (Parmenidean) possibility that what is known truly must be eternal, as goodness and beauty must be assumed to be eternal, for there could be no knowing without unchangeableness. He comments that it is hard to determine whether there is an eternal nature in things or whether things only exist in Heracleitian flux. One cannot trust therefore that names express the real nature of things, since the true nature of reality cannot itself be decided.

The medieval commentator, Ammonius Hermaeus,[1] concentrates upon a distinction made by Aristotle between human words, which change from language to language, and animal sounds, such as a dog barking, which he conceded do have a natural meaning. Ammonius attempted to reconcile Plato and Aristotle by extending Aristotle's animal sounds to include animal-like sounds that humans make, such as groaning, laughing, babies' babbling, and so on. Words, which are indeed conventional, signify mental concepts, whereas animal-like human sounds express emotions and disturbances of the mind and are natural.

When Panurge becomes frightened, as he notably does during a storm at sea in Book IV, chapter 19, his language degenerates into just such animal sounds – 'Bous, bous, bous, paisch, hu, hu . . .', etc. It is extremely expressive of his fear, and also expresses that his cowardice, like his lechery, makes him bestial. The passage is like a 'sound poem' which virtually proves Rabelais' point. Lacking control over his passions, Panurge's language is frequently uncontrollable like this. When Pantagruel first meets him, in Book II, chapter 10, however, Panurge exemplies Aristotle's position on the conventionality of languages by talking in several languages, some invented, to the almost entire mystification of the giant, who cannot share the conventions thus traduced. While natural animal-like sounds may be expressive of base emotions, without convention in proper language there is no intelligent communication. The bestial side of human nature links it with the passions and the bodily change and flux of the lower organs; paradoxically, the sounds associated with this are, because natural, universal. The rational side of human nature is linked with the highest organ, the brain, which looks upwards to the divine and is linked with the fixity of sure concepts; paradoxically the words associated with this are conventional and arbitrary in their ascription to things.

With that background we may look more closely at the structural implications for space and time of the burlesque by Rabelais that I am coming to. Let me talk anecdotally for a moment. I have a presentiment that I want to tell a story about evil; my mind is whirling about with this problem and so I project a character out of this whirling and make him evil. He is already in an emotional tension with whatever in me resists evil; so I project another character to represent this goodness in me and set up a tension in the story between the two characters to represent the tension that had formerly been between me directly and the evil.

The same is true when I try to imagine a fictional space or time. I split off and project from the here and now of writing a fictional space 'there' at a time I'll call 'then'. The same is true when I imaginatively 'inhabit' a character I am creating. Depending on whether I imaginatively enter the standpoint of hero or villain or of minor characters who come into being to represent other tensions, I have secondary 'heres and nows' in the story and secondary 'theres and thens' with a consequent redefinition of the subjective pole each time, since that is normally thought of as the 'here and now'. I have explained the episode from Chaucer's 'Miller's Tale' as an irony of levels of awareness: it is also, of course, an irony involving our sense of space and time – for example, with the husband closed off from awareness in his 'ark' up in the roof, awaiting the flood.

The job of a story is then to resolve the intellectual and emotional tensions that the division into characters, spaces and times has set up.

Once again we shall consider what happens when in the middle of his story a writer for the sake of burlesque collapses back together his major divisions between his 'I' pronoun and the other characters, *and* between his sense of space as divided into 'here' and 'there', *and* his sense of time as divided into 'now' and 'then'. This is seen in Rabelais, who uses an anagram of his own name, Alcofribas Nasier, as narrator.

Alcofribas, like Chaucer the Pilgrim, is a reduced figure of the author and so takes part in an identical narrative structure to that described in my previous chapter. We have a real Rabelais (Rabelais 1), who is unknowable, a 'Historical' Rabelais (Rabelais 2), who is a version we construct from scholarship and imagination, but who should not be confused with the Implied Author Rabelais (Rabelais 3). And we have Alcofribas (Rabelais 4), who every so often reminds us that he is writing the story and is the subjective here and now from which all the 'past places' of the tale are observed.

To what place and time can we assign Rabelais at the time the story was written, say the story *Pantagruel*? Of course, it depends which Rabelais we mean. The Real Rabelais can be assigned almost certainly to Lyon, since letters of his to Erasmus and others survive from that year. And Rabelais, a monk who left cloisters both for intellectual freedom and to practise medicine, was working as a doctor in Lyon in 1532. But we have said we cannot know the 'Real Rabelais', even were he standing beside me as I write. If on the other hand we consider our version of the 'Historical' Rabelais, perhaps we have made a mistake; and in any case there is an enigmatic phrase in the *Pantagruel* prologue which talks of the author's visiting his home pastures, perhaps Rabelais' home near Chinon, about this time. So the 'Historical' Rabelais may be set fairly confidently in Lyon or Chinon at the time of writing this Book II.

But where could the Implied Author (Rabelais 3) be situated?[2]

Let us remember that this figure represents our sense of the unified source of the story. There is a complication, for he talks always through the mouth of Alcofribas, in that extraordinary voice capable of adopting a bewildering variety of tones from measured humanism to sheer babble which has given its name to a whole genre of comic prose. Alcofribas, however, takes part in his own story and also pretends to be outside it writing it. I suppose we cannot say that the Implied Author 'is' anywhere, because we sense his presence by reflecting *back* on the story; he is ambiguously everywhere at once. But Alcofribas has come into being as part of the splitting process between subjective and objective poles. Considered as pretended author, he is always in a fictional 'here and now', presumably Chinon after the events he describes, and structurally set under the subjective pole. If so, that is not the *real* Chinon but the aggrandised, fictional Chinon. Considered as a character in the story, he joins the objective world of Pantagruel's friends but, at those moments when he draws attention to himself, becomes a secondary subjective standpoint under the pole of the objective. We should remember that the logic of these categories, though clear, also will not hold mentally still as we read. Each time Rabelais and hence Alcofribas and hence the reader enter imaginatively into the mind of one of the other characters to make him speak or act, that character becomes a secondary 'here and now' in a secondary division of the objective pole into subjective and objective; this even applies to Alcofribas himself considered as Pantaguel's friend in the story. The structure is constantly in motion, and furthermore the story itself moves in space; the tension in the plot means that the 'here' is under mental pressure to keep moving. Pantagruel is privileged because he is the unifying figure of the band and to an important degree is the universal principle which converts their diversity into wisdom.

As before, I create a simple structure of subjective and objective poles, but including times and places, which are particularly schematic because it is, conveniently, a journey story:

The Real Rabelais (Rabelais 1)	– unknowable
(Proustian gap)	
The 'Historical' (Rabelais 2)	– For Book II, Chinon or Lyon 1532
(gap)	
The Implied Author (Rabelais 3)	– everywhere referred to, all times in the story

Subjective pole *Here* (and now)	*Objective Pole* *There* (and then)	
	Here	*There*
Alcofribas as author (Rabelais 4) – Chinon (but in his storytelling imagination everywhere like Rabelais 3)	*Pantagruel* Alcofribas, Panurge, etc. – successively at all places and times they move as a body down to the underground temple (end of Book V)	Characters the friends meet – usually unmoving, set in the places visited, plus the friends themselves whenever described objectively

Here *There* *Here* *There*

• •

• •

(finer distinctions of time and place according to whose mind we enter)

• •

• •

etc. etc.

If, in Chaucer, collapsing subjective and objective poles together confused our sense of the division into different 'I' pronouns, this time, in Rabelais, one might expect that collapsing these two poles together would also confuse our sense of place and time as well as of the 'I' pronoun.

It is tempting to look towards the end of Book V, when they visit the underground temple, to show this in relation to the form of all four last books, which comprise a continuous story. Alcofribas specifically compares that distant temple to an underground cavern in his own home town, where he is perhaps supposed to be writing the story. 'This entrance reminds me of the painted cellar in the first city in all the world,' he says, by which he means Chinon, which he alleges to have been founded by Cain ('Cainon') of the Cain and Abel legend, as though Chinon was the city from which the other cities were born. (Modern Chinon still has its caves set into the cliff on which the castle stands.) It would be formally neat if at the point where the story resolved its questions of male–female harmony, flux and order, etc., it united our sense of that place and time with the originating place of the story, the birthplace of its narrator, and the figurative beginning of all times and places. I should perhaps not rely upon a book of dubious authorship to illustrate such a speculative supposition.

But as Auerbach has noted, in chapter 32 of the avowedly authentic Book II, *Pantagruel*, Rabelais suddenly brings together the splitting of the author's consciousness into 'here and now' and 'there and then', along with the subjective and objective poles too. He does so by having his narrator, his 'I' pronoun, Alcofribas, recognised by his chief other character, but more than that, literally climb up Pantagruel's huge tongue and walk into the mouth to seek shelter in a rainstorm. The 'I' is now alive inside a giant-like objective pole of the story. Rabelais has throughout made the mature Pantagruel's wisdom such that the giant's mind can resolve in wise behaviour, wise words, the tensions I was describing earlier between passion and reason, flux and form, undesirable language and desirable, male and female principles, and the rest. So let's look at the inside of Pantagruel's body when Rabelais begins, in Kierkegaard's striking phrase, to 'understand life backwards through the idea.'

Alcofribas finds inside a whole second world, beginning with France just on the tongue surface, as though a Chinon complete with phlegmatic French peasant planting cabbages. At this moment the whole space–time of the story involutes. The inside of Pantagruel's body contains what the peasant calls a world older than the 'new world' of Rabelais' story outside, that new world of imagination copying the new world of Renaissance explorations, whose journeys lie outside the giant mouth, and towards whose end the party will travel. Inside, Italy lies just across the Alps of the giant's teeth; other cities lie within the throat, foul airs rise from digestive regions. It is the role of wisdom, in Renaissance philosophy, to harmonise these bodily levels and not to be subject, like Panurge, to the play of flux, appetite and passion. The body and mind of Pantagruel form the textual origin where the widest Rabelaisian virtues are created; from them issue the measured language of convention, the delighted natural laughter, the moderated behaviour – everything that is the correct answer to Panurgian indiscipline but which also includes its element of flux, harmonised into wisdom. This, the Implied Author seems to be saying, is what reality is truly like. To take a quotation that I have always imagined to be one of the sources of Rabelais' enterprise: a great favourite of his, Sir Thomas More, wrote about his Utopians: 'they're even blind to the existence of that notorious Universal, MAN. Now he, as you know, is a pretty conspicuous figure, bigger than any giant you ever heard of.'[3]

But outside the mouth, the new world of story continues from where they are standing, significantly in Pantagruel's birth city in Utopia, or 'no-place'. So this, like Chinon, is a birth city. Outside, the space extends towards the end of the fictional world, created, through the fantastic voyages, perhaps to the far temple of the oracle, also like Chinon. Inside the body, we begin in France and extend to new mythical regions of this giant body, harmonising form and flux. Outside is a time of war, for Pantagruel has been forced to fight the grandiloquent Dipsodes, and the battle continues while Alcofribas shelters; he is safe inside this peaceable giant who only undertakes war in the way Erasmus recommended, reluctantly when absolutely necessary and with utmost generosity after conquest.

For whatever artistic motive, Rabelais has created the natural consequence of joining together the subjective and objective poles of his story. If these two poles are resolved fully into artistic form, the whole story unifies and resolves its contradictions as in an Aristotelian resolution of plot: the form becomes full of resolved content. But when the two poles are collapsed together, the form is entirely destroyed and has to begin again. Here it begins again in the country of its birth, but in the reverse direction, away from Utopia and away from its imaginary world, so that at the very lip of Pantagruel real and fictional become utterly ambiguous in status.

If we ask where we are at this moment, we 'are', as readers, wherever Alcofribas', the author's, imagination is. And the 'there' of the story is where the other characters including Pantagruel are, seen from the outside. So at this swallowing of the subjective by the objective pole, the 'here' and 'there' fuse together too. We are unsure who is 'I', since we are active inside Pantagruel; we are unsure what size we are; and we are unsure where we are: in France, on the tongue of the giant, or in Utopia outside.

So surely Rabelais has found, consciously or not, an extraordinary metaphor for the process by which a story is born: in that moment or moments of birth, the 'here' and 'now' of the act of writing and also of reading are still in a sort of vivid present, what I have called a creative tension, in which they are still ambiguously the same as the 'there' and 'then' of the fictional world and the 'I' is also confused. In Ricoeur's terminology, we have been transported back to the stage of Mimesis I. Only by extending the splitting into the duration of the novel, as in the orthodox work of composition, and then bringing that duration into form, can the form be given unambiguous content, seizable in a single act of conception. Only by conceiving this form as emanating from a notional point do we gain access to its many levels of narrative and so discover the full voice of the Implied Author.

Our sense that Rabelais must in some way have known what he was doing, is why, at this moment, we have a vague presentiment that it is not just the Implied Author but Rabelais himself who nears our own time, and our own consciousness, a larger, more universal figure than we had imagined, but a presence whose mind no longer seems to have definite content beyond the brilliantly empty joke of the burlesque itself.

12

Emotion in Literary Response

Though various aspects of poetry and narrative structure have been tackled, an underlying coherence of view binds the studies together. It remains to draw this out more clearly.

When analysing Chaucer and Rabelais I assumed that narrative form is typically produced by splitting up aspects of a writer's creative mental tension and objectifying them in some literary way. Objectification may include division into places and times, the creation of settings, the choice of point of view or other subjective–objective effects, oppositions of morals, emotions, semantics and other linguistic contrasts and so on, as well as – more evidently – the creation of characters and of the narrative levels in which each of them is implicated. Any of these tensions could theoretically produce a story. (If narratology can reduce these to abstract entities then, as I remarked in Chapter 9, these cannot help us too much in the discussion of performance.) In performing the narrative the reader first encounters the splitting-up, then reads it back towards the Implied Author. As I have suggested in my discussion of poetic stress, all perception of artistic form is, described in 'ideal perfection', instantaneous; the time and space durations of the form are seized in a moment of comprehension.

This may seem far-fetched when applied to the diverse material of the contemporary novel, where there are many 'spots of indeterminacy', to re-use Ingarden's term, in which the discursiveness does not seem tightly related to the whole. But in the best of the modern realists, such as in a novel by V. S. Naipaul, although much of the textual energy seems to go into giving the colour and smell of a real Caribbean or African world, the more vividly we respond to the realism the more vividly we enter the imaginary world of the Implied Author, so that we may experience the overall form yet more strongly. A *nouveau roman* may try to abolish this traditional formal structure – omitting, for example, subjective–objective interplay as far as possible, or endeavouring to refuse reader identification through various kinds of alienation, rejecting any realistic referential function of its language, or making the narrative structure open-ended instead of attempting closure. But such effects are only gained by taking to its limits the traditional story-telling art, with its subjective–objective splitting, its reader identification, its apparent reference to a real world, its formal closures. Suppose we describe the nature of objectivity in Robbe-Grillet's *La Jalousie*, where the normal relation between self and external world is deliberately ruptured in favour of an apparently pure observer eye peering at jalousied windows from the outside. The strange emotional consequences set up between this objectivity and the emotion of jealousy are now a critical commonplace of the *nouveau roman*, but they arise just because we sense we are being denied a normal subjectivity and therefore sense that a pathological state lies behind the observer eye.

Despite the influence of phenomenology and the philosophical deconstruction of 'self' on modern literary experiment, in what follows I shall employ the ordinary, non-philosophical sense of 'self'. There are two unashamedly humanistic principles here: first, the 'I' that arises in the text may be considered, as far as that text is concerned, as no more complex than the 'I' that the author has put into it; second, such an 'I' is likely to find an equivalent response from the reader's 'natural attitude I', to use Husserl's term.

I insist, then, non-conservatively actually, that there is a primary definition of narrative form which underwrites all discursive realism and all modern experiment. It arises from *some process* of splitting the originating creative tension and, in the perception of literary form, these oppositions are rendered satisfactory cohabitants of the form created. Most evidently, when good defeats evil we are emotionally satisfied by their coherence within the one form. With any subtle writer, these oppositions and their resolutions may obviously be of great refinement.

Spatio-temporally, what happens at a moment of the reader's formal perception while reading a novel is essentially the same as what happens when we perceive a poetic stress, because the latter is also an artistic form. One can see the spatio-temporal dynamic of narrative form by examining its inverse, when the form is collapsed inwards on itself. This was the point of studying the burlesques of Chaucer and Rabelais: when the splitting processes that create form are merged, this happens in an apparent instant which is suddenly emptied of content. Rabelais' extension of this instant into an amusing passage of time should not confuse us: he is deliberately playing upon the impossibility of filling an anti-formal instant with content; and he makes the uniting of the subjective and objective poles paradoxically exist *in durational time,* as opposed to coexisting within a notional *instant* of formal perception. If the consequence of collapsing narrative form is to empty the instant of content, the consequence of creating or perceiving an orthodox narrative form in performance must be to fill a notional instant with content. This is just what I supposed poetic stress to do.

Perhaps the reader would find this more convincing if I could positively state that, during the course of reading a novel, any sudden formal insight comes through post-dating narrative significance of some kind and back-dating narrative significance on to that moment of insight. In poetry the medium which creates formal resolution is sound which has rhythmic beats; the resolution into a stress involves only a little of the poem's meaning each time; but as the medium of resolution in the novel is narrative movement, which is itself composed of complex meanings, one little package of meaning–emotion–movement, comparable with a stress (substituting sound for movement), cannot usually be consciously perceived.

All the same, small, point-like moments of formal perception must surely occur in our reading of novels. The usual objection to such a description is rationalist: we form concepts over time, or by bunching operations similar to computers, or by some other time-conquering device. In literary terms, we gradually become aware of the significance of this or that narrative moment. But without individual conceptual moments ('cognitions') we should have no *conscious* gradual awareness. I shall return to novels in a moment, but this is where the examination of poetic stress – apparently such a minute and technical question – is so revealing: a stress is conceptual and its mental dynamic is probably formed in the same way as that of all concepts, including all individual cognitions of artistic form. I have claimed that the most convincing model for how we do so is by a mental mis-timing, where the mind post- and back-dates its information on to a notional moment in the past when the concept is deemed to have 'occurred'.

The following question arises: if a stress and a poetic or narrative form are conceptualised in the same way as any other mental concept, what is their point? Why do we not gain the same satisfaction from just thinking about the problems raised in a work of art as we do from experiencing that work in performance?

Many possible answers to this question may be obvious. I am going to concentrate upon our emotional reasons for wanting to experience art. This is because in studying aesthetic emotion we stand to learn something about emotion in general; and I shall begin by studying it first in terms of poetry.

Research psychologists often compile lists of fairly fundamental emotions or attitudes, but the lists vary and distinguishing between complex emotions and those, if any, which are truly fundamental is difficult (see Lyons, 1980, p. 15). In considering poetry, we may say a melody expresses disgust or joy, providing we recognise that disgust can be very like contempt in its expression, or that there are manifold kinds of joy and that poetry can be emotionally many layered. Much work on the emotional correlates of vocal music, whether in poetry or ordinary speech, depends upon commonsense classifications. Uldall, in a series of studies (for example, 1960, 1961), has explored dimensions of social and emotional meaning conveyed by intonation in both tone languages (such as Thai, in which tones have phonemic significance) and non-tone languages (such as English, where there is no formalisation of their meanings). Her scales include such attitudes or emotional meanings as disapproving–approving, impatient–patient, and so on. Fónagy has also gone some way to showing that certain intonation patterns are linguistic universals capable of expressing such basic or complex emotions as anger, joy, coquettishness, complaint or irony, and he has investigated this cross-culturally in speech, cliché, poetry and music (summed up in Fónagy, 1983). Bolinger (1972, p. 313) has long pointed out there is good evidence that intonation can transcend the usual language-specific connection between meaning and form.

I am not claiming cross-cultural universality in my own work on poetic intonation because I want to retain the language-specific complexity of individual poems in performance. Lieberman and Michaels (1962) found no one single acoustic correlate of the emotional modes they studied, again a mixed list including perhaps basic and certainly complex categories such as boredom, disbelief, fear, happiness, etc. Phonetic content, gross changes in fundamental frequency ('pitch'), the fine structure of the fundamental frequency and the speech envelope amplitude (a summing operation on the vocal wave forms which correlates to 'loudness'), in that order, all contributed to the transmission of the emotional modes. Small perturbations in fundamental frequency appeared to be an acoustic correlate too: when the perturbations were smoothed out confusions between the modes increased. Their finding is expected if, as this book's analyses suggest, tiny details of versification such as consonant duration affect our emotional reaction to a line of poetry – and we should have to add voicing pattern, overall cadence and pause. When we apply such insights to the *literary* analysis of a given poem we have also to remember that other acoustic and non-acoustic factors contribute to emotional significance (including, obviously, meaning).

Fónagy (1976) adds a further complication. For him, what is specific about artistic voice in a poem, as opposed to the voice used in ordinary speech, is that it uses melody in a metaphorical way. As in ordinary speech, the artistic voice may express the content of the text in a 'symptomatic' sense – the intonation may suggest plaintiveness where the textual meaning is plaintive; or it may express the content in a 'symbolic' sense, as in a verse line whose melody suggests restless search or mad running, even as the text expresses the same semantic concept. But artistic voice is specific partly in associating individual melody-metaphors with texts with which they are not usually associated or which they even contradict, thus setting up complex interactions of melody and meaning. The possibility of a plaintive intonation may coexist in a text with the possibility of a harder or more ironic rendition. There may thus be overlays of possible melodies residing within a text, and a given performance may decide to select one of these overlays for special emphasis, giving extra force to the melody's potential for expressing a plaintive content, for example. If there are universal responses to intonation patterns, then the basis of poetic music is universal but the performance (reading or writing) of any given poem is a very fine, language-specific tuner. Despite all that I have said about a 'neutral music' in poems arising from a minimum of interpretation but a natural sense of the musicality of the words, I have also allowed for complex interpretations – 'talented alternatives'. We cannot make a science of it.

Poetically, however, one may speculate. Let us take our well-worn Wyatt lines – 'So unwarely was never no man caught / With steadfast look upon a goodly face / As I of late' – and put them into the mouth of a boring but literate man standing next to us in the pub. His concentration is on rational meaning; so he says, 'I don't suppose anyone can ever have been so unthinking about the effect on him of staring at an attractive woman as I was the other day.' The meaning is laboriously there, but the link between stress, continuous voicing pattern, pause and final syllable in Wyatt's first line that I pointed out in Chapter 2 is obviously quite lost. The miming of the emotional and semantic content, through sound, is gone. There is, however, always a necessary link in *any* given utterance between what is said and its intonation; language cannot avoid it and it is specific to performance. In ordinary speech we judge the honesty or dishonesty of a lover through the smallest hesitations or inauthenticities of tone; we evidently 'just know' that a strict necessity links emotion and the intonation (or prosody) of ordinary speech. In the pub we should know that the man's choice of words was inadequate to the situation and that the matter-of-fact vocabulary, syntax, tone and rhythm did not mime the onset of sudden awareness out of unawareness. Now suppose we were with this man when he looked at the woman and was overcome by his feelings. He says, first, nothing (while he is looking steadily at her) and then 'Hmm!' or even 'Huh-hmm!' Wyatt's concise expression is lost: the period of silence is an equivalent of the continuous voicing pattern of Wyatt's 'So unwarely was never no man' and the final exclamation a meaningless copy of the moment when, for Wyatt, the poet is 'caught' by his own surprise. In the poetry, the concentrated meaning of the words will create a lively conception of the emotion that is fictionally felt. Owing to the necessary link between emotional reaction and intonation, the intonational features will be surprisingly apt too. Which comes first, the creation of the imaginary emotion, the right vocabulary, or the apt prosody, is a nice question. Perhaps they all come together. In everyday life men and women do not often hit poetry like this: one-sided rationality places learnt, conventional expressions into our speech, which becomes too dead to allow us to mime the appropriate emotion; or one-sided *real* emotion makes us as incoherent as Panurge in the storm.

Let's look at the behaviour of the modern-day Wyatt in stages:

(a) Seeing the woman causes the beginning of sexual wonder.
(b) The wonder unconsciously builds up.
(c) He almost involuntarily exclaims with wonder – the emotion is, however, too fast for any verbal precision.

(d) Later, in the pub, he can talk about the wonder when the emotion has, in fact, somewhat subsided.

Of course, we might have imagined a much more emotional man than this, but although stage (d) might be much closer in time to stage (a) and his language more vivid, even so the four stages would not coincide. In real life, there is nearly always a gap between heart and head. The cause must be sought in the nature of emotion.

It is evidently either through sharing a formal conception (a thought) or through the sharing of an emotional field that ordinary intersubjectivity is possible between two people. In a discussion one person suddenly persuades the other of a single point of argument. Identity of awareness that something 'true' has occurred leads to a moment of sharing of consciousness, signalled by a quick nod which attempts, too late, to trap that moment. There could be a feeling of constant agreement, but leaving the emotional aspect of that aside, such constant agreement on the intellectual plane is actually composed of many moments of concord, of similar formal perception. This is because the arrival of an achieved concept into consciousness is always discrete and always a little too late for the instant of time it pretends to represent. I have already cited Cassirer on this point in Chapter 8. Although there may be no break in the totality of knowledge extending forward from the first stages of sensory, perceptual knowledge, the concept must annul 'presence' in order to arrive at representation.[1] What is of interest is the tiny difference in time-scale between direct perception of emotion and concept-formation.

Sudden emotional reactions are evidently more closely linked to gross bodily processes than are conceptual processes. If we are charged by a bull, our stab of fear is faster than our conscious awareness of exactly what is happening. To distinguish such emotions from feelings (sensation of bodily reactions) we probably have to say they are at origin directly cognitive, like perception.[2] There is a bodily link between visceral, glandular, circulatory, etc., activity that seems to lead to this direct form of cognition that is faster than full consciousness. To bring an emotion fully into consciousness we have to form a discrete concept of it. I am getting angry; it is not until I formulate this to myself that I can be said to be consciously angry. But I have already been feeling the bodily sensations and making the cognitive evaluations that partly cause them; my face may already be adopting its appropriate expression from the Darwinian repertoire; I may feel a hot flush, my speech will have been betraying this half-conscious awareness through certain intonation patterns, even if my phrases are apparently polite. (The connection between emotion and intonation is primitive and perhaps universal in this sense: it is faster than the sophistication of thought and more generally shared by people.) I was talking of intersubjectivity. The signs of anger, of course, imply non-sharing of minds; what is shared, however, is that there is continuous awareness, structured by moments of cognition, that someone is losing his temper. All the bodily and intonational signs, the glances away, the staccato speech forms, convey this; it is a willy-nilly sharing of minds. When the shared emotion is more tender the bodily signs emphasise the continuity of concordance, the mutual sighs and murmurs, the intonational expressions of sweetness and continued harmony, the adoption of parallel body postures, and so on; yet still this is structured by discrete cognitions.

Let us think of three kinds of mental concept: of an instant of time, of a 'single moment of the emotional continuum', of a poetic stress sensed within the flow of music. In each case, the concept is too late, as Cassirer has warned us, to trap a moment in the continuum. By the time we conceptualise the second, the stress or the emotion, the clock has ticked, we have tapped the stress, and we have already been angry in some primitive, pre-verbal sense of the word which can yet affect the intonation of our voice.

Emotion in ordinary life cannot fuse perfectly with thought, therefore, because it does not share the same temporal dynamic; it is more evidently continuous than the conscious reflections that constitute thought-acts; and it is quicker, more intimately related to a primary sensory perception, such as sight or hearing. Our daily working assumption (that it is physiologically wrong does not matter because in performing poetry it is our daily working assumptions that we go by) is that sight or hearing are immediate once the visual or auditory signal has arrived; so it is with a stab of fear. Conscious thought can never quite get into the speed of this alternative system that freezes out from the notional present of an event.

Poetry discovers a way to unify the time-scales of emotion, concept, and verbal music. It does so by transforming the emotion itself into a concept, a fiction.

Lerner (1975, p. 217) notes the reappearance down the centuries from Horace of theories about a special aesthetic emotion, and contrasts such doctrines on the one hand with Aristotelian *catharsis*, which would place emphasis upon real emotions being felt through art, and on the other with critics who would prefer not to use the term 'emotion' in respect of art. In fact, we do need to talk about emotion in three senses: first the fictional miming of real emotions that goes on in literary art; second, the real emotion of Horatian–Coleridgean delight in aesthetic form; and third the complex emotional play-off from the fictional effect of the text into our own lives. The third may seem an aesthetic impurity but truly is a necessary part of the response, since I have said earlier that it is a mistake to think that our whole minds lose themselves in the imaginative world of the text.

If the poet were merely to express his real emotions there would be no poetry: the subjective–objective splitting outlined above would be imperfectly achieved; we should be left with a schoolboy scribbling in his notebook. The language would remain specific to the individual, and the power of real emotion to make us partly incoherent would remain.

Look at what happens when this emotion is real, rather than imaginary. Lerner (1975) states that it is generally agreed that any good poem has an element of the specific and individual. The aesthetic problem of Sylvia Plath's last poems, however, is well known. There is something in their vocabulary and intonation that speaks too directly. We could employ a simplified version of the poetic and narrative levels we have considered:

Real Author(Implied Author(Text)Implied Reader)Real Reader

In these poems of Plath, the Implied Author, out of urgent need, is imperfectly split from the Real Author. By immensely fine nuance, the ear can tell that the intonation partly belongs to real emotion, not to imaginary emotion: it lacks a certain delicacy. Because of that the language remains somewhat hoarse and we seem to eavesdrop on personal tragedy. Enough of an imaginative act remains, all the same, for the poet's talent to create a fine poetry, carrying within the beautiful melodies of fictionalised emotion this other trace of a real emotion that otherwise might simply cry out in anger or despair; and we cannot remain unaffected by its motivating power, since our real lives are always entrained in the aesthetic process.

By transforming emotion more fully into the imagination (conception) of it, the poet can make the speed of thought and the speed of imagined emotion coincide, since conceptions share the same time-scale. He distances the real emotion and uses it rather as a painter uses paint; whereas the aesthetic emotional tension may be high. The result is that the quicker speed of real emotion does not trouble his verbal production, and rationality and conceptualised emotionality are freed into the same imaginative realm so that maximum poetic density can be achieved. Intonation cannot mime its reaction to imaginary emotion without copying the necessary relation it has to real emotions; the coding is already there in the usage of language. Sound, meaning and emotional significance will now share the same time-scale, the intonation will modulate perfectly to vivid meaning, and the stresses will be timed exactly right. (This includes even finer details of timing, such as the incidence of consonants in many of Sidney's sonnets, which I have mentioned earlier.) Consequently, our delicacy in perceiving the emotional effect of intonational patterns is even more fine in poetry than in ordinary speech, owing to the more evident patterning.

To return to an example already used in Chapter 8, the exactness of the great jazz drummer is to know just how much time is added by 'feeling' (actually aesthetic emotion) to perfect synchrony (abstract concept of timing) in order to create the best timing to adapt the abstract synchrony to coincide with the flow of the tune. I suspect that the drummer's minute variations of beat interval recognise that form is never perfect but is each time attainable. This is a formal perception itself, to which our access comes through aesthetic emotion. How much the drummer wants to dwell in one interval of aesthetic emotion, between beats, makes him want to delay, slightly, the onset of the next, at the next beat. The exact stroke of it is decided by finding the right end-point of the interval that will most prolong the tension of feeling but not beyond the moment at which tension begins to slacken. It is rather like deciding how long to delay the middle 'ss' in Creeley's 'for / christ's sake', discussed in Chapter 6. The time-scales of all this are infinitesimal.

The poet, as Lerner remarks, is in control of his emotions. As in a poem, much in our dreams does not give us conventional emotional reactions but those very like aesthetic ones; a little does give us real emotion and it is those parts of the dreams that are out of control.

The resolution and control of emotional and conceptional scales of space–time in poetry, therefore, would go like this: the Real Author makes of himself an imaginary Implied Author fit to have imaginary (conceptualised) emotions: thus thought and aesthetic emotion can be brought into temporal consonance. In performance the Real Reader makes of himself an Implied Reader who repeats the process. The Real Reader's experience is not identical to that of the real poet because the engagement of the reader's real world with the imaginary one is affected by differences of personality, real experience, historical epoch, and so forth; but the spatio-temporal dynamics of the text reside in its words and therefore the Implied Reader can imagine he shares experience with the Implied Author (suspension of disbelief). Divisions of mind and emotion which were in discord in the original creative tension with which the poem began, are brought into concord. A difference is that the poet begins with this tension and the reader reconstructs it backwards from his performance. The concord brings delight, like delight at truthfulness; and the delight occurs at minor moments of formal perception as well as at major. With Ricoeur's help, we have compared it in Chapter 8 to the authenticity of unified temporal experience through St. Augustine's 'triple present', which is doubled up so that there is three-fold distension of the soul (past–present–future time as still), allowing the present to have content, and a three-fold intentional driving-onwards of time (time as changing), allowing the present to have dynamic. Similarly, verbal music has its moments of stress in which content and musical movement are by a mental trick of the mind given at least notional unity at a time held in memory.

This is difficult to relate to the resolution of emotions and concepts in the temporal world of the novel because it is now the vague term 'narrative movement' which is the medium of resolution.

We are going to consider drama and novels somewhat together. Ricoeur (1983, p. 85) suggests that the Aristotelian *mise-en-scène* ('fable'), suitably broadened to include all narrative moments, is the inverse replica of the Augustinian distension of soul. By 'inverse' he means that St Augustine was concerned by the existential constraints of temporal discord: how could time *be*? As we have seen, the problem is that the instant has presence but no content, and time passing has content but no presence; whereas Aristotle discerned in the poetic act that created a tragic poem the triumph of concord over discord.

Let me adapt this insight entirely to my own terms. For poetic stress, we could mean by 'discord' the mental filling of one moment of time with a discordancy of content from past and future. But in a novel or play, we can mean by it all those diverging tensions involved in the one originating tension, a divergence that, since it is extensive in time, semiologically complex, and emotionally or intellectually discordant, will not happily share the same temporal unity; it provides the motive for splitting the author's consciousness and knowledges into the different times, spaces and characters. (Again, the modern hermeneutic aspects of this are here set aside.) In formal resolution, these discordant divergencies are going to be united into a single conception whose elements are 'simultaneous'.

In the classical tragedy, this new unity is discovered suddenly, in a *coup de théâtre* as Ricoeur says, through the resolving moments of Aristotle's plot. (I have said that it makes no difference if the realisations are more gradual: a formal concept is always quasi-simultaneous.) These are the reversal of fortune (the *coup*) and recognition (or disclosure) of what has been most importantly ignored in the hero's history. Potts (1968) well describes reversal: in a complex plot it is when 'the movement is first one way and then the other', like the coming full circle of the Wheel of Fortune.

Reversal and recognition are terms abstracted from a limited corpus of classical tragedy: possible resolutions in novels, above all modern novels, are more complex; but we shall keep to this centuries-old model for clarity. Reversal and recognition are alike in holding a mirror up to the division of the splitting processes in the plot. It is rather like bringing a concave mirror up to a pin until the (past) image reverses in a sudden moment which seems to lose coherence altogether until the ('future') image is reconstituted the other way up. In tragic climax, the two sides of good and evil, for example, are impossibly seen both as presented and in reverse (more minor formal resolutions earlier may have given us hints of this). There is an elusive moment of unity between the contradictory functions of good and evil, an instant of time now filled with this contradiction and also driven onwards by it into recognition.

It may be objected that Aristotle concentrated not on character but on the action. This need not detain us long. Paskow (1983) has recently explained that in the Aristotelian *catharsis* action entails character, because it is composed of what characters do. In any case, since Henry James, we know even better how inter-involved the notion of character is with that of action. This is why we can broaden the concept to include narrative movement generally and incorporate into it modern experimental kinds of oppositional tension.

The moment of resolution, if it is to be comparable with the resolution of form in poetry, requires three elements to come into unity: our conceptual knowledge, our emotions, and the formal movement of the narrative, the medium whose dynamism will work the trick. Reversal and recognition are conceptual in nature and arise directly from the narrative movement; so we have consonance of two of the elements we need. What about emotion?

Here, the Aristotelian model is troublesome because it relates to drama, which is an impure art. The presence of actors brings into the 'text' a real human force more easily capable of arousing real emotions in us than the figments of a novel. The real actors present us with real sense impressions which cannot be assimilated entirely into the imagination – the Proustian problem. Perhaps the most perfect actor watched by the most imaginative 'implied spectator' might come near seeing the actor as a spiritual presence; but this extreme is fantasy. I believe this is why the Aristotelian *catharsis* speaks of pleasure arising from the purging of (real) emotion through pity and terror. In the novel it is easier to see that, more purely regarded, the narrative movement arouses imaginary emotions and that the real emotions we experience arise through comparing our real world with the imaginary world of the Implied Reader that we become in order to read the text properly. This comparison is, as I have explained, essential to artistic response all the same, or we just become aesthetes.

Considering the narrative movement along its linear dimension, we find the movement makes 'areas' in the story which have conceptual–emotional–moral–evaluative significance: 'areas' is a deliberately undefined term to include all oppositions of whatever formal 'size' that may cause intellectual or emotional tension, not just characters or character-traits, places, events large or small, good–evil, etc., but also experimental narrative tensions as mentioned above. Each area is a small-scale example of form, which, in an idealised description, contributes to overall form.

If we could freeze these 'areas', stopping their movement in time, we should stop the mental operation that brings thought and emotion (plus evaluation) together. We say 'Captain Ahab = evil at point X'; but the statement remains flat, lacking its actual mobile richness and ambiguity, and there is no emotion in it. To bring the emotion into artistic performance involves two things. First Ahab must be an imaginary, conceptualised figure so that he is of the same temporal scale as the concept 'evil'. Yet again we have Proust's doctrine that in fiction the novelist replaces those impenetrable parts of the soul reported to us through the senses by equivalent immaterial parts that our souls can assimilate. The second requirement is that the imaginary Ahab must be set in motion so that we may experience time's active changing. The driving force is the tendency of the movement to resolve its splitting processes satisfactorily.

The task of literary form, then, whether it be as small in significance as a poetic stress or as large as a great novel, is to fill the instant with content from thought and conceptualised emotion, united through verbal music or narrative movement, so that the result is a permanent working model of experience. The vividness of the instant is thereby more fully discernible in its authenticity. Although I have compared the dynamic to the Augustinian 'triple present', its actual spatio-temporal formation in the unconscious might just as easily accord with some more refined modern mathematical model of the relationship between 'singularity' and extensive space–time: I'm not sure how we could know. My own working beliefs about stress tend towards these more fanciful models, but I am establishing a sort of bunker position: a tactical trench that we can all agree is safe before we go over the hill into the unexpected. Author and reader create, through their own implied personification in the text, a special intersubjectivity – a perfecting of the emotional and semantic fields through a shared experience of space and time, owing to the mystery of artistic form. The process reveals what our everyday experience and speech could be like if, when our emotions were real and not imaginary, our hearts and heads were in temporal consonance. It is a cliché to say that poetry and narrative render perfect what is unsatisfactory in our lives, whether by 'happy' or by otherwise satisfactory endings. But it is through the accord of concept and emotion that a more profound perfection and intersubjectivity are attained, a task that our small-scale investigations of stress, syllable, voicing pattern and melody have shown being performed.

Notes and References

1 Rule and Performance

1. R. D. Cureton has, however, an interesting linguistically-based system of scansion which I shall refer to in Chapter 8. R. D. Cureton (1986) pp. 171–208.

2. Musical Form and Poetic Stress

1. 'Emotional' in a special, aesthetic sense which I shall describe later.
2. Influenced by Rimmon-Kenan (1983) p. 122, and B. H. Smith (1968).
3. Fuller interpretation in, for example, Blamires (1969), Traversi (1976).
4. This and question–answer division adapted from P. Howard (1980).
5. M. Mack and B. Gold (1986).
6. For example, Chatman (1965), p. 127, n. 29; H. Morier (1966).
7. Chatman (1965); and M. E. Loots (1980).
8. More precision in Morier (1966).
9. Critique in T. A. Salthouse (1984).

3. Intonation Contours

1. Surrey, Earl of (1964), Introduction.
2. J. L. Miller, F. Grosjean and C. Lomanto (1984).
3. And see M. A. K. Halliday (1970).
4. Quoted in I. Fónagy (1983).
5. More details in Oliver (1983), (1984).
6. I. Fónagy (1976), (1983).

4 Voicing Patterns and the Pace of Poetry

1. Further detail in D. Oliver (1984).
2. Further detail in D. Oliver (1984).

5 The Music of Translation

1. For example, M. Liberman and A. Prince (1977). D. Bolinger and followers place great emphasis upon intonation. For Cureton's more syntactical analysis see Chapter 8.

7 Eve in the Garden

1. Discussion helped by A. Fowler's notes in J. Milton (1968) pp. 880–1.
2. St Augustine (1945), Book V, chap. IX, p. 153.
3. Quoted and discussed in A. Kenny (1979) p. 81.
4. C. Ricks points out how important such words are here. See J. Milton (1968).

8 Tunes and Instants

1. St Augustine (1930), Book XI, XIII, 16.
2. *Summa Contra Gentiles*, 15, in St Thomas Aquinas (1939) p. 99.
3. St Thomas Aquinas (1963) p. 251.
4. I am aware that I could bring a lot of subtlety into this discussion by employing J. Derrida's theory of the 'differance' and the 'trace', a pure movement in language by which meaning is created. The Derridean 'trace' has much of the ambiguity about spatio-temporal relations of past, present, and future elements in linguistic experience that is required for my following discussion. But the language of Derridean deconstruction is too removed from our ordinary language and too inherently paradoxical about the interrelation of absence and presence ('the disappearance of truth as presence') to be *useful* in describing our everyday belief that we have just had a 'present' experience of a beat in a poem. Anyway, I cannot be sure that a rarefied and 'deconstructed dialectics' best represents the dynamics of ordinary mental processes in response to poetic rhythm. (See my similar hesitance later in this chapter about applying in this present discussion advanced space–time mathematics to descriptions of ordinary mental processes.) Most importantly, the Derridean 'deconstruction' of the presence of the subject and of unity in language cannot quite explain the *confidence* (mentioned later in the chapter) with which in performance we tap a musical or poetic beat as if we had, after all, had 'present' experience of it. That is to say, for all its interest, the Derridean language does not have the right emotional tone for describing this confidence; and people often neglect to consider that emotional tone is part of the evidence for the applicability of doctrine to factual existence. Confidence of that kind is an extra-linguistic, non-abstract emotion, which we ignore at our peril in performance because it is how we judge the truthfulness of what we do. It would overburden my text to go into the considerable complications of Derridean philosophy, which I mention because it has caused such live controversy in schools of literature. Those interested have a wealth of studies to consult, including: J. Derrida (1973), (1967), etc.; J. Culler (1982), (1967); D. B. Atkins (1983); C. B. Leitch (1983); J. Llewelyn (1986); and for some constructive criticism, L. Lerner (ed.) (1983).
5. A related notion in Derrida's 'trace' or 'Differance' theory is that in the linguistic act the 'thing itself' is always deferred, although in

Derrida the context is post-Saussurean linguistics. See Atkins (1983, p. 17).

6. St Augustine (1930), XXVIII, 37.
7. Derrida's dynamics of 'differance' has equivalents to these active and passive aspects.
8. A full bibliography would exceed my confines, but, see R. M. Gale (1968) for the historical questions, and for some modern issues W. H. Newton-Smith (1980).
9. This is related to the mutual exclusivity of phenomenological and cosmological descriptions of time, mentioned by Ricoeur.
10. As in Abercrombian or Hallidayan prosody, for example M. A. K. Halliday (1970).

9 Narrative in Performance

1. See A. J. Greimas (1970), my account helped by S. Rimmon-Kenan (1983). Later work by Greimas (1983).
2. St Augustine (1964) p. 54; see also (1945) p. 339.
3. It is the basis for much in Ricoeur in (1983), (1984).

10 Poles Apart and Together

1. Also see Booth (1983) chap. 1.
2. S. Chatman (1978), quoted in S. Rimmon-Kenan (1983) p. 86.
3. F. N. Robinson (ed.) (1974).
4. Good discussion of these possibilities in M. Budd (1983).
5. Reproduced in D. W. Robertson Jnr (1963).

11 The Universal Giant

1. Description from M. A. Screech (1979).
2. D. G. Coleman (1971) calls it the 'Olympian author' but her structural analysis differs from mine.
3. Sir T. More (1965). The joke refers to the medieval controversy between Realists, who believed that universal had real existence, and Nominalists, who thought that Universals were merely names.

12 Emotion in Literary Response

1. E. Cassirer (1957), Vol. III, p. 307.
2. W. Lyons (1980), who thinks them cognitive–evaluative.

Bibliography

ADAMS, C. (1979) *English Speech Rhythms and the Foreign Learner*, The Hague: Janua Linguarum.

ALEXANDER, M. (trans., ed.) (1977) *The Earliest English Poems*, 2nd edn, London: Penguin.

ALEXANDER, M. (trans., intr.) (1966) *The Earliest English Poems*, London: Penguin.

ALLEN, G. D. (1970) 'The location of rhythmic stress beats in English', *Working Papers in Phonetics, No. 14*, Los Angeles: University of California. Reported in Adams (1979).

ATKINS, D. B. (1983) *Reading Deconstruction: Deconstructive Reading*, University Press of Kentucky.

AUERBACH, F. (1968) *Mimesis*, New Jersey: Princeton U.P. (first paperback edn of 1946 edn).

ST AUGUSTINE (1964) Anna S. Benjamin and L. H. Hackstaff (trans.), *On Free Choice of the Will*, New York: Bobbs Merrill.

ST AUGUSTINE (1945) John Healey (trans.), R. V. G. Tasker (ed.), *The City of God*, London: Everyman.

ST AUGUSTINE (1930) *The Confessions*, London: The Medici Society.

ST AUGUSTINE (n.d.) W. F. Jackson Knight, *St Augustine's De Musica, A Synopsis*, London: The Orthological Institute.

BALDWIN, R. (1955) 'The Unity of *The Canterbury Tales*', in T. Dahl, K. Malone and G. Tillotson (eds), *Anglistica*, vol. V, Copenhagen: Rosenkilde & Bagger. Excerpts in R. Schoeck and J. Taylor (eds), *Chaucer Criticism*, vol 1, London: University of Notre Dame Press, 1960.

BARRY, W. J. (1981) 'Prosodic functions revisited again', *Phonetica*, 38, pp. 320–40.

BARTHES, R. (1977) 'Introduction à l'analyse structural des récits', in R. Barthes, W. Kayser, W. C. Booth, Ph. Hamon, *Poétique du récit*, Paris: Editions du Seuil, Points 78. Originally in *Communications*, 8, 1966.

BLAMIRES, H. (1969) *Word Unheard. A Guide Through Eliot's Four Quartets*, London: Methuen.

BOLINGER, D. (ed.) (1972) *Intonation, Selected Readings*, London: Penguin.

BOOTH, W. C. (1983) *The Rhetoric of Fiction*, 2nd edn, University of Chicago Press.

BOOTH, W. C. (1961) 'Distance and point of view', in *Essays in Criticism XI*, French translation in (1977) *Poétique du récit*, Paris: Editions du Seuil, Points 78.

BUDD, M. (1983) 'Belief and sincerity in poetry', in E. Schaper (ed.), *Pleasure, Preference and Value*, Cambridge University Press.

CASSIRER, E. (1957) R. Mannheim (trans.), *The Philosophy of Symbolic Forms*, Vol. 3: *The Phenomenology of Knowledge*, New Haven: Yale University Press.

CHATMAN, S. (1978) *Story and Discourse*, Ithaca, NY: Cornell U.P.

CHATMAN, S. (1965) *A Theory of Meter*, The Hague: Mouton.

CICERO (1980) C. R. Edmonds (ed.), *Cicero's Three Books of Offices or Moral Duties, etc.*, London: Bell & Daldy, Bohn's Classical Library.

COGHILL, N. (1951) *Chaucer: The Canterbury Tales*, London: Penguin.

COLEMAN, D. G. (1971) *Rabelais: A Critical Study of Prose Fiction*, Cambridge University Press.

COLERIDGE, S. T. (1920) F. Sampson (ed.), Sir A. Quiller-Couch (intr.), *Biographia Literaria, Chaps. I–IV, XIV–XXII*, Cambridge University Press.

COOPER, H. (1983) *The Structure of The Canterbury Tales*, London: Duckworth.

CREELEY, R. (1966) *Poems 1950–1965*, London: Calder & Boyars.

CRYSTAL, D. (1980) *A First Dictionary of Linguistics and Phonetics*, London: Andre Deutsch.

CRYSTAL, D. (1969) *Prosodic Systems and Intonation in English*, Cambridge University Press

CULLER, J. (1982) *On Deconstruction; Theory and Criticism after Structuralism*, Ithaca: Cornell University Press.

CURETON, R. D. (1986) 'Traditional scansion: myths and muddles', *Journal of Literary Semantics*, December.

CUTLER, A. and D. J. FOSS (1977) 'On the role of sentence stress in sentence processing', *Language and Speech*, 20, pp. 1–10.

DANILOFF, R., G. Schuckers and L. Feth (1980) *The Physiology of Speech and Hearing, An Introduction*, New York: Prentice Hall.

DAVENPORT, G. (1984) *The Geography of the Imagination: Forty Essays*, London: Picador.

DAVIDSON, A. (1968) *Edward Lear, Landscape Painter and Nonsense Poet (1812–1888)*, London: John Murray.

DERRIDA, J. (1973) D. B. Allison (trans.) *Speech and Phenomena and Other Essays on Husserl's Theory of Signs*, Evanston: Northwestern University Press.

DERRIDA, J. (1967) *De la Grammatologie*, Paris: Editions de Minuit.

DONALDSON, E. TALBOT (1954) 'Chaucer the Pilgrim', in *PMLA LXIX*, pp. 928–36.

ELIOT, T. S. (1944) *Four Quartets*, London: Faber & Faber.

FÓNAGY, I. (1983) *La Vive Voix*, Paris: Payot.

FÓNAGY, I. (1976) 'The voice of the poet', in *Toward a Theory of Context in Linguistics and Literature* (ed. A. Makkai), The Hague: Mouton.

FÓNAGY, I, and K. MAGDICS (1963) 'Emotional patterns in intonation and music', *Zeitschrift fur Phonetik Sprachwissenschaft und Kommunikationsforschung*, vol. 16, pp. 293–313. Also in Bolinger (1972).

FREUD, S. (1961) J. Strachey (ed.), 'Civilisation and its discontents', in *The Standard Edition of the Complete Psychological Works of Sigmund Freud*, Vol. XXI, London: The Hogarth Press.

FREUD, S. (1955) J. Strachey (ed.), 'The "Uncanny"', *The Standard Edition*, op. cit., Vol. XVII.

FRYE, N. (1957) *Anatomy of Criticism, Four Essays*, Princeton University Press.

FULLER, R. (1977) 'The bum-bum game', *Thames Poetry*, 1, 3 (Winter).

FULLER, R. (1976) 'Boos of different durations', *Thames Poetry*, 1, 1 (Winter).
FUNKHOUSER, L. B. (1979) 'Acoustic rhythm in Randall Jarrell's "The Death of the Ball Turret Gunner"', *Poetics*, 8, pp. 381–403.
GALE, R. M. (1968) *The Philosophy of Time, A Collection of Essays*, London: Macmillan.
GENETTE, G. (1983) *Nouveau discours du récit*, Paris: Editions du Seuil.
GENETTE, G. (1972) *Figures III*, Paris: Editions du Seuil.
GIMSON, A. C. (1973) 'Stress in English', in W. E. Jones and J. Laver (eds), *Phonetics in Linguistics: A Book of Readings*, pp. 94–102.
GREIMAS, A. J. (1983) *Du Sens II*, Paris: Editions du Seuil.
GREIMAS, A. J. (1970) *Du Sens: Essais sémiotiques*, Paris: Editions du Seuil.
IZARD, C. E. (1977) *Human Emotions*, New York: Plenum Press.
HALLE, M. and S. J. KEYSER (1981) 'The iambic pentameter', in D. C. Freeman (ed.), *Essays in Modern Stylistics*, London: Methuen, pp. 206–24.
HALLE, M. and S. J. KEYSER (1975) 'Sur les bases théoriques de la poésie métrique: Le shift sur l'Arabe classique et autres exemples', J. Roubaud (trans.), in J-P. Faye (ed.), *Change de Forme, Biologies et Prosodies*, Paris: Colloque de Cerisy.
HALLE, M. and S. J. KEYSER (1971) *English Stress: Its Form, Its Growth, and Its Role in Verse*, New York: Harper & Row.
HALLE, M. and S. J. KEYSER (1966) 'Chaucer and the study of prosody', *College English*, 28, pp. 187–219. Also in D. C. Freeman (ed.), *Linguistics and Literary Style*, New York: Holt, Rinehart & Winston, 1970, pp. 366–426.
HALLIDAY, M. A. K. (1970) *A Course in Spoken English: Intonation*, Oxford: Oxford University Press.
HAWKING, S. W. and G. F. R. ELLIS (1974) *The Large Scale Structure of Space-Time*, Cambridge Monographs on Mathematical Physics (paperback edn), Cambridge: Cambridge University Press.
HILLMAN, J. (1962) *Emotion, A Comprehensive Phenomenology of Theories and their Meanings for Therapy*, 2nd edn, London: Routledge & Kegan Paul.
HOWARD, P. (1980) *Haydn in London*, Milton Keynes: The Open University Press.
HUSSERL, E. (1973) D. Cairns (trans.), *Cartesian Meditations, An Introduction to Phenomenology*, The Hague: Martinus Nijhoff.
INGARDEN, R. (1973) G. G. Grabowicz (trans.), *The Literary Work of Art*, Evanston: Northwestern University Press.
ISER, W. (1978) *The Act of Reading: A Theory of Aesthetic Response*, London: Routledge & Kegan Paul.
JAUSS, H. R. (1982) M. Shaw (trans.) W. Godzich (intr.) *Aesthetic Experience and Literary Hermeneutics*, Minneapolis: University of Minnesota Press.
JOWETT, B. (trans.) (1970), ed. R. M. Hare and D. A. Russell, *The Dialogues of Plato*, Vol. 3, London: Sphere.
KENNY, A. (1979) *The God of the Philosophers*, Oxford: Clarendon Press.
KIPARSKY, P. (1981) 'Stress, syntax and meter', in D. C. Freeman (ed.), *Essays in Modern Stylistics*, London: Methuen.

KIPARSKY, P. (1977) 'The Rhythmic structure of English verse', *Linguistic Inquiry*, vol. 8, no. 2, pp. 189–247.

LACAN, J. (1966) *Ecrits*, Paris: Editions du Seuil.

LADD, D. R. (1980) *The Structure of Intonational Meaning*, Bloomington, Indiana: Indiana University Press.

LANGER, S. (1969) 'The work of art as a symbol', from *Aesthetic Analysis*, excerpt in J. Hospers (ed.), *Introductory Readings in Aesthetics*, New York: The Free Press, 1969

LEAVIS, F. R. (1963) *New Bearings in English Poetry*, Harmondsworth: Peregrine.

LEITCH, C. B. (1983) *Deconstructive Criticism: An Advanced Introduction*, New York: Columbia University Press.

LERNER, L. (ed.) (1983) *Reconstructing Literature*, Oxford: Blackwell.

LERNER, L. (1975) entry on 'Emotion' in A. Preminger (ed.), F. J. Warnke and O. B. Hardison, Jr (assoc. eds), *Princeton Encyclopedia of Poetry and Poetics*, enlarged edn, Princeton University Press.

LEYRIS, P. (trans.) (1980) G. M. Hopkins, *Poèmes*, Paris: Editions du Seuil.

LIEBERMAN, P. and S. B. MICHAELS (1962) 'Some aspects of fundamental frequency and envelope amplitude as related to the emotional content of speech', *Journal of the Acoustical Society of America*, vol. 34, 7, pp. 922–7.

LIBERMAN, M. and A. PRINCE (1977) 'On stress and linguistic rhythm', *Linguistic Inquiry*, pp. 249–336.

LIST, G. (1961) 'Speech melody and song melody in central Thailand', *Ethnomusicology*, vol. 5, 1, pp. 16–32. Also in Bolinger (1972).

LLEWELYN, J. (1986) *Derrida on the Threshold of Sense*, London: Macmillan.

LOOTS, M. E. (1980) *Metrical Myths. An Experimental–Phonetic Investigation into the Production and Perception of Metrical Speech*, The Hague: Martinus Nijhoff.

LYONS, W. (1980) *Emotion*, Cambridge University Press.

MACK, M. and B. GOLD (1986) 'The effect of linguistic content upon the discrimination of pitch in monotone stimuli', *Journal of Phonetics*, 14, pp. 333–7.

MAILER, N. (1983) *Ancient Evenings*, London: Macmillan.

MEYER, L. B. (1956) *Emotion and Meaning in Music*, Chicago: Chicago University Press.

MEYER-EPPLER, W. (1972) 'Realisation of prosodic features in whispered speech', *Intonation: Selected Readings* (Bolinger, D. ed.), London: Penguin, pp. 385–90.

MILLER, J. L., F. GROSJEAN, and C. LOMANTO (1984) 'Articulation rate and its variability in spontaneous speech: A reanalysis and some implications', *Phonetica*, 41, pp. 215—25.

MILTON, J. (1968) J. Carey and A. Fowler (eds), *The Poems of John Milton*, London: Longman.

MINNIS, A. J. (1984) *Medieval Theory of Authorship: Scholastic Literary Attitudes in the Later Middle Ages*, London: Scholar Press.

MORE, Sir T. (1965) P. Turner (trans.), *Utopia*, London: Penguin.

MORIER, H. (1966) 'Le moment de l'ictus', in M. Parent (ed.), *Le Vers*

Francais au 20e Siècle, Colloque of the Centre de philologie et de littérature romanes de l'Université de Strasbourg.

MORRISON, T. (1977) *The Portable Chaucer*, revised edn, Viking Portable Library, London: Penguin.

NEWTON-SMITH, W. H. (1980) *The Structure of Time*, London: Routledge & Kegan Paul.

NOAKES, V. (1968) *Edward Lear, The Life of a Wanderer*, London: Collins.

O'CONNOR, J. D. and G. F. ARNOLD (1973) *Intonation of Colloquial English*, 2nd edn, London: Longman.

OLIVER, D. (1986) 'A method for comparing the music of English and French poetry', *Franco-British Studies*, Journal of the British Institute in Paris, 1 (Spring).

OLIVER, D. (1984) 'Voicing patterns as one key to the pace of poetry', *Journal of Phonetics*, 12, pp. 115–32.

OLIVER, D. (1983) 'Fundamental frequency studies as a preliminary to the literary criticism of poetry', *Journal of Phonetics*, 11, pp. 1–35.

OLIVER, D. (1979) 'Even poets can have beliefs about poetic stress', *Grosseteste Review*, 12, pp. 12–32.

OLSON, C. (1967) D. Allen (ed.), *Human Universe and Other Essays*, New York: Grove Press.

PANOFSKY, E. (1972) *Studies in Iconology, Humanistic Themes in the Art of the Renaissance*, New York: Icon Editions, Harper & Row.

PASKOW, A. (1983) 'What is aesthetic catharsis?', *The Journal of Aesthetics and Art Criticism*, Fall issue, pp. 59–68.

PIKE, K. L. (1945) *The Intonation of American English*, Ann Arbor: University of Michigan Press.

POPPER, K. R. and J. C. ECCLES (1977) *The Self and its Brain*, London: Routledge & Kegan Paul.

POTTS, L. J. (trans, ed.) (1968) *Aristotle on the Art of Fiction: 'The Poetics'*, Cambridge University press.

POUND, E. (1959) *Selected Poems*, T. S. Eliot (intr.), London: Faber & Faber.

RICARDOU, J. (1978) *Nouveaux Problèmes du Roman*, Paris: Editions du Seuil.

RICHARDS, I. A. (1950) *Coleridge on Imagination*, 2nd edn, London: Routledge & Kegan Paul.

RICOEUR, P. (1985) *Temps et Récit*, t.3, *Le Temps Raconté*, Paris: Editions du Seuil.

RICOEUR, P. (1984) *Temps et Récit*, t.2, *La configuration dans le récit de fiction*, Paris: Editions du Seuil.

RICOEUR, P. (1983) *Temps et Récit*, t.1, Paris: Editions du Seuil.

RICOEUR, P. (1984) (1985) (1986) *Time and Narrative*, vols I, II, III, English translation of *Temps et Récit* by K. McLaughlin and D. Pellauer, Chicago University Press.

RICOEUR, P. (1975) *La métaphore vive*, Paris: Editions du Seuil.

RIMMON-KENAN, S. (1983) *Narrative Fiction: Contemporary Poetics*, London: Methuen.

RITZ, J-G. (trans.) (1980) G. M. Hopkins *Poèmes, 1862–1868: 1876–1889*, Paris: Aubier Montaigne.

ROBERTSON, D. W. Jnr (1963) *A Preface to Chaucer*, Princeton University Press.

ROBINSON, F. N. (ed.) (1974) *The Complete Works of Geoffrey Chaucer*, 2nd edn, Oxford: Oxford University Press.

ROBINSON, F. N. (ed.) (1957) *The Works of Geoffrey Chaucer*, 2nd edn, Boston: Houghton Mifflin Co., Cambridge: The Riverside Press.

SALTHOUSE, T. A. (1984) 'The skill of typing', *Scientific American*, vol. 250, 2.

SANDERS, W. (1985) 'Straddling the Criticism and Creativity Border', *The Listener*, 15th August.

SCREECH, M. A. (1979) *Rabelais*, London: Duckworth.

SCREECH, M. A. (1958) *The Rabelaisian Marriage: Aspects of Rabelais's religion, ethics and comic philosophy*, London: Edward Arnold.

SMITH, B. H. (1968) *Poetic Closure: A Study of How Poems End*, Chicago University Press.

SOLOMON, R. C. (1976) *The Passions*, New York: Anchor Press, Doubleday.

SPEIRS, J. (1951) *Chaucer the Maker*, London: Faber & Faber.

SURREY, EARL of (1964) E. Jones (ed.), *Poems*, Oxford University Press.

TATHAM, M. A. A. (1980) 'Phonology and phonetics as part of the language encoding/decoding system', in N. J. Lass (ed.), *Speech and Language, Advances in Basic Research and Practice*, vol. 3, New York: Academic Press, p. 35.

ST THOMAS AQUINAS (1963) R. J. Blackwell, R. J. Spath and W. E. Thirlkel (trans), V. J. Bourke (intr.), *Commentary on Aristotle's Physics*, London: Routledge & Kegan Paul.

ST. THOMAS AQUINAS (1939) *Summa Contra Gentiles*, in Rev. Father M. C. d'Arcy (ed), *Thomas Aquinas: Selected Writings*, London: Everyman.

TILLYARD, E. M. W. (1972) *The Elizabethan World Picture*, London: Penguin, 1st Pelican Edn.

TODOROV, T. (1978) *Poétique de la Prose*, Paris: Editions du Seuil, Points 120.

TRAGER, G. L. and H. L. SMITH (1957) *An Outline of English Structures*. Studies in Linguistics, Occasional Papers 3, Norman, Oklahoma: Battenburg Press.

TRAVERSI, D. (1976) *T. S. Eliot: The Longer Poems*, New York: Harcourt Brace Jovanovich.

ULDALL, E. (1961) 'Dimensions of meaning in intonation', from *In Honour of Daniel Jones: Papers Contributed on the Occasion of his Eightieth Birthday, 12 September 1961*, ed. D. Abercrombie, D. B. Fry, P. A. D. MacCarthy, N. C. Scott and J. L. M. Trim. Also in Bolinger (1972).

ULDALL, E. (1960) 'Attitudinal meanings conveyed by intonation contours', *Language and Speech*, vol. III, pp. 223–34.

WELLEK, R. and A. WARREN (1963) *Theory of Literature*, London: Penguin (3rd edn).

WIMSATT, W. K. (1971) 'The rule and the norm: Halle and Keyser on Chaucer's meter', in S. Chatman (ed.), *Literary Style: A Symposium*, Oxford: Oxford University Press.

Index